CAROLE A. LEVITT AND JUDY K. DAVIS

Internet Legal Research
on a Budget

Free and Low-Cost Resources for Lawyers

ABA LAW
PRACTICE
DIVISION
The Business of Practicing Law

Commitment to Quality: The Law Practice Division is committed to quality in our publications. Our authors are experienced practitioners in their fields. Prior to publication, the contents of all our books are rigorously reviewed by experts to ensure the highest quality product and presentation. Because we are committed to serving our readers' needs, we welcome your feedback on how we can improve future editions of this book.

Cover design by RIPE Creative, Inc.

Printed in the United States of America.

Library of Congress Cataloging-in-Publication Data

Levitt, Carole A., author.
  Internet legal research on a budget / by Carole A. Levitt and Judy K. Davis.
     pages cm
  Includes bibliographical references and index.
  ISBN 978-1-62722-616-5 (alk. paper)
  1. Legal research--United States--Computer network resources. I. Davis, Judy K., II. American Bar Association. Law Practice Division sponsoring body. III. Title.
  KF242.A1L479 2014
  340.0285'4678--dc23

                          2014007160

Dedication

CAROLE A. LEVITT

I'd like to dedicate this book to my husband, Mark Rosch. In 1999, when I first had the idea of presenting CLE seminars to lawyers on using the Internet to find free and low-budget websites for research, he was the one who encouraged me to launch Internet For Lawyers (IFL). Mark created our company's website by teaching himself HTML and staying up late at night for weeks on end. He also came up with the idea for IFL's online CLE seminars. Together, we have co-authored six ABA Law Practice Division books and thirteen editions of our seminar book, *The Cybersleuth's Guide to the Internet* and given hundreds of CLE seminars all over the U.S. I couldn't have asked for a better husband, best friend, and work partner, all wrapped up into one person. Finally, I appreciate Mark taking on the lion's share of IFL's work during the many months it took me to write this book.

Contents

Chapter 3   Apps for General Legal Research   27

Part II   Legal Portals and Directories   31

Chapter 4   Free Commercial Portals and Directories   35

Chapter 14 Foreign, International, and Comparative Law Resources 235

Part VI Additional Research Sources 249

Chapter 15 Dockets 251

Chapter 16 Social Media 277

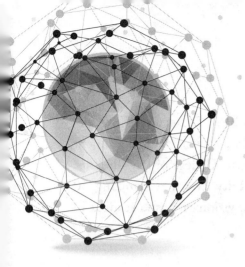

About the Authors

Carole A. Levitt is the founder and President of Internet For Lawyers (www.netforlawyers.com). She is a nationally recognized CLE seminar speaker and best-selling American Bar Association Law Practice Division (ABA LP) author. She is an expert on Internet investigative and legal research; social media research; social media ethics; Google search and Cloud Apps; and technology for lawyers. Carole has been presenting CLE seminars full-time since 1999 throughout the United States.

Carole has co-authored six other ABA LP books with her husband/co-speaker, Mark Rosch, including (1) *Google Gmail and Calendar in One Hour for Lawyers* (2013); (2) *Find Info like a Pro*, Volumes 1, 2, and (3) *Google for Lawyers: Essential Search Tips and Productivity Tools* (2010). She has also co-authored thirteen editions of *The Cybersleuth's Guide to the Internet* with Mark Rosch.

Previously, Carole was a California attorney, a law librarian in Chicago and Los Angeles, and a Legal Research and Writing Professor at Pepperdine University School of Law. She graduated with distinction from The John Marshall Law School in Chicago and was a member of the school's law review. Carole has a Masters in Library Science and a B.A. in Political Science from the University of Illinois.

Carole is an active member of the ABA Law Practice Division, serving on its Publications Advisory Board since 2003 and on its Executive Council from 2006 to

2011. Carole is past Chair of the California State Bar's LPMT Executive Committee and in 2013 became the second recipient of LPMT's Lifetime Achievement Award. Recently, Carole was nominated as a Fellow to the College of Law Practice Management and was a recipient of the 2013 "Fastcase Fifty" award, recognizing "50 of the smartest, most courageous innovators, techies, visionaries, and leaders in the law."

You can reach Carole at clevitt@netforlawyers.com.

 Judy K. Davis is a law librarian and adjunct assistant professor of law at the University of Southern California Gould School of Law. Prior to coming to USC, she worked at the University of San Diego Pardee Legal Research Center. Earlier in her career, she also practiced law before a wise person showed her that her true calling was to be a librarian. She currently teaches legal research to USC law students, works in the law library's reference department, and gives lectures and training sessions on legal research and related topics. When not writing books about legal research or imparting knowledge to future attorneys, she likes to spend as much time as possible outdoors in beautiful Southern California.

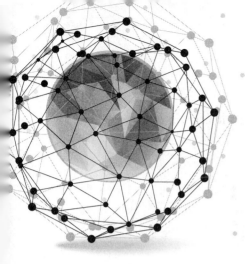

Acknowledgments

CAROLE A. LEVITT

First, I would like to thank my co-author, Judy Davis. It would have been a daunting task to write this book on my own, but with Judy's help, this book was brought to fruition. Despite never having met in person, we were able to successfully collaborate on this book using the magic of e-mail and Google Hangouts.

The amazing ABA LPD Publishing staff members (Denise Constantine, Lindsay Dawson, and Laura Bolesta) are next in line to thank. They are a joy to work with.

My sincere appreciation goes to my Project Manager, Jennifer Ellis, and also to all the peer reviewers for their quick turnaround over the Christmas/New Year's Eve holiday season: Jennifer Ator, Renay Bloom, Kathleen Havener, Blair Janis, Cookie Lewis, and Tom Mighell.

For inspiring me to become a law librarian in 1976 and teaching me all about print legal research, I owe my gratitude to my University of Illinois library science legal research professors, Carol Boast and Nancy Johnson. I'm also grateful to my fellow law librarian, Cindy Chick, for introducing me (and many other law librarians) to the Internet and how we could use it for free legal research.

JUDY K. DAVIS

I would like to thank everyone at the USC Law Library for the support that allowed me to take on this project. Thank you for your advice when I needed it and for your patience when I didn't take it. Many thanks to Carole for your confidence in me, and for your willingness to work with this new author. And finally, thank you Pavan, for being there, for believing in me, and for entertaining the cat while my attention was elsewhere.

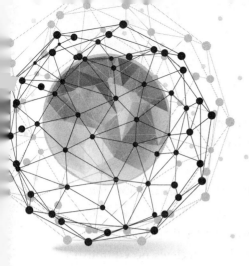

Foreword

ROBERT J. AMBROGI

"Imagine instant access to virtually unlimited sources of legal information. Imagine receiving court decisions within hours of their release. Imagine consulting experts in any legal field, anywhere in the world, and having their answer within minutes. Imagine having statutes, bills and government documents at your fingertips. Imagine huge files of legal forms and pleadings at your disposal.

"Now imagine that this is all free and available to you right in your office, no matter how small or remote. No travel to distant libraries. No expensive search fees."

It seems laughable now, but when I wrote those words in 1995, in an article introducing lawyers to the Internet, the legal research landscape I described was a pipe dream. Then, much of the Internet still consisted solely of text. Navigating it required knowledge of archaic and confusing commands and interfaces with names such as Gopher and Telnet.

Hyperlinked navigation of the Internet—what came to be called the World Wide Web—was invented in 1991 and only began to find broader use in 1993 with the development of the first two viable web browsers. Notably, one of those browsers, Cello, was developed specifically with lawyers in mind by the Legal Information Institute at Cornell Law School.

Back then, neither Westlaw nor LexisNexis were accessible through the Internet. Researchers could access them only through a dial-up terminal. Only a handful of courts had begun to publish their opinions on the Internet, and only newly released ones—there were no extensive archives to search. The vast majority of legal research was still done as it long had been, by trudging to the law library and poring over hard-copy books.

Fast forward two decades and that pipe dream is a reality, and then some. Every federal and state appellate opinion can be found online at no cost. Federal and state statutes are online, as are growing bodies of other primary legal materials, from federal regulations to municipal ordinances. Traditional law reviews now publish online while legal blogs are creating new forms of legal commentary and analysis. Search technology has become so sophisticated that we forget how difficult a search used to be. All of this is available to us wherever we are, in the office or on a mobile device sitting outside a courtroom.

This glut of legal research materials on the Internet is a good thing, of course. But it is also a mixed bag. Paid research services compete with free ones. Established publishers go against start-ups. So many resources are available that some of the most useful ones can be lost in the crowd. Even professional legal researchers have a hard time keeping score.

I will confess that I am a cheapskate. Way back when, when I started using the Internet, I was hoping to save a buck. I had just started my own practice. I did not want to pay the high cost of a Westlaw or LexisNexis subscription or invest in a library of hard-bound reporters. I went on the Internet to see what free resources I could find there.

All these years later, I am as budget-conscious as ever. *Internet Legal Research on a Budget* is written for any lawyer or legal researcher who is similarly budget-conscious—and I am willing to bet that most of us are. Carole Levitt and Judy Davis have scoped out the terrain. They have tested and evaluated a host of free and low-cost legal research sites and identified the best. Not only do they show you the sites, they provide detailed instructions on how to use them.

Much as I imagined twenty years ago, the Internet today offers legal professionals seemingly unlimited sources of legal information—much of it free. But that abundance can be daunting. Think of *Internet Legal Research on a Budget* as a roadmap to the best of what is out there. It will guide you to what you need, and save you a buck along the way.

ROBERT J. AMBROGI, ATTORNEY AND TECHNOLOGY WRITER
WWW.LAWSITESBLOG.COM
@BOBAMBROGI

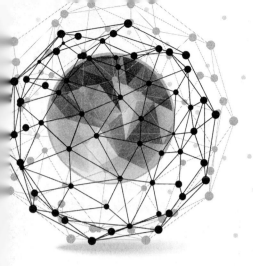

Introduction

WHY A BOOK ABOUT FREE ONLINE LEGAL RESEARCH?

According to the American Bar Association's 2013 Legal Technology Survey Report,[1] 96 percent of respondents report they conduct legal research online but that they are less satisfied with free resources than with fee-based resources. The 2012 Research Intelligence Group's "New Attorney Research Methods Survey"[2] found that new associates (five years or less) spend about 31 percent (14.5 hours per week) of their time conducting legal research. For those in practice less than two years, the percentage rises to 35 percent. The new associates (5 years or less) reported that they used fee-based online resources for eight of their 14.5 hours of legal research per week while spending four hours per week using free or low-cost online resources. Fee-based resources are used more often by large firm associates (74 percent frequently/always) than small firm associates (46 percent).

---

1   Legal Technology Survey Report, *Online Research*, Vol. 5 (ABA Legal Technology Resource Center 2013) (http://linkon.in/ltrcsurvey).

2   Steven A. Lastres, "Rebooting Legal Research in a Digital Age," available at http://www.llrx.com/files/rebootinglegalresearch.pdf. Mr. Lastres's article is based on results from the "New Attorney Research Methods Survey," a survey of 190 law firm associates independently conducted by The Research Intelligence Group (TRiG) during December 2012. Funding was provided by LexisNexis®. The survey may not be available to the public. The statistics we refer to in this preface are derived from Mr. Lastres's article. In the survey, 190 young attorneys (equally represented by large and small law firms across a variety of practice areas) were asked questions about their legal research methods. Nearly 40 percent of the respondents were 28 or younger, in practice for five or fewer years, and a quarter of the respondents were recent law school graduates from the class of 2011 or 2012.

With cost-conscious clients scrutinizing legal bills, lawyers cannot afford to depend on fee-based resources the way they used to, especially if there are reliable free resources available. This book[3] was written to help lawyers quickly find reliable free (or low-cost) resources online and to learn to use the resources effectively so they can become more satisfied using free resources. Our goal was to write a book that would save you time and money and help you avoid frustration. We wanted to share what we have learned about the best legal research sites we have "scoped out." We have tested and evaluated each site, described how to actually use the site (often step-by-step), and included numerous screen shots to better illustrate the steps.

WHAT IS LEGAL RESEARCH?

While we know that a lawyer's research involves both investigative/background research and "pure" legal research (cases, statutes, dockets, ordinances, etc.), this book focuses primarily on "pure" Internet legal research. For those who want to learn about free and low-cost investigative/background Internet research, please read books on that topic written by Carole Levitt and Mark Rosch.[4]

THE AUTHORS OF THIS BOOK ARE UNIQUELY QUALIFIED TO WRITE THIS BOOK

The authors of this book share a common background that uniquely qualifies them to write this book: We have both have had careers as lawyers as well as law librarians. Carole worked as a law librarian at corporate legal departments, law schools, and law firms in Chicago and Los Angeles, while Judy currently works as a law librarian at the University of Southern California (USC) Gould School of Law and previously at the University of San Diego Pardee Legal Research Center. We have also both taught Legal Research at law schools (Judy currently teaches at the USC Gould School of Law and Carole taught at Pepperdine University School of Law). In 1999, Carole founded Internet For Lawyers (IFL) to teach Internet research to lawyers and paralegals at CLE seminars throughout the United States. She is still running IFL today.

---

3 Some of the chapters of this book are an update and expansion of a few chapters from *The Cybersleuth's Guide to the Internet* (IFL Press 2013), and some chapters are unique to this book.

4 *The Cybersleuth's Guide to the Internet* (IFL Press 2013), *Find Info Like a Pro, Volume 1: Mining the Internet's Publicly Available Resources for Investigative Research* (ABA LPM 2010), and *Find Info Like a Pro, Volume 2: Mining the Internet's Public Records for Investigative Research* (ABA LPM 2011).

Because of this background, we understand how lawyers think when it comes to legal research, so we decided to put our heads together to write a current book on Internet legal research, discussing government, academic, and commercial (free and pay) websites as well as apps, blogs, Twitter feeds, and crowdsourced sites.

IS FREE ALWAYS BEST?

We know, as it is with most anything, that price is a major consideration when deciding between alternative research resources—and we all agree that all other things being equal, free is better. That said, we do make note of pay databases when they have more useful features than the free sites. Sometimes it makes sense to pay for data—especially if the pay databases have something the free ones are lacking (content or functionality), or when using the pay databases can simply save you time, and thus money.

IF YOU DIDN'T RECEIVE FORMAL ONLINE LEGAL RESEARCH TRAINING AT YOUR FIRM OR ENOUGH IN LAW SCHOOL...THIS BOOK IS FOR YOU

Fifty-six percent of the surveyed associates[5] indicated that their employer expected them to have strong legal research skills but did not provide any formal training. Only 29 percent of respondents said they received some formal training, and that percentage falls to a mere 12 percent for those in small firms. Nearly half surveyed (49 percent) feel that legal research should be a larger part of the law school curriculum. And, eight in ten feel that there was at least one area of legal research that should have been given more time. Statutory research, administrative law, and public records searching topped the list for specific areas that deserved more time or exposure.

We hope this book fills in some of the legal research training that the 190 surveyed young attorneys (and many other attorneys) felt was missing from their law firm and law school training and that it empowers you to become a more efficient and effective researcher.

---

5   Lastres, *supra* note 2.

HOW THIS BOOK IS ORGANIZED

This book is primarily organized by type of material. For example, there are chapters about websites for statutes, cases, dockets, and so on. One chapter is organized by practice area, from advertising law to trademark law. That chapter includes both websites and blogs. Finally we have a chapter about general legal research (such as where to find free law review articles, forms, court rules, etc.). That chapter includes websites and apps.

We only show you the best sites. We begin each chapter with the most useful or comprehensive site for a specific topic and then discuss a few alternative sites. We include tips about the most useful aspect of each site (content and functionality) and let you know if there are any hidden functions.

CONVENTIONS USED IN THIS BOOK

Throughout the book we will use boldfaced type to indicate exact text that appears on a web page (links, buttons, dropdown menus, etc.), and italics to indicate the exact text of search terms/keywords used in sample searches we conducted to evaluate the sites we discuss.

Website URLs are accurate and up to date as of March 2014.

Part I

GENERAL RESEARCH

Part I will focus on free and low-cost general legal research sites, blawgs (law blogs), and apps.

Chapter 1

WEBSITES FOR GENERAL LEGAL RESEARCH

When conducting legal research, lawyers are usually searching for primary law, such as court opinions, statutes, and regulations. But, sometimes it is easier and quicker to begin your research project using secondary law, such as articles, sample pleadings, and briefs, because these resources explain and analyze primary law and point you to the primary law relevant to your project. For that reason, we will begin this book discussing secondary law websites. We will also discuss websites that contain neither primary nor secondary law, but contain important pieces of the legal research process, such as court rules, jury verdicts, and expert witness directories.

ARTICLES

Journals and Magazines (General)

- Before using any pay sites, visit your public library's website to see if it provides library card holders with free remote access to pay databases that include articles from journals, magazines, and newspapers. See also information about free (and pay) articles via Google Scholar in Chapter 6.

- **IngentaConnect** (http://www.ingentaconnect.com) allows visitors to advance search (by keyword, author, publication, etc.) the full text of articles from over 12,000 professional and academic publications. The article abstract results can be viewed free of charge, but to read the full text of most articles, visitors must pay via credit card (prices vary, but tend to be quite expensive).

- In addition, sometimes you can find a free article by simply entering the title as a phrase into a general search engine's (e.g., Google or Yahoo!) search box.

Articles (Legal)

- **Washington & Lee Law School's Current Law Journal Content (CLJC)** site (http://linkon.in/b2SGVV) ceased being updated May 13, 2011, but the site is still useful to search for older law review/law journal articles. The site offers tables of contents from almost 1,600 journals back to the year 2000 for most U.S. law reviews and back to 2005 for other English language law journals. You can view the table of contents by one or more of these options: publication year, country (or all countries), or a specific review/ journal. You can also search for an article by author, title, journal name, or keywords, but you will only be searching the article's citation (not the full text) as listed in the table of contents. Links to the full text of articles may be provided, but not always from a free source, and sometimes you will only be linked to a catalog record of the review/journal, and not to the actual article. Wildcard searching and Boolean searching are available (for search tips, see http://linkon.in/a3xGvR).

- The **ABA Legal Technology Resource Center** (http://tinyurl.com/5talf2d) provides a Google-powered search engine to keyword search (for free) full-text articles from 400 online law reviews and law journals (mostly U.S., but some foreign and international). The database also includes some academic papers and publications such as Congressional Research Service reports. Coverage dates and online availability of the full text of articles varies from publication to publication. Some of the journals are online-only journals. In addition, if you scroll down the page, you will find a list of journal titles that are not part of this searchable database but can be searched/browsed individually at each journal's site (by clicking the title's link).

COURT RULES

Links to federal and state local court rules can be found at **LLRX** (LLRX.com):

- Federal local court rules: http://linkon.in/fedlocalcourtrules
- General federal court rules (e.g., Federal Rules of Civil Procedure) and state court rules can both be found at http://linkon.in/courtrules1

DOCKETS

For Docket information, see the section on Samples of Pleadings/Briefs/Oral Arguments in this chapter, as well as Chapter 15 for an in-depth discussion of docket websites.

EXPERT WITNESSES

See Jury Verdicts.

FORMS: COURT, AGENCY, AND TRANSACTIONAL

Numerous federal agency forms can also be found at **USA.gov** (http://www.usa.gov/Topics/Reference-Shelf/forms.shtml). The forms are listed alphabetically by agency name. On the left-hand side of the page, you will find links to tax forms (federal and state). Using the search box at USA.gov, you can also keyword search state, local, and federal forms (both agency and court).

For access to over 2,000 generic and state-specific business and personal forms, from quitclaim deeds to employment agreements to wills and name change forms, see **Publiclegalforms.com**, a product of the **Internet Legal Research Group** (ILRG) site (http://www.ilrg.com/forms). You can browse by topic or enter a keyword into the search box on the home page and then select a state from the drop-down menu. You will be able to view a free preview of the form, but it won't be usable because it has a watermark. If you decide the form is useful, you will need to pay to download their "Professional MS Word and PDF formatting" version (at $9.99 per form), which is editable and reusable.

The **'Lectric Law Library's Forms Room** (http://www.lectlaw.com/form.html) also offers free law practice, business, and general forms, but read their "Extreme Caution" warning below, which should probably be heeded for any free forms site.

"*Exercise Extreme Caution* when using many of our free forms—or any legal material. While they may provide general ideas on format & content, validity requirements *can and do vary greatly from state to state.* Many *MUST be Properly Modified* for your own location and circumstances. (Hint: If in doubt it's *usually* safer to include unneeded clauses than to leave out necessary ones. . . . but it's even safer to consult a competent source or use current, state-specific ones like ours mentioned below.)"

The "state-specific ones" noted above will link you to pay forms at **Rocket Lawyer** (http://www.rocketlawyer.com) or **U.S. Legal Forms** (http://www.uslegalforms. com). Another popular pay form site is **LegalZoom** (http://www.legalzoom.com).

For court and transactional forms (free and pay), visit the **LexisNexis Communities Portal** (http://linkon.in/yORjKu) to access 6,000 free Matthew Bender forms that can be browsed by topic or by jurisdiction. The forms can also be keyword searched if you scroll down the page. To use the interactive HotDocs software to fill in the forms, you will need to set up a free account. (Note that HotDocs only works with Internet Explorer.) Once filled in, forms can be saved in either Word or WordPerfect. Click on the **Pay Forms** link if you don't find the necessary form in the free section. The Pay Forms require you to purchase a subscription to an interactive HotDocs forms package.

LawInfo (http://legalforms.lawinfo.com/) provides access to about 100 free forms in categories like Business & Corporation; Wills & Estate Planning; Debt & Finance; Trademarks, Patents & Copyrights; Family Law; Real Estate & Landlord Tenant; as well as a few general forms. After you select a form and click **Get Started**, you will be asked to register with your e-mail address.

We used to use **LLRX** for links to federal, state, and local court forms (http://www.llrx.com/courtrules), but many of the links no longer work, so it's best to visit the specific official federal, state, or local court web site and click on their forms link or visit **LexisNexis Communities Portal** noted earlier and browse by jurisdiction.

To access federal tax forms and tax publications (back to 1864), visit the **IRS** website (http://www.irs.gov/formspubs/index.html) and choose **Current Forms & Pubs**, or **Prior Year Forms & Pubs**, or **Accessible Forms & Pubs** for those using assistive technology such as screen reading software, refreshable Braille displays, and voice recognition software. After selecting one of these three options, you can search by one keyword in the **Title** (such as *airline*), a **Product Number** (such as 15-A), or the **Revision Date** (enter a specific date or a year). You can re-sort the results by clicking on the column headings (**Product Number, Title, Revision Date**, or **Posted Date**). There is an **Advanced Search** link located to the right of the search box in the upper right-hand corner of the home page where you can enter one or more keywords or phrases into various search boxes. You can also limit the search to **Forms, Instructions,** or **Publications** (among other choices) or limit results to a specific File Format (e.g., PDF). Many forms can be filled in online and saved to your hard drive. For those forms that are not fillable, you can fill them in and save them to your hard drive if you own the full professional version of Adobe Acrobat, which allows you to "typewriter enable" most any document.

For links to states that have tax forms online for free, see the **Federation of Tax Administrators'** site (http://linkon.in/xnWbiS) and click on a state (or Puerto Rico) from the map of the United States.

JURY INSTRUCTIONS

In 2007, Jan Bissett and Margi Heinen published an article, *Reference from Coast to Coast: Jury Instructions Update*, with links to publicly available electronic versions of state jury instructions (http://www.llrx.com/columns/reference53.htm). Although it hasn't been updated, the links will often take you to current state jury instruction web pages.

JURY VERDICTS AND EXPERT WITNESSES

Researching verdicts and settlements of cases similar to your case might help you assess a case's worth and also find experts.

MoreLaw.com (http://www.morelaw.com/verdicts) provides a free jury verdicts and settlements database. To locate experts who have previously testified in cases similar to one that you are handling, search by keywords describing your case and limit the search to the **expert** field. To research verdicts/settlements, search by keywords describing your case and limit the search to the **case description** or **verdict** field. You can further limit any of your searches by state.

Law.com has a pay database of jury verdicts at **VerdictSearch.com** (http://www. verdictsearch.com). Annual subscription prices are based on law firm size. Day passes are available to any practitioner for $349 to view up to 75 cases.

JuryVerdicts.com (http://www.juryverdicts.com) is maintained by The National Association of State Jury Verdict Publishers (NASJVP).

While the site does not offer a searchable database of verdicts, it links to the sites of its members that publish jury verdict summaries throughout the United States. You must follow the links to the publisher(s) that cover the jurisdiction(s) in which you're searching. Fees to access summaries of the cases, jury verdicts, or awards in which the experts testified vary from publisher to publisher. Access to the site's expert witness directory (culled from jury verdicts) is free. However, it is only browseable by the last names of experts and includes an area of expertise with a link to the jury verdict publisher so you can contact them to purchase a copy.

Jurispro.com (http://www.jurispro.com/) allows you to search for an expert witness by name or by expertise to get background information about the expert. Most experts' profiles include the expert's photo, C.V., list of published articles, references, and a link to their website. Some have even placed an audio or video file on their profiles so you can listen to their voice or watch them in action to decide if you want to contact them.

SAMPLES OF PLEADINGS/BRIEFS/ORAL ARGUMENTS

Instead of drafting pleadings and writing briefs from scratch, consider searching for samples to speed these tasks along. Samples can also serve as research guides to the leading cases and statutes on the topic. Some courts, government agencies, professional associations, and law firms offer access to case documents (some free and some for a fee) which, in turn, you can use as samples.

Check the website of your professional association to see if it posts any sample pleadings or has a brief bank. For example, **The American Association for Justice** (http://linkon.in/aajdocs) provides its members with access to its **AAJ Exchange and Litigation Packets** service.

PACER's federal court docket site includes complaints, answers, and sometimes briefs (each document is capped at a low cost of $3) from federal district, bankruptcy, and appellate court cases, and can be searched topically using the NOS code or by party name if you know of a case similar to your case.

Various state and local courts also provide access to these case documents. For instance, for a fee, the Los Angeles Superior Court offers access to case documents at its **LA Court Online** site (https://www.lasuperiorcourt.org/onlineservices/ LAECourtOnlineIndex.htm).

The **ABA Preview of U.S. Supreme Court Cases** provides the current U.S. Supreme Court term's merit and amicus briefs for free (http://www.americanbar. org/publications/preview_home/alphabetical.html) while **FindLaw** posts select merit and amicus briefs from 1999–2007 (http://supreme.lp.findlaw.com/ supreme_court/briefs/index.html). **Oyez** (http://www.oyez.org/cases/) provides free access to many of the Supreme Court's oral arguments back to 1955, which can be accessed by legal issue or alphabetically by plaintiff (you must choose a year first).

Stanford Law School's **Securities Class Action Clearinghouse** database (http:// securities.stanford.edu/index.html) contains copies of more than 42,800 complaints, briefs, filings, and other litigation-related materials filed in federal class action securities fraud lawsuits since 1995. You can search by litigant's name, type of litigation (e.g., *any*, *mutual fund*, etc.), ticker symbol, and a host of other options.

Chapter 2

WEBSITES BY PRACTICE AREA

This chapter will focus on traditional Internet resources that are practice area-specific. A practice area-specific legal site focuses on one area of law (such as advertising law) and either provides content at its site or links to other sites that focus on that practice area. Because there are so many areas of practice, we will discuss only a few practice areas.

ADVERTISING LAW

The law firm of Reed Smith originally created an advertising and marketing law website, which was updated bi-weekly, but it has now morphed into a blog, **Adlaw By Request** (http://www.adlawbyrequest.com), which is updated more frequently. From the left-hand column labeled **Topic**, select a topic (such as **Children's Advertising, In the Courts, Cloud Computing, Legislation, Regulatory**, etc.), to focus on specific types of advertising law. The blog's keyword search engine is also located in the left-hand column. The firm also has other topical blogs.

The law firm of Arnold & Porter sponsors a consumer protection and advertising law blog, **Seller Beware** (http://www.consumeradvertisinglawblog.com). You can read the most recent posts or read all posts pertaining to one specific category by clicking on one of the categories listed on the right-hand side of the blog's home page. Categories range from **Children**, the **FTC**, and **Green claims** to **Sweepstakes/**

Promotions, **Telemarketing**, and more. The blog also provides a search engine to search posts by keyword.

For other advertising law blogs, see the list at **Justia's BlawgSearch** (http://blawgsearch.justia.com/blogs/categories/advertising-law).

BANKRUPTCY LAW

The **American Bankruptcy Institute** (ABI), which was founded in 1982 to provide Congress and the public with unbiased analysis of bankruptcy issues, has a site at http://www.abiworld.org for its members. Useful information (some of which is restricted to members, such as the membership directory) can be found by clicking on the **Online Resources** link located at the top of the site's home page. The **Consumer Bankruptcy Center** link (also located at the top of the site's home page) offers a section for nonmembers (click the **For Consumers** tab) and another section for members (click the **Consumer Bankruptcy Professionals** tab). The site (http://law.abi.org/) allows members and nonmembers to keyword search the Bankruptcy Rules and Code or browse them by Code or Rule number, but you need to be a member to view Bankruptcy case summaries. ABI offers a 30-day trial.

Naturally, the information on the ABI site is U.S.-centric, so for links to international and foreign bankruptcy law sites, in addition to U.S. sites, see **HG.org** at http://www.hg.org/bankrpt.html.

For information about Bankruptcy Courts and opinions, see Chapters 4 and 5 on Free Case Law and for information about Bankruptcy dockets, see Chapter 15 on Dockets.

For other Bankruptcy law blogs, see the list at **Justia's BlawgSearch** (http://blawgsearch.justia.com/blogs/categories/bankruptcy).

CLASS ACTION LAWSUITS

Timothy E. Eble, a contributing author to a leading treatise on class actions (*Newberg on Class Actions*), is the site owner of **Class Action Litigation Information** (http://www.classactionlitigation.com). The site contains the full text of the *Federal Class Action Practice Manual—Internet Edition* (1999), by Timothy E. Eble (http://linkon.in/IDt3gA) and links to class action articles, legislation, and more.

Despite focusing mostly on their own firm's class action cases, the sites of two big players in this arena, **Robbins Geller Rudman & Dowd LLP** (http://www.rgrd-law.com/) and **Milberg** (http://www.milberg.com), each provide some useful research information about their cases. At the Robbins' site, you can click on **Cases** to get details about settled and pending cases, including documents such as complaints and settlement agreements. (See the section on Securities Law on page 22 for a Securities class action site.)

For other class action blogs, see the list at **Justia's BlawgSearch** (http://blawg-search.justia.com/blogs/categories/class-action).

COPYRIGHT LAW

See Intellectual Property.

CORPORATE/BUSINESS LAW

Since many corporations are incorporated in Delaware, attorneys researching corporate law may find it useful to visit the **Delaware State Court** site (http://courts.delaware.gov). As the site explains, "The Delaware Court of Chancery is widely recognized as the nation's preeminent forum for the determination of disputes involving the internal affairs of the thousands upon thousands of Delaware corporations and other business entities through which a vast amount of the world's commercial affairs is conducted. Its unique competence in and exposure to issues of business law are unmatched." On the right-hand side of the **Court of Chancery** home page (http://courts.delaware.gov/Chancery/index.stm), there are tabs for **Administrative Directives and Standing Orders**, the **Court Calendar**, **Guidelines for Practitioners**, and **Opinions**, among other items.

The **Opinions** database is keyword searchable with coverage back to 2000. To browse or keyword search the opinions, click the **Opinions** and choose a year. To find the search box, scroll all the way over to the right. There are no instructions on how to search, and our test searches were inconclusive. For example, sometimes a phrase search (enclosing two words in parentheses) worked and sometimes it didn't. Be sure to click **Clear** when you want to enter a new keyword/phrase into the search box. Simply typing over the prior keywords with your new keyword doesn't work. To browse, select any of the column headings (e.g., **Date, Parties/Caption, Number**, etc.).

For a better keyword search experience, use other free or member-benefit case law databases such as Google Scholar, Casemaker, or Fastcase, which are discussed in Chapters 6, 8, and 9, respectively.

From the court's home page (http://courts.delaware.gov/Chancery/), you can link to a private vendor, **File and ServeXpress**, which handles e-filing and a docket and pleadings repository for the court. There is a fee to use this service.

The M&A Law Prof blog (http://lawprofessors.typepad.com/mergers/#) is written by two law professors and a practicing attorney. You can read their posts, which focus on mergers and acquisitions, or search by keyword.

For blogs about various areas of business/corporate law, see the list at **Justia's BlawgSearch** (http://blawgsearch.justia.com/blogs/categories/business-law). Blog titles range from the **Delaware Corporate and Commercial Litigation Blog** to **Indian Corporate Law.**

CRIMINAL LAW

The **Kent State University College of Arts and Sciences Department of Sociology's** site (http://linkon.in/HDqGO4) provides links to federal and international criminal justice agencies, as well as informational links to corrections, professional associations, employment sites, and Ohio state and local criminal justice links.

The **Association of Federal Defense Attorneys (AFDA)** is a members-only Internet group which offers online education and other resources for the federal defense bar and professionals who provide services to defense counsel (http://www.afda.org).

The **National Association of Criminal Defense Lawyers'** (NACDL) site (http://www.criminaljustice.org) has information about criminal law in general, but mostly from the defense point of view. Some information is available free to nonmembers (e.g., articles from the association's magazine, *The Champion*) while other information is available only to members, such as the **Brief & Motion Bank**.

For prosecutors and researchers interested in the prosecutorial point of view, see the **National District Attorneys Association's (NDAA)** site (http://www.ndaa.org). While most of the site is for members only, there are some free publications listed at http://www.ndaa.org/publications.html. For example, you can read current and past issues of the **Child Sexual Exploitation UPDATE** (http://www.

ndaa.org/ncpca_cse_archive.html) or download a PDF of the book, *Civil Gang Injunctions.*

For blogs about various areas of criminal law, see the list at **Justia's BlawgSearch** (http://blawgsearch.justia.com/blogs/categories/criminal-law). The areas range from mortgage fraud to sex offenders to DUI.

EMPLOYMENT AND LABOR LAW

The **Employment Law Information Network** (**ELIN**) website (http://www. elinfonet.com) includes articles, sample personnel policies and forms, summaries of federal and state employment cases, and an attorney directory. The site is aimed at management-side employment lawyers, in-house employment lawyers, and human resource staff. The content is supplied by affiliates of ELIN, which include various law firms, one corporate affiliate, the University of Pennsylvania's Wharton School of Business, and Cornell University, School of Industrial & Labor Relations (http:// www.elinfonet.com/employment-law/membership).

HG's **Employment** page (http://www.hg.org/employ.html) links to articles, organizations, lawyers, websites, laws, and government agencies (e.g., the U.S. Department of Labor and the labor departments in all fifty states and the District of Columbia) dealing with employment/labor law for both the employer and the employee. In addition, HG includes international and foreign labor law links.

For links to hundreds of U.S. and foreign labor unions' sites, see the Yahoo! **Labor Union** page (http://linkon.in/cTWYAf).

For blogs about various areas of employment/labor law, see the list at **Justia's BlawgSearch** (http://blawgsearch.justia.com/blogs/categories/employment-law). The blog titles range from **New York Public Personnel Law** to **Connecticut Employment Law Blog**.

FAMILY LAW

DivorceNet (http://www.divorcenet.com), a site created by Nolo (publisher of do-it-yourself legal guides), includes a family law blog, articles, and referrals to attorneys and experts. The site also provides some state-by-state family law links, such as **Best Interests of the Child State-by-State** (http://www.divorcenet.com/

topics/divorce-and-children) and **Divorce and Property Laws by State** (http://www.divorcenet.com/topics/divorce-who-gets-what).

Also useful is **Cornell's Divorce Law Overview** (http://topics.law.cornell.edu/wex/divorce), with links (click the **Resources** tab) to uniform laws and recent federal cases about divorce and related family law issues. For links to all fifty states' divorce laws, visit http://www.law.cornell.edu/wex/table_family.

Illinoisdivorce.com (http://illinoisdivorce.com) has over 100 articles about Illinois divorce available for free on its site (http://illinoisdivorce.com/family_law_articles/). This site is an example of e-lawyering. Everything is handled online. For $500 they will handle an uncontested divorce (from filing the papers to representing clients in court), and for $185 they will fill out paper work and coach clients to file their own papers and represent themselves.

FOREIGN AND INTERNATIONAL LAW

See Chapter 14.

INSURANCE LAW

Although **Insure.com** is a commercial site that provides instant quotes from insurers and insurance brokerage, it also provides useful articles about various lines of insurance at http://www.insure.com/ (click on the **Life, Health, Car, Home**, and **Other Insurance** tabs) and links to every state insurance department (http://www.insure.com/articles/statesinsurance).

For blogs about various areas of insurance law, see the list at **Justia's BlawgSearch** (http://blawgsearch.justia.com/blogs/categories/insurance-law). The blog topics range from reinsurance to coverage and many also focus on the insurance law of a specific state.

INTELLECTUAL PROPERTY—COPYRIGHT, PATENTS AND TRADEMARKS

The **U.S. Copyright Office** (http://www.copyright.gov), a department of the Library of Congress, provides online access to forms, regulations, and laws relating to copyright; it also posts a primer about copyright.

In addition, there is a user-friendly searchable database of over 20 million copyright records dating back to 1978 (http://cocatalog.loc.gov/). The catalog includes registrations and pre-registrations for books, music, films, sound recordings, maps, software, photographs, art, multimedia, periodicals, magazines, journals, newspapers, and so on. Also included are records for assignments, transfers, and miscellaneous documents relating to copyright ownership. To search the database, click the **Search the Catalog** link. This link leads to the **Basic Search** page, where you can search by **Title, Name, Keyword, Registration Number, Document Number**, or **Command Keyword** (Boolean, phrase, and wildcard searching). Sample searches are located on the search page and should be referred to before beginning a search. For more detailed searching, click the **Other Search Options** link.

To access 1870–1977 records, a researcher would need to use the copyright card catalog at the **Copyright Office** in Washington, D.C., or fill out a form (http://www.copyright.gov/forms/search_estimate.html) to request a search for $165 per hour.

Stanford University Libraries are the name sponsors of the **Copyright & Fair Use** site (http://fairuse.stanford.edu), but the site is supported pro bono by Justia. com. Tabs in the site's **What's New** section (scroll down the page to see it) link to copyright-related **Opinions, Dockets, Legislation, Regulation, News, Copyright Blogs**, and **Our Blog** (the university's own **Fairly Used** blog at http://fairuse.stanford.edu/blog/).

For other Copyright law blogs, see the list at Justia's **BlawgSearch** (http://blawgsearch.justia.com/blogs/categories/copyright).

Visit the **U.S. Patent and Trademark Office** (USPTO) site (http://www.uspto.gov) to search U.S. (and some other countries) patent and trademark text and image databases. (The USPTO does not handle copyrights. See the section on Copyrights discussed earlier in this chapter.)

The USPTO offers a database of patents back to 1976 at http://www.uspto.gov/patents/process/search/index.jsp. The **Quick Search** allows you to search full-text, using keywords with Boolean connectors and fields. You can also conduct a **Number Search** and an **Advanced Search**. The Advanced Search allows users to search with keywords and phrases and to include fields (e.g., inventor's name). You can select to search 1976 to the present or 1790 to the present.

However, the patents from 1790–1975 are searchable only by Issue Date, Patent Number, and Current U.S. Classification. The database also includes full-page images (http://patft.uspto.gov/netahtml/PTO/patimg.htm) that can be searched only by number.

Patent applications are searchable back to March 2001 using the same **Quick Search, Number Search**, and **Advanced Search** as described above for searching patents (http://www.uspto.gov/patents/process/search/index.jsp).

In addition to U.S. patents, the USPTO now includes the **Global Patent Search Network** (GPSN) to search the full text of Chinese published applications, granted patents, and utility models from1985 to 2012 (http://gpsn.uspto.gov/). It includes full text Chinese patents, English machine translations, and full document images. This collection will eventually include other countries' patents. The USPTO site also links to international and other countries' IP offices (http://www.uspto.gov/faq/other.jsp).

Google's Patents Search (http://www.google.com/patents) uses Google's familiar search interface to provide access to over 7 million patents dating back to 1790. Google Patents' **Advanced Search** page (http://www.google.com/advanced_patent_search) allows for keyword and phrase searches similar to those on the Google Advanced Search page. Additionally, you can search for information in specific areas of the patent document, such as Patent number, Title, Inventor, Assignee, and more.

Google and the USPTO have entered into an agreement to make the following USPTO products available as bulk downloads to the public at no charge: Patent data (grants, published applications, assignments, classification information, and maintenance fee events) and Trademark data (registrations, applications, assignments, and Trademark Trial and Appeal Board proceedings) at http://www.google.com/googlebooks/uspto.html.

Patents and patent articles can also be retrieved via **Google Scholar** (http://scholar.google.com) searches.

For trademark research, use TESS, the **Trademark Electronic Search System** (http://www.uspto.gov/trademarks/index.jsp), to search over 4 million pending, registered, and dead federal trademarks at the USPTO site. Click the Trademark Search tab on the left-hand side of the home page. There are three search options: (1) the **Basic Word Mark Search (New User)** allows you to search word marks; (2) Word and/or Design Mark Search (Structured) allows you to search word and/or design marks (but you must first look up relevant Design Codes in the **Design Search Code Manual** at http://tess2.uspto.gov/tmdb/dscm/index.htm; and (3)

Word and/or Design Mark Search (Free Form) allows you to search word and/or design searches with Boolean operators and multiple search fields.

For patent and other IP resources, see the **American Intellectual Property Law Association**'s (AIPLA) website (http://www.aipla.org). The AIPLA is an association of 17,000 attorneys who deal with national and international intellectual property issues. Portions of its site are member-only. Use the search box on the right side of the home page to search the site. Results could include books, abstracts of articles (only members can view the full text of the articles), and AIPLA's advocacy statements, briefs, and testimony submitted to Congress, executive agencies, federal courts, and international organizations and governments (which anyone can view full-text). You can also browse the advocacy statements, etc. by selecting the IP **Policy & Advocacy** tab from the home page.

For blogs about various areas of IP, see the list at **Justia's BlawgSearch** (http://blawgsearch.justia.com/blogs/categories/intellectual-property-law). The blog titles range from **Likelihood of Confusion to IP Dragon** (covering IP law in China, Hong Kong, etc.)

LEGAL ETHICS AND PROFESSIONALISM

The **ABA Center for Professional Responsibility** (C.P.R.) site (http://www.abanet.org/cpr) describes itself as "[p]roviding national leadership in developing and interpreting standards and scholarly resources in legal and judicial ethics, professional regulation, professionalism and client protection." CPR posts the Model Rules (with comments), its Table of Contents, and its subject index for free (http://linkon.in/cshkzE).

The Model Rules of Professional Conduct are now available for Apple iOS devices (iPad, iPhone, and iPod) for $24.99 (https://itunes.apple.com/us/app/rulebook/id454619081?mt=8).

The C.P.R. site also links to **State Ethics Rules** and an **Alphabetical List of States Adopting Model Rules** among other state ethics related topics (http://linkon.in/stateethicslinks).

Anyone can read summaries of recent Formal Opinions for free (http://linkon.in/d6kqER). ABA members can access opinions for free for one year from the opinion's date of release while C.P.R. members have full-text access to all opinions from all years (back to 1984). The opinions are organized by date of issue and by subject. Archived opinions can be purchased online for $20.00 each.

ETHICSearch is another service offered on the ABA site to any ABA member; it provides free initial consultations to ethics inquiries (http://linkon.in/ethics-search). From the left-hand column of this page you can also link to the **Ethics Tip of the Month** and ethics articles.

Use this URL for links to all of the above-mentioned ABA resources from one place: http://linkon.in/aJvYt8 and for links to Professionalism topics, such as state and local bar associations' Professionalism Codes.

The **LegalEthics.com** blog (http://www.legalethics.com), updated by Professor David Hricik of Mercer University School of Law and Peter Krakaur, used to be a general ethics blog but now is dedicated to the "Ethics of technology use by legal professionals." However, the site has maintained its links to each state's ethics opinions and model rules if they are available online (select a state from the column on the right side of the home page). The site includes brief annotations about new technology-ethics articles, ethics opinions, and court cases (often with links to the full text). The site can be keyword searched or browsed by topic (listed on the right side of the home page). Topics include **Advertising, Confidentiality, Domain Names, Social Networking**, and more. Archived material is available back to 1995. There are useful links to other ethics resources such as the **Directory of Lawyer Disciplinary Agencies**, the **Judicial Ethics Forum**, and **NOBC** (National Organization of Bar Counsel).

MEDICAL MALPRACTICE AND PERSONAL INJURY LAW

The **American Medical Association** (AMA) site (http://www.ama-assn.org) is a good starting point to find information about nearly every one of the 814,000 licensed physicians in the United States. Unfortunately, it takes about six click-throughs to actually reach the search page where we can search the information we want. First, select the **Patients** link on the top-right side of the site's home page. Second, select the **DoctorFinder** link located on the right side of the page. Third, enter the words or numbers you see in the Captcha image (Captcha is used to determine whether the user is a human or just automated software). Fourth, scroll down and click on the image labeled **For Patients**. Fifth, click on the **DoctorFinder** link. Sixth, read the disclaimer and click **Accept**. You can search by **Last Name** or by **Specialty** (a ZIP code or State is required for both searches). Adding a First Name or a City is optional. Basic background and contact information is provided.

You won't find any discipline information at the AMA database, but you might find some if you visit the **Association of State Medical Board Executive Directors DocFinder** site (http://www.docboard.org/docfinder.html). This site simultaneously searches nineteen states' physician license databases and two osteopathic license databases. Discipline information is sometimes included. There are also links to the other states' licensing boards, and there you might find discipline information.

To conduct medical-related research, we used to search several National Library of Medicine (NLM) databases simultaneously by using **NLM's Gateway** site (http://gateway.nlm.nih.gov/gw/Cmd). However, in December 2011, that changed because, as the NLM website explains, "Although NLM has invested in and supported the NLM Gateway for eleven years, based on current budget limitations and the results of evaluations of the use of NLM Gateway, the Library has decided to discontinue this service and transition to a new pilot project site ... from the Lister Hill National Center for Biomedical Communications (LHNCBC)." The individual databases once housed at NLM are listed (with links) on the **NLM Databases & Electronic Resources** page (http://linkon.in/wYULqK). Probably the most useful individual NLM database to lawyers who are researching medical issues is **PubMed** (http://www.ncbi.nlm.nih.gov), which provides over 23 million citations from MEDLINE, life science journals, and online books. Some of the citations link to full-text content from PubMed Central or publishers' websites, and they are free. A search box at the top of the home page can be used to keyword search for medical articles.

For blogs about various areas of Medical Malpractice and Personal Injury Law, see the list at **Justia's BlawgSearch** (http://blawgsearch.justia.com/blogs/categories/medical-malpractice). The blog titles can range from very narrow topics such as **Military Medical Malpractice Legal Network Blog** and **Podiatry Malpractice Blog** to the more general, like **Nursing Law Blog**.

PATENT LAW

See Intellectual Property.

REAL ESTATE AND PROPERTY LAW

See **Cornell LII's Property – State Statutes** page (http://www.law.cornell.edu/wex/table_property) for links to each state's real property statutes.

For "quick and dirty" price estimates of over 110 million U.S. homes, including homes for sale, homes for rent, and homes not currently on the market, see **Zillow.com** (http://www.zillow.com).

For blogs about various areas of Real Estate and Property Law, see the list at **Justia's BlawgSearch** (http://blawgsearch.justia.com/blogs/categories/real-estate-and-property-law). The blog titles vary from **inversecondemnation.com** to **Florida Foreclosure Defense Lawyers Blog** to **Massachusetts Land Use Monitor**.

SECURITIES LAW

The **U.S. Securities and Exchange Commission's (SEC)** site (http://www.sec.gov) has reams of SEC documents online that can be accessed either by entering keywords/phrases into the SEC documents search box on the upper right-hand side of the home page or by selecting one of the tabs listed on the top of the home page (**Divisions, Enforcement, Regulations, Education, Filings, News**). Each tab offers a drop-down menu with more selections. For instance, from the **Enforcement** tab's drop-down menu you can select **Litigation Releases, Administrative Proceedings**, and so on.

From the **Filings** tab's drop-down menu, you can access free "real time" SEC company filings using the **EDGAR** database. Originally, EDGAR was not full-text searchable, but since 2006, EDGAR has offered full-text searching (http://searchwww.sec.gov/EDGARFSClient/jsp/EDGAR_MainAccess.jsp). Unfortunately, you can only full-text search the most recent four years of filings. If you click the **Advanced Search Page** link you will be allowed to narrow down your keyword search by Company Name, Central Index Key (CIK) (which is the unique identifying number the SEC assigns to each company), or Standard Industrial Classification (SIC) number, the U.S. government's numerical classification system that describes a company's line of business. For earlier years' filings, you can search by Company or fund name at http://www.sec.gov/edgar/searchedgar/companysearch.html and also by ticker symbol, CIK, file number, state, country, or SIC number (if you click the **More Options** link).

SEC Info (http://www.secinfo.com) offers free, full-text searching of U.S. Securities and Exchange Commission filings. The following search options are available: **Name, Industry, Business, SIC Code, Area Code, Topic, CIK, Accession Number, File Number, Date**, and **ZIP Code**. Additionally, although not listed as one of the available criteria next to the Search box, you can also search by NAICS (North American Industrial Classification System numbers—the government's newer numerical classification system that describes a company's business, adopted to replace the SIC Codes). While you can search the site (and receive a list of results) without registering, free registration is required to view full-text filings and to receive new filing e-mail notifications.

For those who need to keyword search filings from earlier years, you will need to subscribe to a pay database such as **Morningstar Document Research** at http://www.10kwizard.com (this site was formerly known as 10kWizard). It offers real-time, full-text searching of current U.S. Securities and Exchange Commission EDGAR filings, archival EDGAR filings back to 1994, and pre-EDGAR filings back to 1966. The following search options are provided: Company Name, Industry, Keywords, Phrases, CIK, SIC, Type of Form, and Date Restrictors. Automated company alerts are also available. When launched, the site offered free access to these searches and was one of the first sites to do so. Access is available through three different subscription packages (pricing used to range from $419 to $1,339 per year but is no longer shown on the site). There is a free seven-day trial.

To obtain dockets for over 3,700 class action securities fraud matters filed since 1995, with the full text of nearly 43,000 complaints, briefs, and orders, see **Stanford Law School Securities Class Action Clearinghouse** (SCAC), a site created in cooperation with **Cornerstone Research** (http://securities.stanford.edu). The SCAC also contains opinions, articles, settlement news, reports, and charts about securities litigation.

The SCAC offers the following ways to search or browse its collection:

- Keyword-search the entire collection by using the search box on the top right-hand side of the homepage.
- Click the grey **Menu** button on the top left-hand page of the homepage and then click the **Filings Database** button to:
  - Browse filings in reverse chronological order or
  - Type a filing name or company into the search box on the right-hand side or

- View charts, statistics, and lists relating to **Heat Maps & Related Filings, Top Ten, Key Stats, Filings by Year**, or **Filings by Circuit** by clicking any one of their buttons
- Click the grey **Menu** button again, then click the **Resources** button, and then click the **News & Blogs Excerpts, Academic Articles, Related Sites, or Conferences & Sem**inar buttons to browse these materials or use the search box to keyword-search **News & Blogs Excerpts.**
- Click the grey **Menu** button again and then click the **Litigation Activity Indices** (e.g., **The Median Lag Time index** shows the number of days between the end of class periods and the filing dates from 1997-2013).
- Click the grey **Menu** button again and then click **Clearinghouse Resources** to read research reports about filings and settlements.

Check out your broker's background at the **Financial Industry Regulatory Authority (FINRA)** site's free **BrokerCheck** database (http://brokercheck.finra. org). Note: FINRA was formerly known as the National Association of Securities Dealers (NASD). You will be able to find BrokerCheck Reports for brokers currently registered with FINRA, registered with FINRA within the past 10 years, or whose registration terminated over 10 years ago. Report summaries provide overviews of brokers, their credentials, listings of current registrations or licenses, industry exams passed, and registration and employment history.

FINRA also provides two other databases: **FINRA Disciplinary Actions Online** (http://disciplinaryactions.finra.org/) and **FINRA Arbitration Awards Online** (http://finraawardsonline.finra.org/).

For blogs about various areas of Securities Law, see the list at **Justia's Blawg-Search** (http://blawgsearch.justia.com/blogs/categories/securities-law). The blog titles range from **The Race to the Bottom** (includes postings from professionals, law faculty, and law students about corporate and securities law) to **Stockbroker Fraud Blog** to **Hedge Fund Law Blog.**

TAX LAW

The **IRS** site (http://www.irs.gov) provides tax forms and publications online for free. The U.S. Tax Court's **TC and Memorandum Decisions** (September 25, 1995–present) and its **Summary Decisions** (2001–present) are available online in a searchable database at the **U.S. Tax Court** site (http://www.ustaxcourt.gov/

UstcInOp/asp/HistoricOptions.asp). Searches can be done by one or more of the following criteria: **Text Search** (keywords), **Date Search, Case Name Keyword, Judge,** and **Opinion Type** (choose **All Types, TC, Memorandum,** or **Summary**). Dockets are also online for cases filed on or after May 1, 1986, and can be searched by **Docket Number, Individual Party Name** (a state and year can be entered to narrow the search), or **Corporate Name Keyword** (http://www.ustaxcourt.gov/docket.htm). Some case documents, such as a stipulated agreement, may also be online.

For blogs about various areas of Tax Law, see the list at **Justia's BlawgSearch** (http://blawgsearch.justia.com/blogs/categories/tax-law). The blog titles include **Taxable Talk, Texas State & Local Tax Law Blog,** and **Tax Trials.**

TRADEMARK LAW

See Intellectual Property.

Chapter 3

APPS FOR GENERAL LEGAL RESEARCH

App is short for *software application*. Apps are designed to run on smartphones, tablet computers, and other mobile devices, not desktops. They are usually obtained from the Apple App Store (for iOS mobile devices—iPads, iPhones, and sometimes iPod Touch), Google Play (for Android mobile devices—phones and tablets), or the Windows Phone Store. Sometimes there are also Apps for Blackberry devices. For each App listed below, we will indicate if it is currently available for iOS or Android devices. It's always a good idea to go online and check to see if any of the iOS Apps we mention are now available for the Android and vice versa.

To search for and download Apps, locate the "App Store" icon on your device. You usually have to know the exact name of the App, so they are not that easy to find. To help you find useful Apps, we have listed a sampling in this chapter by topic or practice area and have also listed sites and books where you can find more.

- UCLA Law Library's free **Mobile Applications for Law Students and Lawyers**: This is an alphabetical by title annotated list of law apps (http://linkon. in/uclalawapps). You can scan the list to find useful Apps or better yet, keyword search the list. For example, to find court rule Apps, use your Find function (**Control F** for PCs or **Command F** for Apple devices) and enter keywords into the Find search box. Many of the Apps in this chapter were first found by browsing the UCLA list.

- For a $50 subscription (for one year of access), see the **Mobile Apps for Law** site (http://www.informedlibrarian.com/MobileAppsforLaw/index.cfm).
- You can also find legal apps by reading Tom Mighell's book, *iPad Apps in One Hour for Lawyers* (ABA, 2012) (http://linkon.in/ipadappslaw) or Daniel J. Siegel's book, *Android Apps in One Hour for Lawyers* (ABA, 2013) (http://linkon.in/androidappdan). Both are also available as an e-book at http://linkon.in/ipadappslawebook   and   http://linkon.in/androidappebook, respectively.

COURT RULES

- **Litigator** (iOS): mobile access (search by keyword or rule number) to the Federal Rules of Appellate, Civil, and Criminal Procedure; the Federal Rules of Evidence; the Supreme Court Rules of Procedure; Title 18; Title 28; and Local Rules for federal courts for $14.99.
- **Rulebook** (iOS): mobile access to federal and state court rules using full-text searching. You can highlight text, add notes, copy, print, and/or bookmark text. The app and the Federal Rules of Evidence are free, but it will cost anywhere from $1.99 to $4.99 to purchase other rules.
- **dLaw** (Android): free federal court rules that allow users to search, bookmark, copy, share, and annotate text. Other apps are available for purchase (state codes, U.S. Code, U.S. Supreme Court cases, Code of Federal Regulations, Manual of Patent Examining Procedure (MPEP) and the Uniform Commercial Code.
- **LawStack** (iOS): claims to be a "legal library in your pocket." The free app includes the U.S. Constitution and various Federal Rules. For $1.99 you can also purchase California, New York, and Texas Civil Codes.

DOCKETS

- **LexisNexis CourtLink** (iOS): a "free" app to those already subscribing to CourtLink; it can be used to set up alerts to follow specific cases or find recently filed cases in a specific practice area or involving certain parties.

LAW DICTIONARIES

- **Black's Law Dictionary** (iOS and Android): $54.99.
- **Nolo's Plain English Law Dictionary** (iOS and Android): The iOS App is free, but Nolo's Droid version is $16.19.

CASE LAW

- **PushLegal** (iOS, Android, and Blackberry): search annotated case law (linking to Google Scholar), statutes (California, Delaware, Florida, New York, and Texas), and court rules. There is a 30-day trial. Law students have free access.

- **Fastcase** (iOS and Android): free even to non-subscribers, but they will need to register with Fastcase to use the app. The app allows you to search cases and statutes by keyword or citation and limit the search by jurisdiction and date. The Authority feature is also available on the app. If you mark a case as a **Favorite** when researching from your computer, your favorites will automatically be synced to your iPhone, iPad, and Android Fastcase App. If you **Save** a document when you are researching from the Fastcase App, that document will be synced to your computer and all your other mobile devices. You can print the document when you later log into your Fastcase account on your computer by clicking **My Library** and then clicking **Go to Recent Documents.**

  See Chapter 9 to learn about using Fastcase on your computer.

- **Casemaker** (BlackBerry, iOS, and Android): free only to subscribers who register for the mobile app using their iPhone or Android mobile devices. See Chapter 8 on Casemaker to learn what's available and how to search.

CODE OF FEDERAL REGULATIONS

See **dLaw** and **LawStack**, discussed in this chapter under the Court Rules section.

CONGRESSIONAL RECORD

- **Congressional Record (CR)** (iOS): The Library of Congress offers the CR for free from 1995–present. Using your iPad, iPhone, or iPod touch, you can keyword search the CR, copy text, save text as a PDF, and e-mail it.

THE U.S. CONSTITUTION

- **Constitution of the United States** (iOS): includes the text and audio versions of the Constitution for the iPhone, iPod Touch, and the iPad for $0.99. Google Play also has apps relating to the U.S. Constitution.
- See also **LawStack** in the Court Rules Section of this chapter

STATE STATUTES

- See **LawStack** noted earlier in the Court Rules section in this chapter.
- See **Casemaker, PushLegal**, and **Fastcase** noted earlier in the Case Law section in this chapter.

UNITED STATES CODE

- **U.S.C.** (iOS): a free iPad app to search the United States Code by keyword or citation. You can bookmark sections and even forward sections through email.
- See also **LawStack** in the earlier Court Rules section in this chapter.
- See also **Casemaker, PushLegal,** and **Fastcase** noted earlier in the Case Law section in this chapter.

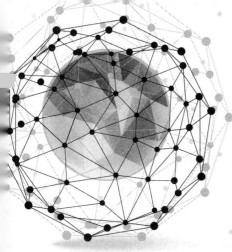

Part II

LEGAL PORTALS AND DIRECTORIES

Legal directories attempt to categorize websites by areas of law, jurisdiction, or both, and then provide links to those legal content websites. Legal portals, while also providing directories, go a step further and provide "added value," such as a full-text keyword searchable database of court cases or subject-specific articles about an area of law. Thus, portals are more than a directory of links to other legal content sites because they include substantive legal content right on their sites. Even with this "added value," most portals are still free (or partially free) because advertisers (and other alliances) support the cost of running the site.

Portals and directories are quite different from a search engine. Search engines return their results via automated programs that do not rely on human intervention. In contrast, legal portals and directories employ humans to create their product. These humans (usually law librarians or lawyers) have the subject expertise to be able to categorize the sites (just as a librarian would catalog a book by subject) and to judge whether a site is reliable before adding it to the portal or directory. This ensures that you will be able to easily pinpoint relevant and reliable sites.

Free legal portals and directories are usually sponsored by one of five different groups, all of which have their own reasons for sponsorship: (1) commercial entities, which support the free portion of their site through advertising or by selling related paid products or services (such as FindLaw or Justia, which both advertise their lawyer website businesses on their free portals); (2) law firms, which are using their sites to attract clients; (3) governmental entities, which are using their sites to make government documents and services more accessible to the public; (4) academic institutions, which are using their sites for scholarly reasons; and (5) associations, which are using their sites to offer value to their members (and sometimes to educate the general public).

ASSESSING LEGAL PORTALS AND LEGAL DIRECTORIES

If you want to use a portal or directory that we have not mentioned in this book, you will need to assess its quality before relying upon it. A high-quality, useful legal portal or directory should do the following: (1) include a subject (or practice area) directory and preferably also include a jurisdictional directory, (2) include an internal search engine so you can search the site with keywords, (3) be user-friendly (intuitive), (4) link directly to many relevant sites, (5) include "added value" (and make it easy to access this "added value"), and (6) be reliable—by which we mean it's credible, up to date, and objective. An example of a legal portal that meets these qualifications is **Justia** (http://www.justia.com) (see Figure II.1).

Figure II.1   Justia Home Page

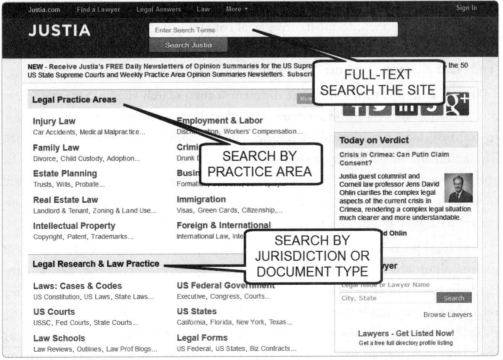

As you review the Justia home page, it's easy to see that it meets most of our "quality" tests by (1) having a practice area directory and a jurisdictional (and document type) directory, (2) offering a keyword search box, (3) being user-friendly (intuitive) by providing an easy-to-read and easy-to-navigate home page, (4) linking directly to many relevant sites that appear once you start clicking on the practice areas or jurisdiction links, and (5) offering "added value." Some examples of added value are Justia's **Supreme Court Center**, a searchable database of all U.S. Supreme Court decisions since the 1790s, and links to **Recall Warnings**, the **Stanford Copyright and Fair Use Center**, and **Free Law Firm Web Sites**, all located at the bottom of the home page, beneath **Public Interest and Pro Bono Projects** (not shown in the figure). Also of note on the home page is the recent addition of Latin American legal research resources. Unfortunately, as it continues to redesign its site, Justia has made it less easy to access some of its other "added value" resources by hiding them behind the **more** drop-down menu at the top of the home (e.g., Justia's Federal Dockets database).

Justia also meets the final criteria of the quality test—our three-pronged reliability test. Scroll down the home page to locate the **Company** link. Clicking this link and then selecting the **About Justia** link helps you decide that. As to the first prong of our reliability test, credibility, Tim Stanley is listed as the leader of the Justia team. Tim is well-known in the Internet legal research field and is the former CEO and co-founder of FindLaw. To add to the credibility of the company, the **Contact Us** page prominently displays Justia's address and toll-free number which means you can actually contact them with questions or comments.

As to the second prong of our reliability test, objectivity, "Justia works with educational, public interest and other socially focused organizations to bring legal and consumer information to the online community" (http://lawyers.justia.com/organization/justia-inc-16302). As to the third prong of our reliability test, being up-to-date, cases and dockets are added to Justia's database on a daily basis.

THE TOP LEGAL DIRECTORIES AND PORTALS

Some of the top legal directories and portals are FindLaw, Justia.com, Nolo.com, Law.com, HG.org, LLRX, USA.gov, Cornell Law School's Legal Information Institute (LII), the American Bar Association, and VISALAW, each of which will be discussed in the following two chapters. We'll divide them into the following categories: Free Commercial, Law Firm, Governmental, Academic, and Legal

Association. Chapter 4 will discuss Free Commercial and Law Firm portals. Chapter 5 will discuss Governmental, Academic, and Legal Association portals.

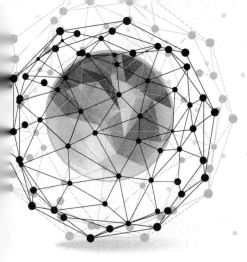

Chapter 4

FREE COMMERCIAL PORTALS AND DIRECTORIES

JUSTIA

Justia (http://www.justia.com) is a free legal portal that offers a directory to help researchers find legal research websites and also offers free "added value" databases. Justia does not require registration. Figure 4.1 shows the following features:

- A Google-powered search box to full-text search Justia with keywords and phrases (and Boolean connectors). (Justia's **Legal Web** search engine, which locates legal-specific information on the web and is also powered by Google, is described later in this chapter.)

- Two directories (located below the search box) for those who prefer to browse rather than keyword search. The first directory, **Legal Practice Areas**, can be browsed by legal topic (e.g., **Family Law**). The second directory, **Legal Research & Law Practice**, can be browsed by jurisdiction (e.g., **U.S. Federal Government, U.S. States**, etc.) or by document type (e.g., **U.S. Constitution, U.S. Laws, Legal Forms**, etc.).

- The **Lawyer Directory, Legal Answers**, and **more** tabs.

- The **more** tab provides a drop-down menu to search other added-value Justia resources. From this tab, you can select to search some of the same material you find listed on the home page, but there are also some materials not listed on the home page, such as **Federal Dockets**.

Figure 4.1   Justia's Features

Because so many sites include an internal Google-powered search engine, let's review some Google search syntax.

- Google, like all search engines, uses Boolean connectors, so you can instruct the search engine how to connect your keywords and phrases. The default Boolean connector is AND. Leaving a space between words automatically connects your keywords/phrases with the AND Boolean connector so there is no need to type the word AND.
- Google also offers phrase searching if you surround your phrase(s) with quotation marks.
- Google offers the Boolean connector OR but requires you to place it in upper case: *nevada OR Oregon.*

If you are excluding a word, you would place a minus sign before the word without any space. Google does not recognize the Boolean connector NOT: *"homeland security" nevada -oregon.*

Justia's Legal Web Search

One of Justia's most notable features is a sophisticated search engine, **Legal Web**, which locates legal-specific information on the Web. It is powered by Google's search engine technology.

To actually run a Legal Web search at Justia, do not enter any keywords into the search box at Justia.com. Instead, click the **Search Justia** button to the right of the search box on the home page, while leaving the search box blank (see Figure 4.2).

Figure 4.2   Justia's Search

Then a **Legal Web** tab will appear over the search box (see Figure 4.3). After selecting **Legal Web**, enter your search into the search box and click the **Search Legal Web** option.

Figure 4.3   Justia's Legal Web Tab

Below your search results (see Figure 4.4), a group of suggestions is displayed to help you refine the initial results list—although they tend to be less than helpful because they seem to be the same for every search. Also, depending on your browser, the search results page may display paid Google Ads above the suggested refinements.

Figure 4.4   Justia's Legal Web Search Results

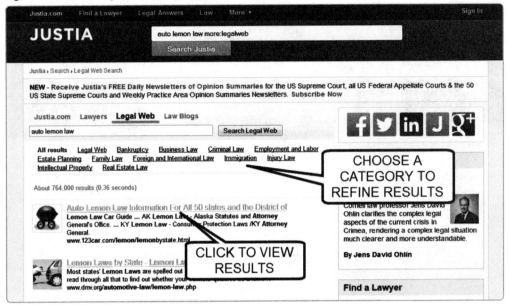

Justia's Free Court Opinion Newsletters

Justia offers free daily court opinion summary newsletters for all federal appellate and all state supreme courts, as well as weekly practice area newsletters. They can be received by e-mail or news feeds (http://law.justia.com/about-daily-summaries).

The following specific features of Justia will be discussed in the chapters indicated:

- **Justia's Free Online Case Law Databases.** See Chapter 6, Free Commercial Online Case Law Databases, for a discussion of Justia's free online case law database.

- **Justia's U.S. Regulation Tracker.** See Chapter 12, Federal Executive and Administrative Law.

- **Justia's Free Federal Court Docket Database.** See Chapter 15, Dockets for a discussion of Justia's federal court docket database.

- **Justia's Free Latin America Law Links.** See Chapter 14, Foreign, International, and Comparative Law Resources.

FINDLAW

The **FindLaw** (http://www.findlaw.com) portal is one of the oldest legal portals, dating back to 1995. It started as a simple list of Internet resources compiled by computer engineer/attorney Tim Stanley and attorney Stacy Stern (now owners of Justia) for a workshop of the Northern California Law Librarians Association. It grew into a full-blown legal portal under Stanley and Stern's watch. Eventually, Thomson/West (now Thomson Reuters) purchased FindLaw. Although it is still a free portal, there are now links to Thomson Reuters pay services, such as Westlaw and KeyCite. It includes directories and "added value" resources ranging from full-text searchable case law databases and a brief bank of U.S. Supreme Court briefs to e-newsletters and more.

> **CAVEAT:** Certain services that were once free are no longer available, or are not being kept up-to-date, or have been changed to such an extent that they are not as useful. Other services, such as free full-text case law databases for selected courts (which we'll point out in Chapter 6), are not as easy to find and sometimes don't work properly. We've pointed out these problems to FindLaw and have been assured that they are working on a fix, thus we are keeping FindLaw in this book, but with this caveat.

FindLaw focuses on two audiences—the legal professional and the public—and is divided into those two categories. If you use the direct URL http://www.findlaw.com, you will find yourself on the consumer side of the site. (Probably the most useful data on the consumer side for both consumers and legal professionals is FindLaw's Lawyer Directory.)

To reach the site created for legal professionals, click on the link at the top of the home page labeled **Visit our professional site** or use this URL: http://lp.findlaw.com (see Figure 4.5).

Figure 4.5   FindLaw's Home Page

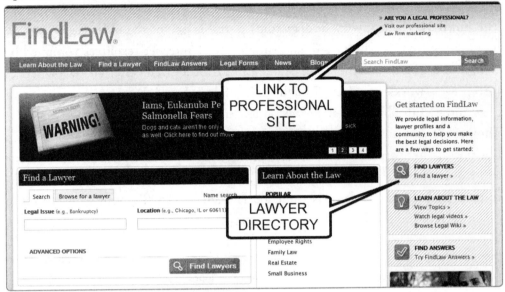

Figure 4.6   FindLaw for Legal Professionals

The FindLaw Legal Professionals site's home page (see Figure 4.6) has a lot going on. Much of its information can be accessed by clicking the tabs located in one of the two rows of tabs running horizontally beneath the FindLaw logo, such as **Cases & Codes** on the top row (left side) or **Forms** or **Law Technology** on the second row (left side). The **Forms** tab takes you to free sample business contracts and free forms (and also pay forms). Beneath the **Browse Research Materials** section, notice the links to browse **by Research Type**, **by Jurisdiction**, and **by Practice Area**. The **Cases & Codes** section contains links to state, local, and federal resources (constitutions, statutes, cases, ordinances, and more). This section and the **Research the Law** section both offer access to free FindLaw-created case law databases and will be discussed in detail in Chapter 18.

LAW.COM

Law.com (http://www.law.com) is a legal portal owned by ALM (American Lawyer Media) and describes itself as "the premiere source for trusted and timely legal news and analysis." It provides content from online legal publications such as *The American Lawyer*, *The National Law Journal*, *New York Law Journal*, *Legal Times*, and others. News from its legal publications is arranged by **Practice Areas** and various segments of **The Legal Industry**, as indicated by the first two tabs across the top of the site. In addition to news, Law.com offers other services to lawyers, such as Reports and Studies, Rankings, a legal dictionary, and other resources, located under the **Insights** and **Resources** tabs (see Figure 4.7).

Figure 4.7 Law.com's Home Page

The tabs include drop-down menus and/or links to various publications and services. Some of these are free, some are free with registration, some are partially free, and some are fee-based. For example, selecting **Post a Job** from the **lawjobs.com** link under the **Resources** tab will cause a pricing menu to appear, but selecting **Find a Job** opens a page to free job searching. The **Resources** tab offers links to various services such as **ALM Experts**, which is a free database of experts that includes resumes.

If you scroll to the bottom of the page and click the **+SHOW** box, a drop-down menu appears with links to various ALM legal newspapers, some of which are free, some offering only select stories for free, and others requiring pay subscriptions.

You can register to receive numerous free e-newsletters (http://www.law.com/jsp/law/newsletters.jsp), such as Law.com's **Newswire** or **International News Alert** (featuring the day's top legal news and stories culled from various ALM publications, with clickable links to the full stories). Law.com's keyword search engine **Quest** (accessed by clicking the magnifying glass on the top right-hand side of the home page), offers a free search and free abbreviated results, but a paid subscription is often necessary to read the full story. Users can filter results by date, practice area, industry, and document type.

It is unclear until after you've clicked on an article in the results list whether you will receive the full story or a message that states, "Sign Up & Start Your 30-Day Trial. Access to Law.com Practice Areas is for subscribers only." This is one of our main beefs with Law.com. On the other hand, we do find Law.com useful for keeping us up-to-date with the legal field.

HG.ORG (FORMERLY HIEROS GAMOS)

HG.org (http://www.hg.org) was one of the very first online law and government sites, founded in January 1995 by Lex Mundi, a network of independent law firms. HG.org is a bit of a mix between Law.com, FindLaw, and Justia. Like Law.com, HG.org provides an expert witness directory (free) and an employment search.

Like FindLaw and Justia, HG provides a lawyer directory and a directory of law-related websites arranged by subject and jurisdictional categories. Scrolling down to the **About Laws** section and then clicking on **all law guides** takes you to a page with over seventy "core areas of law" and 260 "sub areas of practice." HG explains that, "The Center provides information on US (Federal and State), European and International Laws. An abundance of information dealing with the specific area of law is also integrated into each page, including: Publications, Articles, Organizations, Resources, Attorneys and Law Firms." When we chose Bankruptcy Law, HG displayed links to websites (primarily U.S.) explaining bankruptcy, the U.S. Bankruptcy Code, the U.S. Bankruptcy Courts, organizations related to bankruptcy, bankruptcy lawyers, and articles about bankruptcy.

There is a Google-powered search box on the top right-hand side of the home page to keyword search the site (see Figure 4.8). Searching the two words *Dubai escrow* returned several results, with the top one being an article titled "Property Development and Escrow Law in Dubai." We especially like HG for its foreign and international links.

Figure 4.8 HG.org's Home Page

LLRX.COM

LLRX (http://www.llrx.com) is a cross between an e-magazine and a portal. The e-magazine portion provides Internet research articles that discuss websites and then links directly to them. There are also articles and news items about emerging Internet issues and lawyer-related technology. The portal portion of the site is illustrated by LLRX's database of 1,400 links to state, federal, and local court rules, forms, and dockets. This database can be browsed by type of court (e.g., bankruptcy), by jurisdiction (e.g., federal or state), or searched with keywords. The database was last updated in 2011, and consequently, a few of the links are broken; most of them still work, however. There is a Google-powered search box on the top of the home page to keyword search (1) LLRX.com, (2) LLRX.com together with beSpacific (a blog by the founder of LLRX), or (3) the Legal Web. To learn when new articles are added to LLRX, subscribe to its e-mail list, or follow it on a number of social media sites.

NOLO PRESS

In addition to offering access to online ordering of legal books, software, and forms, **Nolo's** portal offers free information useful to both legal professionals and the general public (http://www.nolo.com). To read free legal articles, select a topic (ranging from **Accidents** to **Wills**) listed under the **Get Informed: Free Legal Information** drop-down menu on the home page (see Figure 4.9). Also at Nolo, you will find the following free resources:

- **Lawyer Directory** (http://www.nolo.com/lawyers)
- **Law Dictionary** (http://www.nolo.com/dictionary)
- **State Law Resources** (http://www.nolo.com/legal-research/state-law.html)
- **Federal Law Resources** (http://www.nolo.com/legal-research/federal-law.html)
- **Law Blogs** (http://www.nolo.com/law-blogs)
- **Law Podcasts** (http://www.nolo.com/podcasts/podcasts.html)

Figure 4.9   Nolo's Home Page

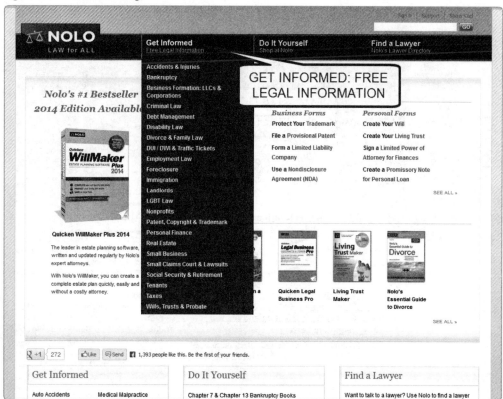

ZIMMERMAN'S RESEARCH GUIDE

Zimmerman's Research Guide, hosted at the LexisNexis InfoPro site (http://law.lexisnexis.com/infopro/zimmermans), is a free, handy, annotated subject guide that links to various websites (both free and pay), print resources, and even specific libraries that have collections on the subject you are researching. It is keyword searchable and can also be browsed by subject (legal and non-legal).

VISALAW.COM

Siskind Susser's **VISALAW.com** (http://www.visalaw.com) was probably the first law firm-sponsored website. In addition to promoting the firm itself, the site offers enormous amounts of free information about immigration law, from articles and forms to links to government sites, and several free e-newsletters, such as Siskind's **Immigration Bulletin** (see Figure 4.10).

Figure 4.10   Siskind's Immigration Bulletin

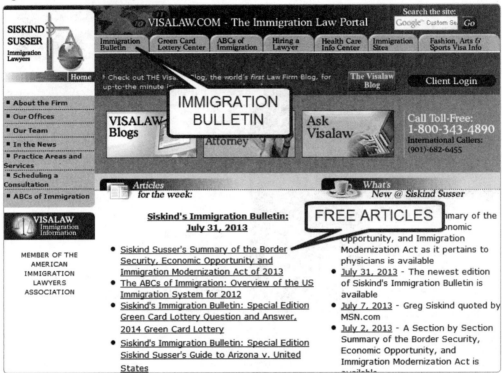

There are many other law firms offering free information on their sites, including **Illinoisdivorce.com** (http://illinoisdivorce.com).

Chapter 5

GOVERNMENT, ACADEMIC, AND ASSOCIATION PORTALS AND DIRECTORIES

This chapter continues the previous chapter's explanation of legal portals and directories and will discuss Governmental, Academic, and Legal Association portals. For an overview of the characteristics of legal portals and directories, as well as a detailed discussion on assessing their quality, see the introduction to Part II.

GOVERNMENT PORTALS AND DIRECTORIES

USA.GOV

USA.gov (http://www.usa.gov), formerly FirstGov.gov, is the federal government's document search portal. USA.gov searches millions of web pages from all levels of the United States government: federal, state, local, tribal, the District of Columbia, and the U.S. territories (see Figure 5.1). Although results occasionally bring back court opinions, this is not the right site to search for them. Instead, see Chapters 3 (Legal Portals and Directories), 8 (Casemaker), and 9 (Fastcase), where free case law research is discussed.

Figure 5.1   USA.gov's Home Page

In addition to offering keyword searching, USA.gov offers the ability to browse by a government service, topic, agency, or government contact. To browse (instead of keyword searching), select one of the five tabs listed below the search box on USA.gov's home page: **Services**, **Blog**, **Topics**, **Government Agencies**, and **Contact Government**. Once you select one of these tabs, such as the **Government Agencies** tab, for example, a drop-down menu appears where more links are revealed.

If you select the **Services** tab, you will see that USA.gov also serves as a forum in which to conduct business online with government agencies. For instance, you can change your address, apply for a passport, shop government auctions, e-file your taxes, and more.

USA.gov's internal search engine (the search box on USA.gov's home page) is powered by **Bing**. You can use the search box to keyword or phrase search government documents. Unfortunately, USA.gov provides no search tips about how to construct a search and use Boolean connectors and we were unable to find any at Bing (at least not easily).

However, on USA.gov's **Advanced Search** page (which you can only find once you run a search or if you visit http://search.usa.gov/search/advanced), there is a link to Bing's search tips. To find the tips on USA.gov's **Advanced Search** page you will need to scroll down to the bottom of the page and click the **You can also use advanced search operators to help limit and focus your searches** link. Then you will be taken to the **Advanced search keywords** page at Bing. But that page only explains how to use various instructions such as how to limit your search to a specific file type (http://onlinehelp.microsoft.com/en-us/bing/ff808421.aspx). The more useful help page, where you learn how to search with Boolean connectors, is found by clicking the **advanced search operators** link at the bottom of the Advanced search keywords page, or just use this URL: http://onlinehelp.microsoft.com/en-us/bing/ff808438.aspx (see Figure 5.2). We will provide a brief Bing/USA. gov tutorial.

Figure 5.2   Bing's Advanced Search

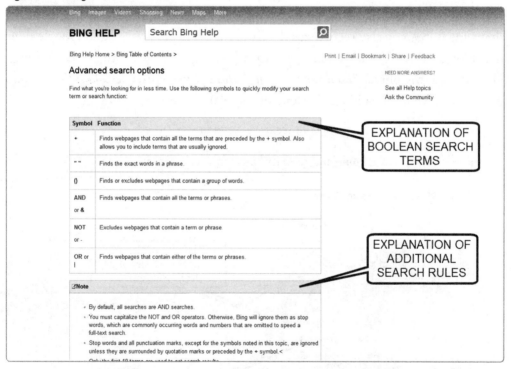

Just like Google, Bing/USA.gov uses Boolean connectors to link keywords and phrases, and the default Boolean connector is *AND*. Leaving a space between words automatically connects your keywords/phrases with the *AND* Boolean connector so there is no need to type the word *AND*. And, just like Google, Bing/USA.gov offers phrase searching if you surround your phrase within quotation marks.

The OR Boolean connector must be upper case at Bing/USA.gov and Google, but Bing/USA.gov treats the Boolean connector *OR* differently than Google in one instance only: when you are combining your *OR* search with other Boolean connectors in a search. For example, to search for the phrase *"homeland security"* and the keywords *nevada OR oregon*, Bing requires you to enclose your *OR* terms in parentheses (Google does not). Your search would look like this:

"homeland security" (nevada OR oregon)

If you are only searching the keywords *nevada OR Oregon*, your Bing/USA.gov search would be the same as a Google search and would look like this:

nevada OR oregon

If you are excluding a word at Bing/USA.gov, you would place a minus sign(-) before the word without any space, just as you would at Google. One difference is that Bing/USA.gov also recognizes the Boolean connector *NOT*, and Google does not. However, *NOT* must be in upper case (see Figure 5.3). So to search at Bing/USA.gov for the phrase *"homeland security"* and the keywords *nevada NOT oregon*, your search would look like either one of these examples:

"homeland security" nevada -oregon

"homeland security" nevada NOT oregon

Figure 5.3   USA.gov Simple Search Results

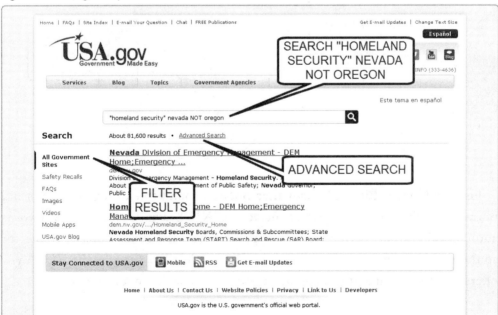

The link to the **Advanced Search** was taken off the home page a number of years ago, much to our disappointment, and it is only visible after you run your search and receive results (as shown in Figure 5.3), or it can be reached directly at http:// search.usa.gov/search/advanced. To use the feature, click **Advanced Search** after you have run an initial search (see Figure 5.4). You must enter something into the search box, or you will receive an error message telling you to enter search terms until you do so.

Figure 5.4   USA.gov Advanced Search

Once you reach the **Advanced Search** at Search.USA.gov, you will then be able to construct your search in the following ways:

- Enter keywords into the following search boxes:
  - **All of these words**
  - **This exact phrase**
  - **Any of these words**
  - **None of these words**
- Select the **File Type** drop-down menu to limit search results to the following formats:
  - PDF
  - Excel

- PowerPoint
- Word
- Text

> If you are looking for a quick overview about a topic, sometimes limiting your search results to a PowerPoint presentation is a useful tactic.

FDSYS (FEDERAL DIGITAL SYSTEM)

The **Government Printing Office** (GPO) maintains a website called the **Federal Digital System** (**FDsys**), which is a database that provides free online access to official publications from all three branches of the Federal Government. The FDsys website arranges its database into Collections, which include **Budget of the U.S. Government, Code of Federal Regulations, Congressional Bills, Congressional Hearings, Federal Register, Statutes at Large, U.S. Code**, and **U.S. Court Opinions**, among others.

The same search protocols (keyword/phrase/citation searching and Boolean and proximity connectors) are used throughout the FDsys Collections. Results can be displayed and sorted in the same way throughout all of the Collections, so we will use this section to explain how to search FDsys, in general. However, a different menu of search criteria options appropriate for each Collection will pop up after you choose to search a specific Collection. For example, if you choose the **U.S.C. Collection**, its search criteria would include a search by **Title, U.S. Code Amendment**, or **U.S. Code Future Amendments** (among others), while the Collection of **U.S. Court Opinions** would include much different search criteria options, such as **Party Name** or **Court Name** (among others). Because of these differences and because there are Collections that focus on different topics, we will discuss them individually in later chapters and then refer you back here for a refresher on general FDsys search protocol strategies.

FDsys researchers can keyword or phrase search through all of FDsys's Collections from the search box on FDsys's home page at http://www.gpo.gov/fdsys/search/home.action. Another option is the **Advanced Search** at http://linkon.in/y2uMZC. Researchers can also browse Collections or retrieve a document by citation via links available on the home page.

Whether you are performing a simple or Advanced Search, you can create simple or complex queries. We will highlight some of the search queries available at FDsys, but for more detailed information and examples, see the **FDsys Help** page (http:// linkon.in/I6uqKF).

According to the documentation at FDsys, its simple queries are similar to "typical search engine such as Google" because FDsys uses the same Boolean connectors (*AND, OR*, and a minus sign) and phrase searching (using quotation marks) as Google. There are some differences, though: (1) FDsys researchers can use the Boolean connector *AND* or leave a space in between words (but Google scolds you if you type *AND* in between words), (2) Boolean connectors are case insensitive at FDsys (while the *OR* Boolean connector must be in uppercase at Google), (3) FDsys researchers can also use *NOT* instead of the minus (-) sign—they are interchangeable at FDsys (but not at Google), and (4) FDsys allows for additional types of complex queries not found at Google such as:

- Proximity connectors (near/#, adj, before/#)
  - *adj* specifies that one word is adjacent to another.
  - *before/#* (e.g., *handgun before/3 protection*) specifies that the first word is within whatever number of words that you select of the second word and that the first word must precede the second word.
  - *near/#* (e.g., *handgun near/10 protection*) specifies that the first word is within whatever number of words that you select of the second word and in any order.
- Wildcards, which are indicated by:
  - the question mark symbol (?) to replace one character before, within, or after a search term.
  - the asterisk symbol (*) to replace one or more characters before, within, or after a search term.
  - Typing *int*city* into the search box indicates a search for any word that begins with *int*, is followed by any two characters, and then ends with *city*. The search results might include the words *intercity* or *intracity*, or both words.
  - Typing *amend** into the search box indicates a search for the word *amend* and any word that begins with *amend*, such as *amendment, amending,* or *amends.*

- Parentheses, which should be used when creating complex searches such as those where you use multiple proximity connectors and/or multiple Field operators. The following is an example:

(congressional OR executive) AND hearing AND (member:mcconnell)

Figure 5.5 shows a simple search and a simple query. We have entered two keywords (*negligence entrustment*) separated with a space into the simple search box. This will search all of the FDsys Collections together for both words.

Figure 5.5   FDSys's Simple Search

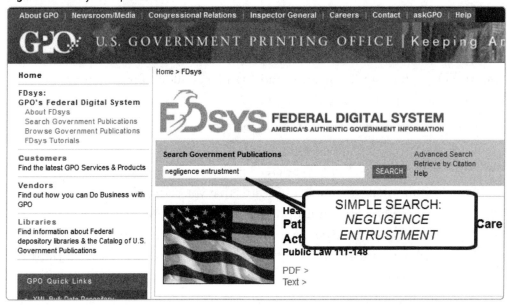

FDsys also allows you to construct a complex query on the simple search page by using Field operators. Field operators, which allow you to restrict your keywords to specific metadata fields (parts of a document), such as:

- Congress Member: To search by this field, enter your search this way: *member:mcconnell*
- President: To search by this field, enter your search this way: *president:Obama*
- You can search using multiple Fields, such as *title:homeland* and *member:smith*

Commonly used field operators that apply to all or most of the Collections can be found at http://linkon.in/HvLIjA (and links to each Collection's unique Field operators can also be found at this URL if you scroll down to **Metadata Fields and Values by Collection**).

Figure 5.6 shows how your search results are displayed, and how you can do the following:

- **Narrow Your Search** by re-sorting results by **Collection, Date Published, Government Author, Organization, Person, Location**, or **Keyword** (see the left-side column).

- Search **Within Results** by clicking into the box to the right of the search box. This allows you to enter one or more keywords and re-run your search within your original search results to narrow down your search further.

- **Sort by Relevance, Date** (New to Old or Old to New), or **Alphabetically** (Z to A or A to Z).

Figure 5.6   FDSys's Simple Search with Complex Query

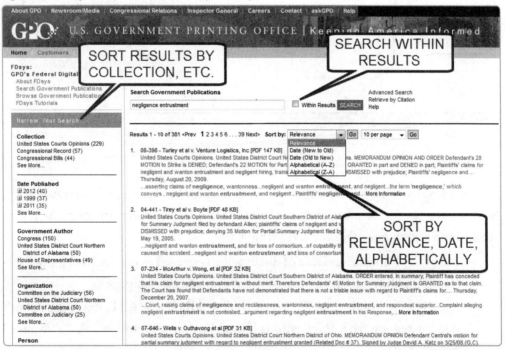

The **Advanced Search** page (http://linkon.in/y2uMZC) is illustrated in Figure 5.7.

Figure 5.7   FDsys's Advanced Search

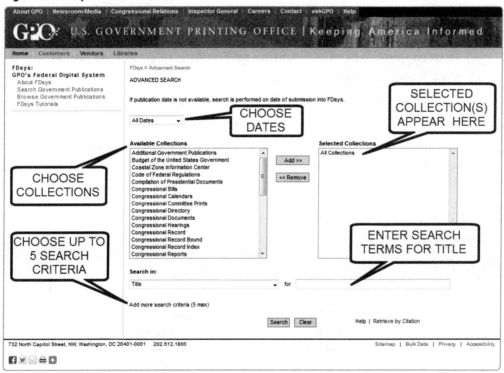

According to FDsys's **Help** page (http://linkon.in/fdsysadvsearch), the Advanced Search page "uses a form based on metadata (information about the documents) to construct a search query" in the following ways:

- Limit the Publication Date of documents retrieved in results (using the **Publications Date** box at the top of the Advanced Search page).

- Broaden the Publication Date by selecting **All Dates** (All Dates is the default date listed on the Publications Date box at the top of the Advanced Search page).

- Accept the **All Collections** choice already displayed in the **Selected Collections** box (it is the default) if you want a broad search. If you choose another collection(s), the **All Collections** choice will be replaced. Limit the search to one (or multiple) Collections from the **Available Collections** dropdown menu.

- Conduct a broad keyword search by selecting **Full Text of Publications and Metadata** from the **Search in** drop-down menu.
- Conduct a narrower search by selecting up to five search criteria. In Figure 5.7, we have chosen **Title** as our search criteria. We could also change this to **Branch, Category, Citation, Government Author, Series,** or **Sudoc Class Number** from the **Search in** drop-down menu. (Remember, the search criteria noted here is for the **All Collections** search but will vary from Collection to Collection if you narrow your search to just one Collection.) By clicking **Add more search criteria** (see bottom left-side of Figure 5.7) you can choose up to four more of the criteria listed above (**Branch,** etc.).

If you opt to search multiple (or all) Collections, you will only be able to use a limited number of generic search criteria options (e.g., ones that are not Collection-specific).

Those who prefer to search by a known citation should choose the **Retrieve by Citation** link from the FDsys home page (to the right of the search box in Figure 5.5). From the **Retrieve by Citation** page, you must first choose a Collection from the **Collections** list. For example, in the Figure 5.8, we chose the **Code of Federal Regulations** Collection.

After choosing the **Code of Federal Regulations Collection**, the search menu that is appropriate for searching that particular Collection is displayed.

Figure 5.8   FDsys's Retrieve by Citation Collection

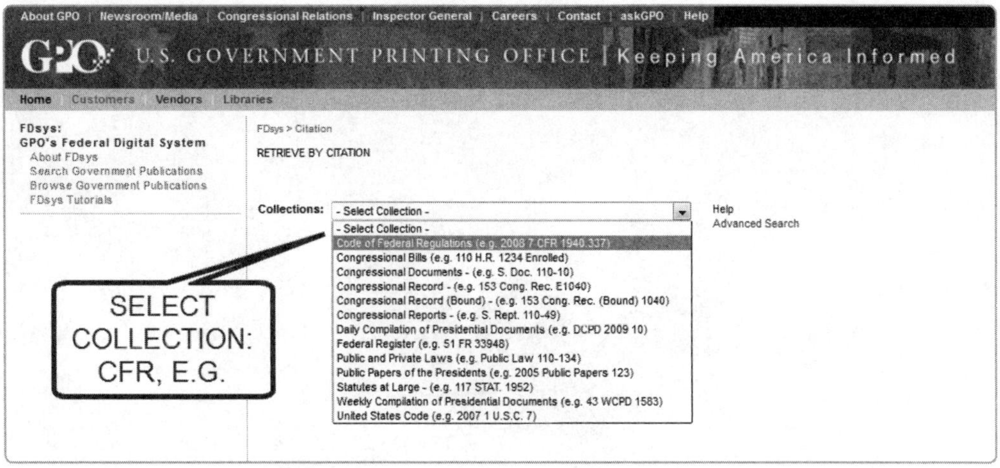

To browse specific FDsys Collections, click the **Browse All** link on FDsys's home page (see Figure 5.5). The **Browse Collections** page also offers four browsing options: **Collection, Congressional Committee, Date,** and **Government Author** (See Figure 5.9).

Figure 5.9   FDsys's Browse Collections

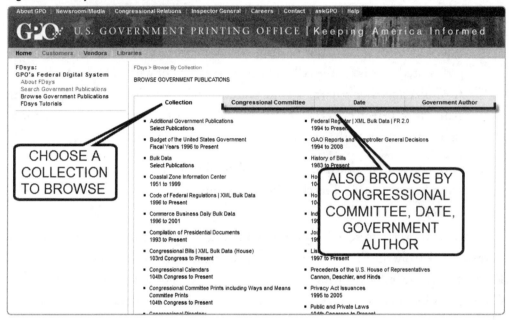

ACADEMIC PORTALS AND DIRECTORIES

There are many excellent academic portals and directories for Internet legal and government research, with most created by law school librarians. Academic portals are particularly useful for linking to their own state and local legal research and government websites; you will probably want to visit your state's law schools' sites for local links. For a list of all law school websites, see **FindLaw** (http://stu.findlaw.com/schools/fulllist.html). Once you link to the relevant law school, you will most likely need to locate the library's page to find its list of legal research and government links.

CORNELL'S LEGAL INFORMATION INSTITUTE

One of the better law school websites for legal professionals is the **Legal Information Institute** (**LII**) portal created by Cornell Law School at http://www.law.cornell.edu. Like FindLaw and Justia, Cornell's LII provides links to material available from other Internet sites, but it has also created a good deal of "added value" with its collections of searchable legal databases hosted on LII's own servers. Many of these databases and outside websites can be accessed by clicking on the links found at the top of the home page beneath tabs labeled **Get the Law** and **Legal Encyclopedia**, or by conducting a keyword search from the home page's search box see Figure 5.10).[6]

Figure 5.10 Legal Information Institute (LII) Home Page

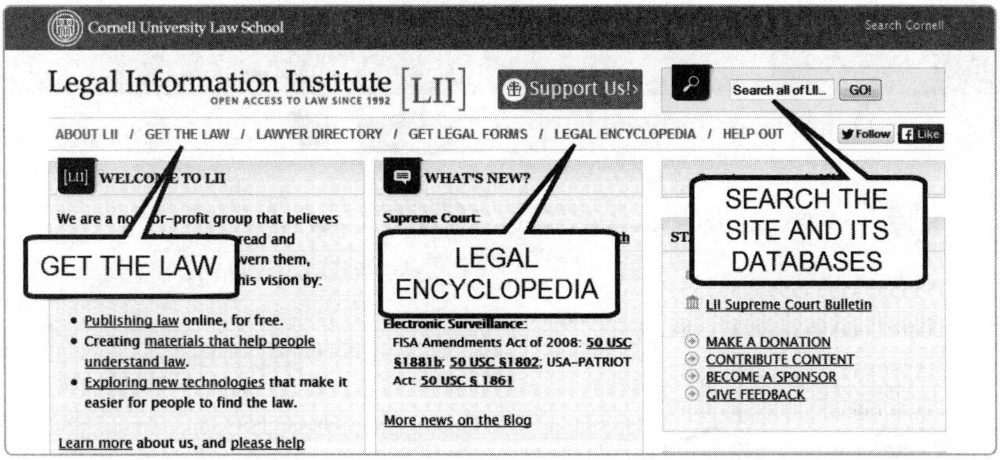

---

6   LII is in the process of redesigning their search to be more user-friendly. These instructions are accurate as of March 2014, but the site may be changing in the near future.

Beneath the section labeled **EXPLORE OUR LEGAL COLLECTIONS** (see Figure 5.11) on the **Get the Law** page (http://www.law.cornell.edu/lii/) you will see a list of links to the following resources, many of which are searchable databases, such as:

- **Federal law** (Among other resources, this is where you will find the searchable database of U.S. Court of Appeals decisions where you can search all circuit court opinions or select just one circuit to search.)
- **Constitution**
- **U.S. Code**
- **C.F.R.**
- **Supreme Court**
- **Federal Rules**
- **State law resources**
- **State statutes by topic**
- **U.C.C.**
- **Uniform laws**
- **World law**

To search these topics, first conduct a keyword search from the home page's search box, then use the filters that appear on the left side of the search results page to see only results for a specific database. See the Wex description below for additional details.

Figure 5.11   LII's Get the Law Resource Links

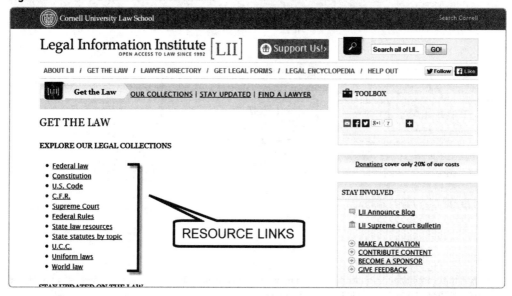

When you click on the **Legal Encyclopedia** link, you'll gain access to **Wex** (http://www.law.cornell.edu/wex), a free legal dictionary and encyclopedia sponsored and hosted by the **LII** (see Figure 5.12).

Figure 5.12   LII's WEX: Free Legal Dictionary and Encyclopedia

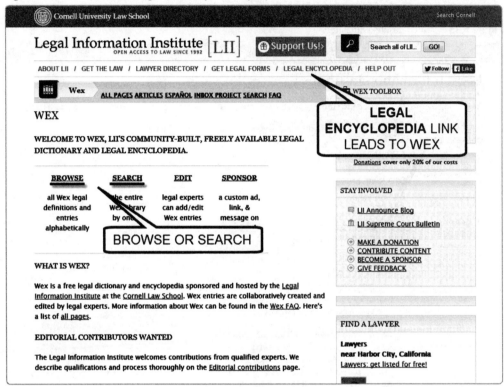

Wex entries are collaboratively created and edited by legal experts. You can search all Wex legal definitions and entries by browsing alphabetically, or search by keyword. When searching by keyword, you first search all of LII and then limit your search results to Wex entries by using the filters that appear on the left side of the search results, as indicated in Figure 5.13. This is the same method you would use to search LII's other databases, as well; after searching, just click the link for the resource you want to see, such as the following:

- CFR (Code of Federal Regulations)
- Supreme Court
- US Code
- Wex page (Wex entries)
- TOPN (Table of Popular Names)

- LII Bulletin Preview (The LII Supreme Court Bulletin)
- Uniform Commercial Code
- Federal Rules of Civil Procedure
- Federal Rules of Bankruptcy Procedure

Figure 5.13 Search Results with Filters

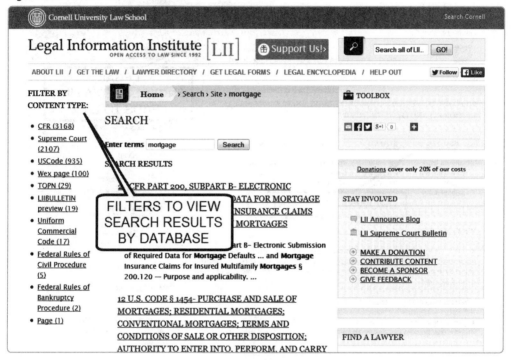

After you have filtered your results to a particular resource, you can return to all search results by using the links that appear above the search results. Figure 5.14, for example, shows results that have been filtered to Wex entries. You would click **mortgage** to return to the full set of search results. You could then browse all results or apply a different filter.

Figure 5.14 LII's Filter Search Results

If you view filter results to a particular resource, a search box will appear at the top of the filtered results list. By checking **Retain current filters**, you can run a search in the resource you have selected. For example, in Figure 5.15, the user could now search in the Table of Popular Names database.

Figure 5.15 Search within Filtered Results

Another highlight of LII is its **State Statutes by Topic** database (http://topics. law.cornell.edu/wex/state_statutes), which links to all fifty states' statutes on topics ranging from **Agriculture** to **Water Code** (see Figure 5.16). Not every state's statutory scheme is organized in a topical breakdown similar to this database. Thus, some topics will display a state's name with a link to the home page of that state's statutory database. A link to a list of all state statutes on the web is also available on this page.

Figure 5.16   LII's State Statues by Topic

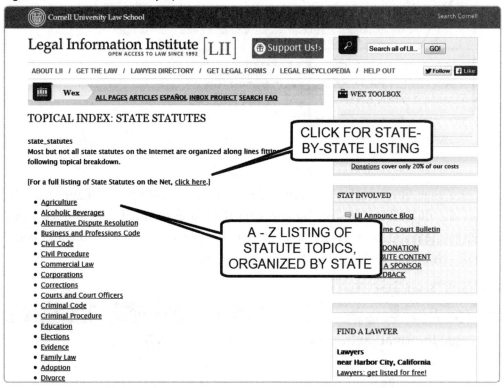

UNIVERSITY OF SOUTHERN CALIFORNIA GOULD SCHOOL OF LAW

The University of Southern California (USC) Gould School of Law's **Asa V. Call Law Library** (http://bit.ly/HWahF9) provides a website with tabs for **General Research Links, Federal Research Links, California Research Links,** and **Foreign & International Research Links** (see Figure 5.17).

Figure 5.17   USC's Gould School of Law

LEGAL ASSOCIATION PORTALS

Many legal associations have created websites that not only provide information about the association, but also provide links to law-related websites that relate to the association's area of focus and that may be of interest to their members. Many have also added original content such as online seminars and discussion groups. Even when association sites are restricted to members only, they often make some information available to the public.

AMERICAN ASSOCIATION FOR JUSTICE

Anyone can access the list of **Related Resources for Attorneys** at the American Association for Justice (AAJ) site (formerly The Association of Trial Lawyers of America; http://www.justice.org/cps/rde/xchg/justice/hs.xsl/485.htm). But only AAJ members have access to the full archive of *Trial* magazine online (and other publications) and to **AAJ Exchange** (http://www.justice.org/cps/rde/xchg/justice/hs.xsl/678.htm), an online, full-text searchable database for members to share over 155,000 documents (pleadings, verdicts and settlements, court strategies, and information about experts).

AMERICAN BAR ASSOCIATION

The **American Bar Association** (http://www.americanbar.org), like AAJ, has information on its website available to members and non-members. Legal research links from the ABA Legal Technology Resource Center's **Lawlink: The Legal Research Jumpstation** are found (free) at http://linkon.in/IbjlF9 (see Figure 5.18).

Figure 5.18   ABA's Lawlink

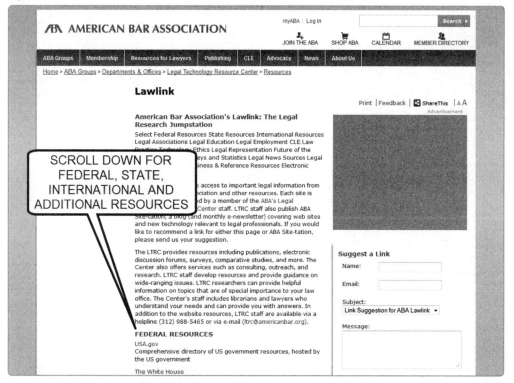

For useful state and local legal website links, check your state or local bar associations for their lists of links. To find links to legal-related associations and bar associations, see the **ABA's State and Local Bar Associations** list (http://linkon. in/adcRDE).

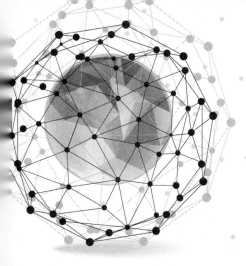

Part III

CASE LAW DATABASES

In Part III, we will discuss a variety of free case law databases. Most free case law databases are limited in some way; they may have limited dates of coverage, only provide cases from certain courts, provide a browse function but no search function, or lack other features that paid databases provide. Probably no databases (even including paid ones) are 100 percent reliable, so researchers must always cite-check their cases. With that said, even the cite-checking databases are not 100 percent infallible.

Chapter 6 will focus on free commercial websites that provide online case law databases, including those found in the various legal portals discussed in Chapter 4 (e.g., Justia and FindLaw). We will also discuss free commercial "stand-alone" case law databases such as The Public Library of Law (PLoL), FindACase Network, The Free Law Reporter (FLR), Google Scholar, and Casetext. Chapter 7 will focus on free government websites that provide free case law.

Casemaker and Fastcase, which are case law databases that are free to many lawyers as a bar association "member benefit," will be discussed in Part IV's Chapters 8 and 9.

(If you have free access to them, we would recommend using Casemaker or Fastcase over all other free databases. They offer more search functions and provide access to more than just case law--such as statutes, regulations, etc.)

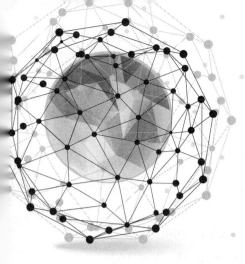

Chapter 6

FREE COMMERCIAL ONLINE CASE LAW DATABASES

This chapter will discuss free commercial websites that provide online case law databases, including those found in the various legal portals discussed in Chapter 4 (e.g., Justia and FindLaw). We will also discuss free commercial "stand-alone" case law databases such as The Public Library of Law (PLoL), FindACase Network, The Free Law Reporter (FLR), Google Scholar , and the "crowdsourced" Casetext. We will begin our discussion with Google Scholar, not because it's the best database or the most reliable, but only because: (1) it offers more court and date coverage than the other free database we will discuss in this chapter and (2) it also includes articles (some free and some pay) and not just case law.

GOOGLE SCHOLAR

ALL FEDERAL AND ALL STATES ONLINE CASE LAW AND ARTICLES

Late in the evening of November 17, 2009, a Google employee tweeted that something was new at Google Scholar and challenged readers to figure out what it was. It turned out that Google had launched a free case law and legal articles database (Legal Opinions and Journals), which was added to its Scholar database of non-law articles. In this chapter, we will only focus on the case law portion of Google Scholar. It can be reached from the Google.com home page by clicking the Apps icon, selecting the **More** tab from the pop-up, then selecting **Even More** and finally selecting

Scholar. Better yet, you can go directly to Scholar with this URL: http://scholar.google.com (we recommend you bookmark it if you use if often).

The cases come from a variety of sources, such as Cornell LII, Justia, Public. Resource.org, and official court sites. Scholar contains opinions from the following courts:

- All U.S. state appellate and state supreme courts back to 1950
- U.S. federal district, appellate, tax, and bankruptcy courts back to 1923
- Court of Claims from 1929 to 1982 (when the court was abolished)
- Court of Customs and Patent Appeals from 1929 to 1982 (when the court was abolished)
- Customs Court from 1949 to 1980 (when it was replaced by the Court of International Trade)
- Court of International Trade from 1980 (when it replaced the Customs Court) to the present
- Board of Tax Appeals from 1924 (when it was established) to 1942 (when it became the Tax Court)
- Tax Court from 1943 (when it replaced the Board of Tax Appeals) to the present
- U.S. Supreme Court back to 1791

Google states that it does not guarantee its coverage to be complete or accurate. The Customs Court and Tax Court, for example, do not appear to be complete for all years, especially for older years. It would be a good idea to double-check your research in another database if possible, especially for older cases. If a particular case is not available online for free in full-text format, Google Scholar search results will only include a citation.

Searching Google Scholar

There are three ways to search case law using Google Scholar. To use any of the three methods, first select the **Case law** (radio button under the search box). Three pre-filtering options will then appear—a **Federal Courts** radio button, a radio button for the state you are in (or the jurisdiction you have saved in a previous search), and a **Select courts** link (see Figure 6.1).

Figure 6.1 Google Scholar's Case Law Search

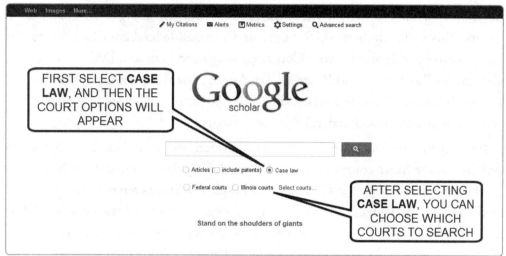

After you have selected **Case law**, you can search in one of three ways: 1) enter your search terms directly into the search box, which will search all jurisdictions; 2) enter your search terms into the **Advanced search** feature, which we will explain below; or 3) pre-filter your search by selecting certain courts to search, such as **Federal courts** or **Illinois courts,** or by using the **Select courts** link, as in Figure 6.1. If you use the first or second methods (and enter your search terms now), you may still want to filter the results by court or other criteria afterward. We will discuss how to do this below.

If you click **Select courts** (see Figure 6.1), a screen containing all the courts Google Scholar covers will appear. You can then use the checkboxes to choose any combination of courts to search (see Figure 6.2).

Figure 6.2 Google Scholar's List of Courts

For example, for a customized all federal courts opinions search, you would click the **Select all** link just to the right of the **Federal courts** heading to select all federal courts. This will include the U.S. Supreme Court, all federal appellate courts, the 1st Circuit Appeals and District Courts (through the 11th and D.C.), the Federal Circuit, the Tax Courts and Board of Tax Appeals, Bankruptcy Courts, and so on. Or, you could search one federal court or multiple (instead of all) federal courts. You could also mix and match federal and state courts.

For a customized all state court opinions search, you would click the **Select all** link beside the **State courts** heading. To search only the state courts of Nebraska, on the other hand, click the **Clear all** link beside the **State courts** heading (as well as the one beside **Federal courts**, if you had selected any) and then check the box next to Nebraska. If you only want the Nebraska Supreme Court but not the Nebraska Court of Appeals, simply click the **Court of Appeals** box to uncheck it. (This will also uncheck the main Nebraska box, as well.) When you are finished making your court selections, click **Done** to close the courts screen.

When you click the **Select courts** link to use the check boxes to select jurisdictions before entering a search (Figure 6.2), clicking **Done** takes you to a screen with a single Google Scholar search box and the instructions **Please enter a query in the search box above** (see Figure 6.3). If you wish to use the **Advanced search** feature at this point (which we recommend), you may click the small arrow to the right of the **My Citations** button, as shown in Figure 6.3. A drop-down menu will appear and you can select **Advanced search.** (**My Citations** is a recently added feature that helps authors track citations to their own publications.)

Figure 6.3   Query in Google Scholar

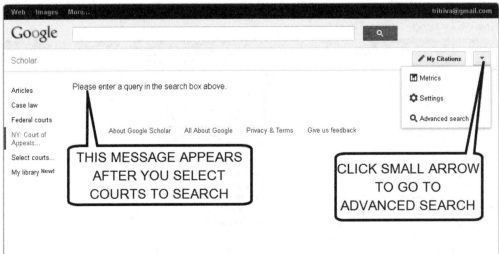

You can also access the **Advanced search** from Google Scholar's home page (in one of two ways, depending on your browser). Most users can access the **Advanced search** option by clicking a small downward-facing arrow in the right side of the search box. This arrow does not always appear, however, and some users may need to access the feature by clicking an **Advanced search** link at the top of the Google Scholar home page. Both options are illustrated above. Regardless of how you access the **Advanced search**, the menu will look the same, as illustrated in Figure 6.4. Before selecting the **Advanced search**, be sure you have changed the **Articles** default to **Case law** if you want to search case law.

Figure 6.4 Access Google Scholar's Advance Search

Google frequently updates its features, and one of these recent updates includes the removal of the separate **Advanced search** page with four sections, which was known as the "old venerable" look. Researchers must now use the "modern" version which essentially consists of a pop-up box containing two of the four sections that had been available with the venerable look. Despite its simplified format, however, you can still create better and more targeted searches with the **Advanced search** than without it.

Searching Google Scholar is similar to searching Google.com as far as Boolean, keyword, and phrase searching are concerned, but proximity searching does not seem to work all the time.

Although there are some Google Scholar-specific search tips (http://scholar.
google.com/intl/en/scholar/help.html#searching), which explain how to use the
Advanced Search menu, they focus primarily on how to search for articles. To com-
pensate for Google's lack of documentation about how to search the case law portion
of Google Scholar and its Advanced search, we have run a number of test searches
to offer searchers some guidance.

The Google Scholar **Advanced search** menu (see Figure 6.5) is labeled **Find
Articles**, but it should be labeled "Find Articles and Opinions" because this is where
researchers enter words and phrases to also search Google Scholar's opinions database. The first four search boxes in this section are similar to the Google.com
Advanced Search page, but there are some differences, such as the the drop-down
menu labeled **where my words occur**. You can use this drop-down menu to select
either **in the title of the article** (this should really be labeled "in the party names of
the case", such as *roe wade* to search for *Roe v. Wade*) or **anywhere in the article** (this
should really be labeled "anywhere in the case").

Figure 6.5   Google Scholar's Advanced Search Menu

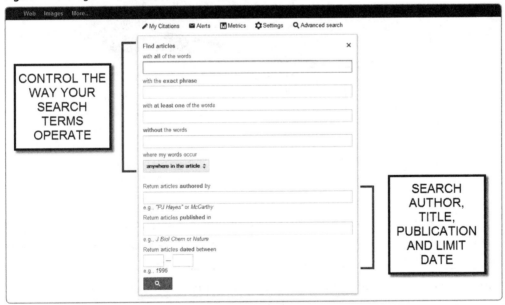

The **Find articles** section provides keyword/Boolean connector field boxes for
you to enter your search terms into and a phrase field box:

- **With all of the words** (This is the *AND* Boolean connector field, so all
  words entered here will appear in your search results.)

- **With the exact phrase** (All of your search results must include this exact phrase. If you enter only one phrase into this field, there is no need to surround the phrase with quotation marks. However, if you enter more than one phrase, each will require quotation marks.)
- **With at least one of the words** (This is the *OR* Boolean connector field, so at least one of the words entered will be included in the search results.)
- **Without the words** (This is the *NOT* Boolean connector field so all words or phrases entered into this field will be excluded in the search results.)

In addition these fields allow you to create searches that are unique to opinions. For example, to force a search by citation, enter the citation (in Bluebook style) into the exact phrase search box. Even though a case citation is not an "article," the results will include cases.

To force a case search by party name, first limit the results to a specific court (e.g., the U.S. Supreme Court) if you know which court decided the case. Next, enter the party names (e.g., *Roe v. Wade*) into the exact phrase search box, making sure to use *v.* and not *versus* or *vs.* Finally, from the **where my words occur** drop-down menu, select **in the title of the article.** This search brought back one opinion. It did not bring back any articles because choosing a court eliminates articles in the search results (see Figure 6.6).

Figure 6.6   Google Scholar's Case Search by Party Results

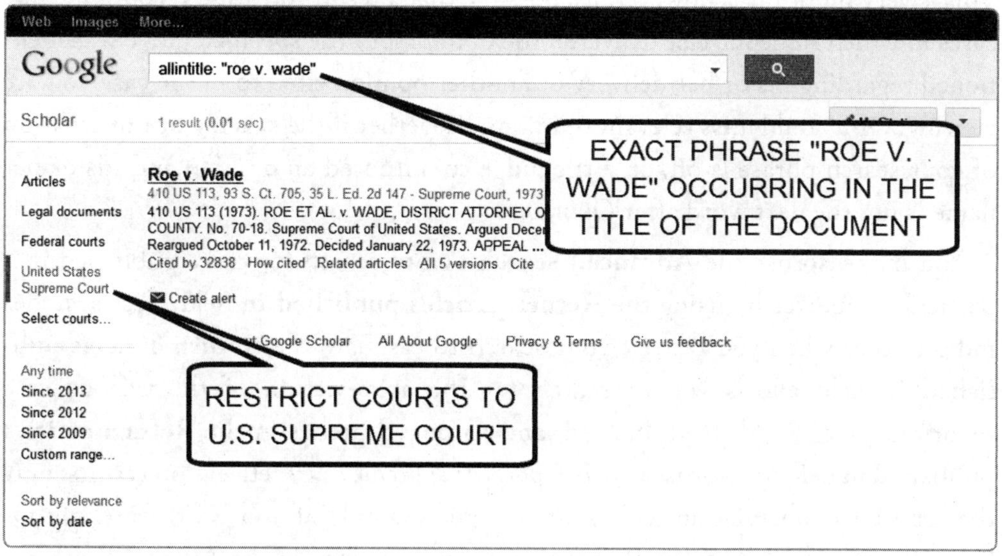

If you wanted to research how specific federal and state courts have cited to *Roe v. Wade,* you would first select the courts you want to search from the **Select courts**

page. Then enter the party names as a phrase (e.g., *Roe v. Wade*) into the **with the exact phrase** search box under **Find articles**. From the **where my words occur** drop-down menu, select **anywhere in the article** to bring back cases that include the phrase "Roe v. Wade" anywhere in the opinion and not just in the case title, (unlike the previous search). This should return a list of cases that have cited to your case. The preceding techniques are also useful for the party name cite check-ing technique.)

The remainder of the **Advanced search** box provides search fields for **Author, Publication,** and **Date**. The label **Judge** could be substituted for the **Author** label because this is where a judge's name can be entered when researching opinions. Test searches indicate that this field does not necessarily return opinions (or concur-rences or dissents) authored by the judge searched, however. Any case in which the judge's name appears (i.e., if he or she heard the case, but did not author the opin-ion) can appear in the search results.

You can try to force a search to return a judge as **Author**. If you want only cases in which a specified U.S. Supreme Court Justice delivered the opinion, for example, you would first select that court and then add the justice's name and the word "deliv-ered" into the search box labeled **Find articles with all of the words**. For other jurisdictions—Arizona, for example—you can try with the exact phrase, using a search such as *opinion Eckerstrom*, if you wanted opinions written by Eckerstrom. This is very hit or miss, however. It's possible that a result (or results) could include cases in which someone else delivered the opinion but the specified judge was men-tioned regarding his or her delivery of another opinion cited to in the case you are viewing. Or it could miss relevant opinions altogether if the spacing or punctuation of your search phrase is off, or if the judge co-authored an opinion and his or her name is not the next word after *Opinion*.

You may also use the **Advanced search** box to search for cases published in a particular reporter by using the **Return articles published in** field. Test searches indicate that when you restrict your search to case law, the **Return articles pub-lished in** field allows you to search for the abbreviation of the various case reporters—e.g., A.2d, P.3d, NY 2d, and so on. (Searches in the **Return articles published in** field for words such as *reports* or *supreme court* retrieve no results; only the reporter's abbreviation will work.) So for example, if you were searching for *Smith v. Jones* and only knew that the case was published in the Atlantic Reporter, you could still search for *Smith v. Jones* in the exact phrase box and enter A.2d, (or A.3d, etc.) in the **Return articles published in** field.

The Collections and Legal opinions and journals sections that were available on the "old venerable" page, which allowed you to search law journals and cases together, have been removed and can no longer be accessed. However, a legal researcher can still approximate this function with Google Scholar's post-search filters, which we will now describe.

When beginning your research, always be sure to select the **Case law** radio button on the main Google Scholar page. Doing so will help ensure that your search results are within the legal field, although this feature is not infallible. (Unfortunately for researchers in other disciplines, law is now the only subject—or "collection"—for which Google even attempts to pre-filter search results in this way.)

Search Results in Google Scholar

Once you have selected which courts to search and entered your search terms, you will receive the list of results, much like any other list of search results. However, Google Scholar now provides search result filtering options for legal document searches, and you can use these to refine your research even more. You will find the filtering options in a sidebar on the left side of the search results page. (See Figure 6.7.)

Figure 6.7 Google Scholar's Filtering Options

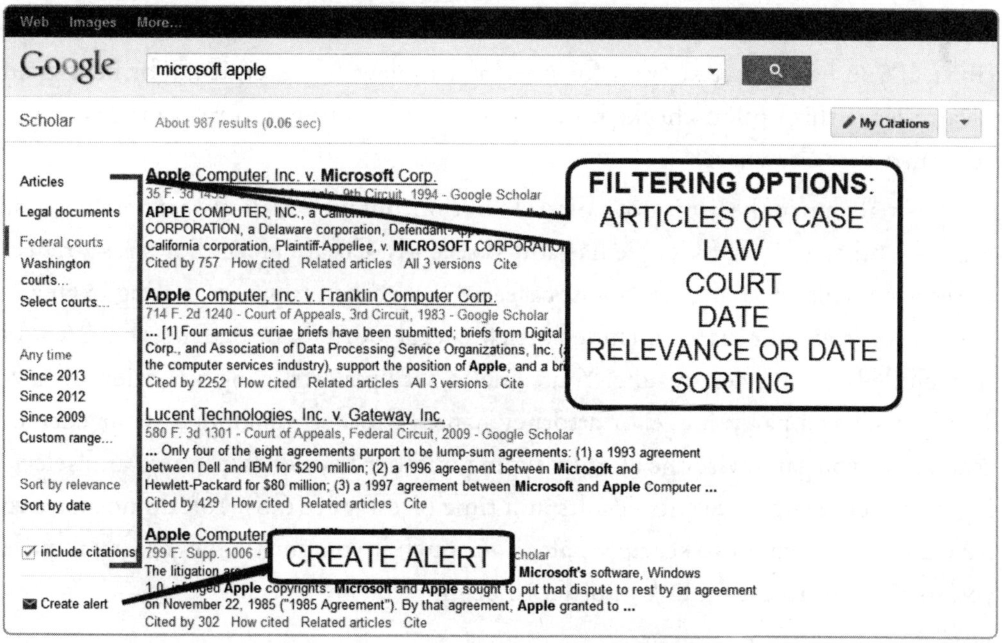

We will discuss the filters from top to bottom as they appear on the search results page. To switch between cases and journal articles that contain your search terms, click the **Articles** and **Case law** links at the top of the sidebar. Clicking these links will refresh your results list to show the relevant type of documents.

Although you may have already selected the jurisdictions you wished to search by before you reached this page, you can now adjust them while retaining your search terms. The court links are the same ones that appeared on the original Google Scholar search page, but you can click them here to see your search results in different courts.

The next two filters are for date. The first one allows you to restrict the dates of the documents that you are viewing. You may want to find more recent cases (or journal articles), and the filters allow you to select **Any time**, various dates in recent years, or your own custom date range. If you click the **Custom range** link, two boxes will appear beneath the link. You enter the four-digit beginning and ending years of the dates you wish to include in your search results and then click the Search button that appears below the two boxes. The next filtering option allows you to sort your search results by date, with the newest items appearing first.

The next link in the list of filtering options is **include citations**. As mentioned above, Google will search cases that include your search terms but to which it (and you) may not have full-text access. If you only want to see search results that inlcude the full text of cases, then you will want to uncheck the box next to **include citations**. If you have other sources for viewing case law, however, it might be a good idea to leave this option checked, in case there are citations to relevant cases that you can access elsewhere.

The final item in the list is not a filtering option, but we will discuss it here because it is a useful feature that Google has added recently. **Create alert** allows researchers to receive regular e-mail alerts about cases on any chosen topic emanating from any chosen court. If your search included articles, legal journals, or patents, those would be included in your alert results. You can also set up alerts using a citation or keywords, such as a party, judge, or attorney name. The alert defaults to your current search, but you can revise the alert by typing in other keywords/phrases and selecting up to ten or up to twenty results at a time (see Figure 6.8). You do not have to have a Google account to set up an alert, although if you don't, Google may require you to click a verification link in order to begin receiving alerts.

Figure 6.8 Google Scholar's Create an Alert

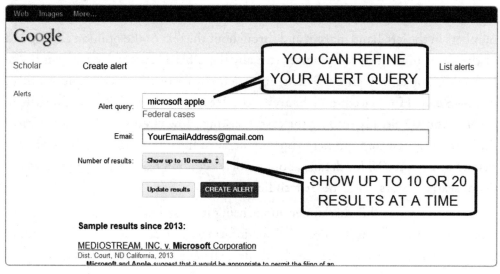

Once you have executed a search and refined your results, you will begin review-ing the cases you have found. Figure 6.9 shows what you will see when you click a search result link to view a full-text opinion with Google Scholar.

Figure 6.9 Google Scholar's Full-Text Option

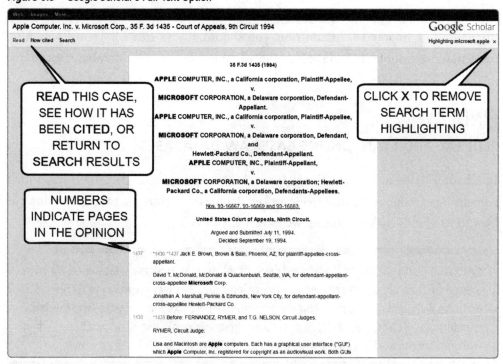

Keywords are automatically highlighted in pale yellow, but you can remove the highlighting by clicking the small *X* in the upper right corner of the screen. Page numbers in the left-hand margin and throughout the text of the opinion correspond to the pages in the printed reporter (usually the official reporter), as shown in the Federal Reporter in Figure 6.9. The upper left corner of the screen contains three links—**Read, How cited**, and **Search**. The **Read** link is inactive on this screen because you are already reading the case. Clicking **How cited** will show other cases that cited this case and can help you conduct a rudimentary citation check of your case. (See Chapter 18 for details about Google's citation features.) To return to the list of search results, click the **Search** link.

Google provides this disclaimer about using its case law database: "Legal opinions in Google Scholar are provided for informational purposes only and should not be relied on as a substitute for legal advice from a licensed lawyer. Google does not warrant that the information is complete or accurate." (http://www.google.com/intl/en/scholar/help.html#coverage). Disclaimers like this can even be found at official courts' websites where they are providing a database of their own legal opinions. As with any case law research, it's imperative that you determine that you are using cases that have not been overruled or reversed by using the citation features at Google Scholar (see Chapter 18); or by conducting a citation check at a pay database such as KeyCite, Shepard's, or Casemaker; or by using free alternatives, discussed in Chapter 18. In addition, you should always run a keyword search by party name to double check Google's and all other free/low cost databases' citations.

FINDLAW

FEDERAL AND STATE ONLINE CASE LAW DATABASES

In Chapter 4, we noted that **FindLaw** is classified as a portal because it has added something of value at its site: free case law databases. Before we take a close look at how to use FindLaw's databases, we have a CAVEAT.

> **CAVEAT:** In our test searches, we found many problems with FindLaw's databases. We have alerted FindLaw about the problems and were informed they were working to fix the problems. We will point out the problems in case they have not fixed them by the time this book is published. We considered deleting FindLaw from our book, but their databases, when working, are the next best databases after Google Scholar.

FindLaw's Opinion Summaries Archive

FindLaw's **Opinion Summaries Archive** includes summaries of cases written by FindLaw staff. The summaries are uploaded soon after the cases are released. After reading the summaries, click **Read** to read the full-text of a case. The Summaries Archive covers opinions from the U.S. Supreme Court and all thirteen U.S. Circuit Courts of Appeals, but only six states (the supreme and appellate courts of California and Illinois, the supreme courts of Delaware, Florida, and New York and the supreme and criminal appeals courts of Texas). Each court must be searched individually. The Archive's date coverage only reaches back to September 2000. (To search further back in time and to search all states' cases, see the section on U.S. Supreme Court, Federal Circuit Courts of Appeals, and Individual States' Case Law Databases: FindLaw later in this chapter.)

The **Opinions Summaries Archive** can be accessed from two places: from the **Cases & Codes** tab on the top left-hand side of FindLaw's home page at http://lp.findlaw.com or from the **Research the Law** search box in the middle of the home page (see Figure 6.10). The only difference between the two points of access is that **Research the Law**'s search menu includes tabs labeled **Search for a Contract** and **Search Articles** (see Figure 6.10), while the **Cases and Codes** search menu does not include these two tabs.

Figure 6.10   FindLaw's Home Page

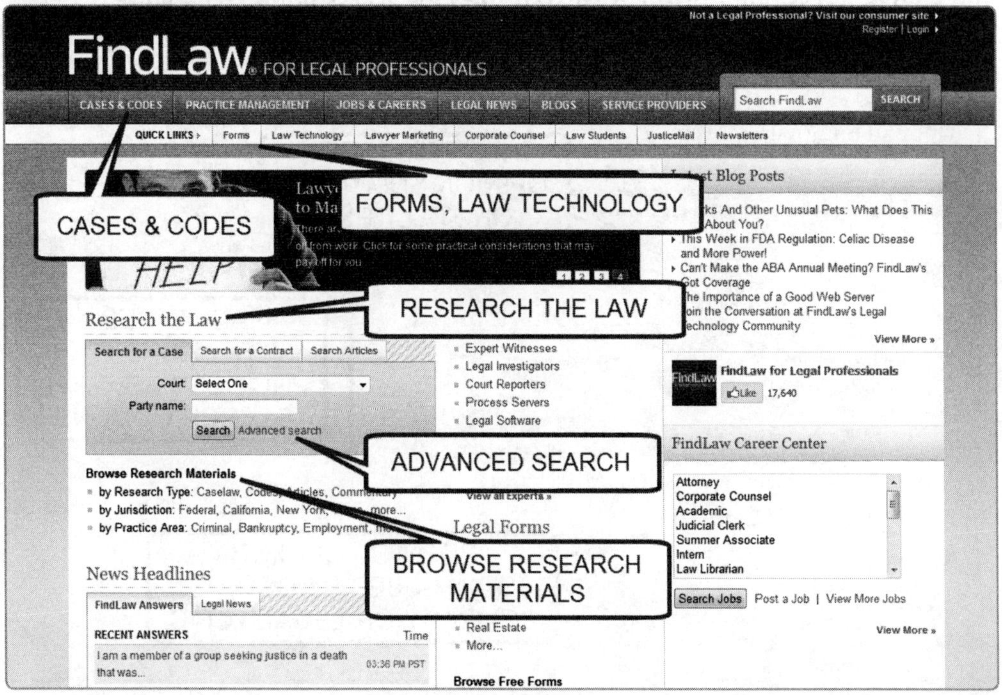

Clicking the **Cases & Codes** tab takes you to a **Cases and Codes** basic search menu page, which offers a choice of (1) searching a specific **Court** by **Legal Topic** (see Figure 6.11) or (2) searching with the **Advanced Search** feature.

Figure 6.11   FindLaw's Cases and Codes Basic Search

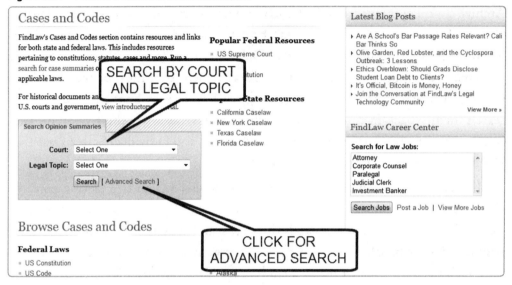

This **Advanced Search** link takes you to the exact same **Opinion Summaries Archive** page at http://caselaw.findlaw.com/summary whether you use the **Cases and Codes** access point or the **Research the Law** access point (see Figure 6.12).

Figure 6.12   FindLaw's Opinion Summaries Archives

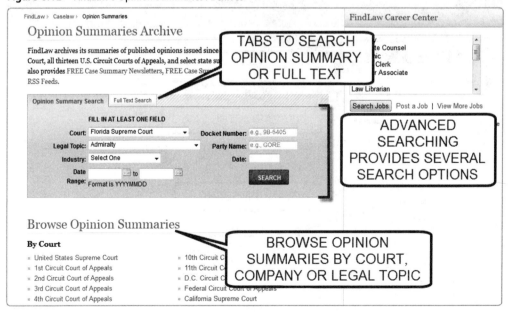

Thus, the researcher views the same **Advanced Search** menu with the same search fields (**Court, Legal Topic, Industry, Docket Number, Party Name, Date, and Date Range**).

The **Advanced Search** menu also offers keyword searching, which is reached by clicking the **Full Text** tab (see Figures 6.12 and 6.13). The full text searching is supposed to work in conjunction with the search fields (such as **Date Range** and **Court**) found on the **Advanced Opinion Summary Search** menu. If it did work, you would be able to filter your full text search by **Date Range** and **Court** and then click the **Full Text Search** tab to refine the search with keywords.

CAVEAT: The **Full Text** function described above was not working at the time we wrote about it. By the time you read this book, it may be working correctly.

Using the **Full Text Search** without also selecting any options from the **Advanced Search** menu returns results in reverse chronological order, without regard to jurisdiction.

Figure 6.13   FindLaw's Full Text Search

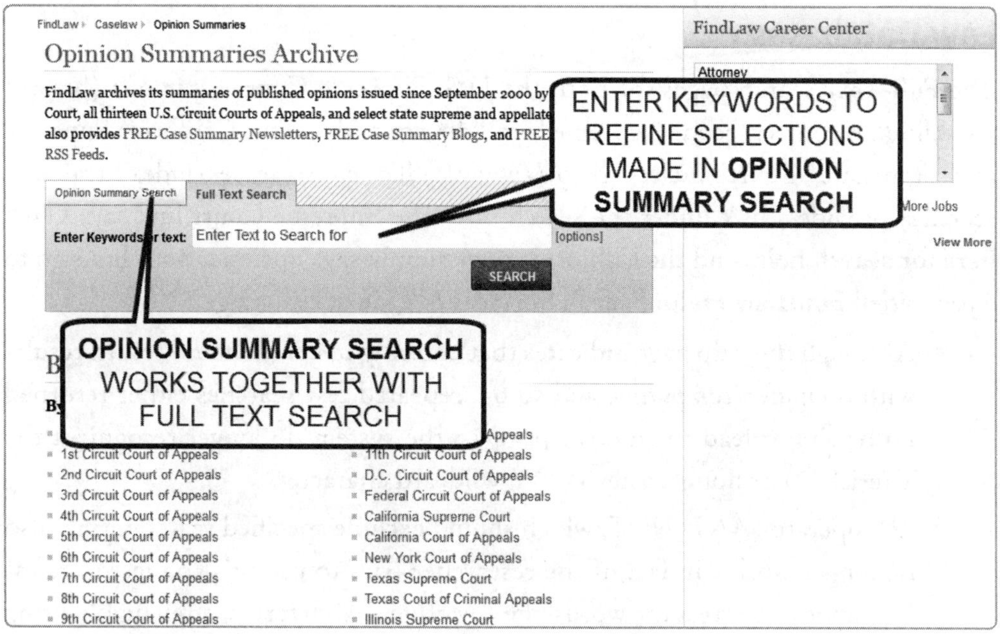

Underneath the **Advanced Search** menu (see Figure 6.12), notice the **Browse Opinion Summaries** section, where you can also browse opinions **By Court, By Company**, or **By Topic**.

After you run your search, there will be a results list displaying summaries of the cases. Click a case name and then click the **Read** link to view the full text of the case. For some cases, when you click the **Read** link you may receive a message that states "FindLaw is currently processing this opinion. In the meantime, you can access a copy of the opinion here." The **here** link will take you to the slip opinion of the case.

> **California Differences:** For some California cases, FindLaw only has a PDF version (and not an HTML version) of the full-text of the case. These PDF cases will not open in a browser and you will be prompted to download or save.

The California and U.S. Supreme Court cases have some additional features not found at the other jurisdictions' databases that we will discuss later in this chapter.

Full-Text Search Tips for FindLaw's Federal and State Case Law Databases

The **Full-Text** search pages for both the U.S. Supreme Court Opinions (http://www.findlaw.com/casecode/supreme.html#dirsearch3) and the California Supreme and Appellate Court Cases (http://www.findlaw.com/cacases/index.html#dirsearch2) provide a link under the search box. The Supreme Court link says **Click here for search help**, and the California page simply says **options**. Both links go to a page titled **FindLaw Help: Search Services & Query Language**.

- Although the help page indicates that entering *comput** should return results with *computer, computing,* and so on, repeated test searches either returned no results or lead to an error page, so the system no longer recognizes the asterisk (*) or double asterisk (**) wildcard characters.

- The operator *AND NOT,* which should exclude specified search terms, also no longer works. In fact, if the researcher tries to use this connector, Find-Law appears to treat the words like any other search terms, often highlighting them in bold throughout the search results along with the term that the researcher intended to exclude.

Some search connectors do still appear to work, however:

- The Boolean operators *AND* and *OR* and the proximity operator *NEAR* (which places words on the same page, "close together," according to the help page) can still be used to connect keywords and phrases. Note that the above operators must be in all capital letters; otherwise the search engine will treat them as regular search terms. Even when the connectors appear to be functioning correctly, FindLaw often highlights them in results, as if they were regular search terms.

- To search for an exact phrase, enclose it in quotation marks. (Although this technique will locate cases containing the phrase, the individual terms will also be highlighted in the cases.)

CAVEAT: Although the **FindLaw Help: Search Services & Query Language** page provides several search tips for Boolean and proximity connectors as well as wildcards, many of the search tips do not seem to work, so we advise using caution when attempting to run a full-text search in FindLaw. We have alerted FindLaw to these issues and by the time you read this, hopefully they will have been fixed.

U.S. Supreme Court, Federal Circuit Courts of Appeals, and Individual States' Case Law Databases in FindLaw

To find U.S. Supreme Court and Circuit Courts of Appeals case law databases that go further back in time than the Opinion Summaries Archive's database and to find each of the fifty states' individual case law databases (instead of the six available at the Opinion Summaries Archive's database), select the **Cases & Codes** tab on the upper-left side of FindLaw's home page at http://lp.findlaw.com (see Figure 6.14) and then:

- Scroll down to the **Browse Cases and Codes** section.
- Select the U.S. Supreme Court, one of the Circuit Courts of Appeals, or one of the states and territories listed beneath State Resources.
- See the description at the beginning of this section for information on how to perform full-text and other searches.

Figure 6.14   FindLaw's Expanded Search Options

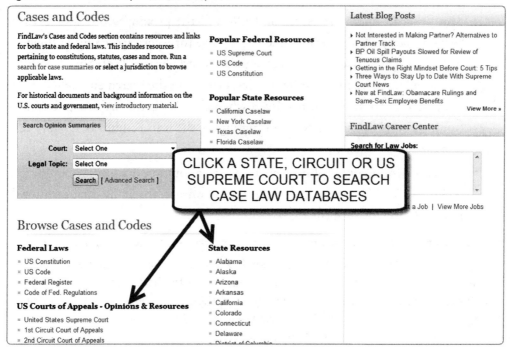

U.S. Supreme Court and Circuit Courts of Appeals Online Case Law Databases in FindLaw

After clicking the **U.S. Supreme Court** or the **Circuit Courts of Appeals** links found at http://www.findlaw.com/casecode, case law database search menus will appear. FindLaw's U.S. Supreme Court Opinions database goes back to 1893 (http://www.findlaw.com/casecode/supreme.html). (See Chaper 4 for information about Justia's Supreme Court Center, which offers additional resources for researching the U.S. Supreme Court.)

As shown in Figure 6.15, the Supreme Court cases can be searched by choosing a tab to perform a **Citation Search** (using the official U.S. Reports citation), a **Party Name Search**, or a **Full-Text Search** by keywords and phrases.

Figure 6.15   FindLaw's Supreme Court Case Search

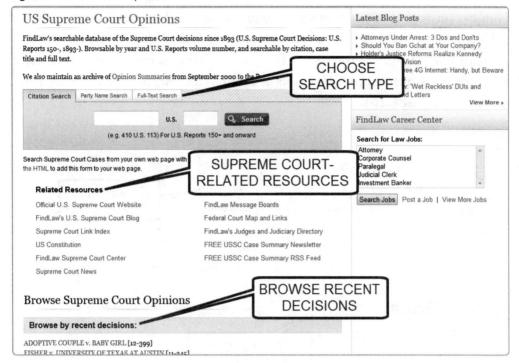

U.S. Supreme Court opinions have links to **View enhanced case on Westlaw** and **Keycite this case on Westlaw.** When the user clicks either of these links, however, a screen appears that states that Westlaw by Credit Card is no longer available. Links are then provided to WestlawNext and Westlaw Classic, both of which require subscriptions. (Westlaw used to offer a separate subscription to Keycite without having to subscribe to a full Westlaw account.)

For the most recent nine years, the Supreme Court cases can also be browsed by selecting a year. Cases will be listed in alphabetical order by the first party's name; to view the alphabetical listing by second party name, click the **Revert** link at the top of the list of cases.

For FindLaw's **Circuit Courts of Appeals Cases** database (http://www.findlaw.com/casecode), dates of coverage vary by circuit, with most going back to 1995. However, the First Circuit goes back to 1984.

The circuit courts' cases can be searched by a **Free Text Search** (this is the same as the **Full-Text Search** shown in Figure 6.15; we pointed out the inconsistent labels to FindLaw and they say they will address this inconsistency and use the same label for each database), **Party Name Search** (unlike the U.S. Supreme Court database, the **Party Name Search** includes counsel and judge names), and **Docket Number** (instead of the citation search found at the U.S. Supreme Court database). A **Date Range** can also be added to the preceding searches (the U.S. Supreme Court database does not offer this option). The Circuit Courts search menu also contains a **Browse by Court** tab, which displays opinions in reverse date order by year/month (see Figure 6.16).

Figure 6.16   FindLaw's Browse Circuit Courts

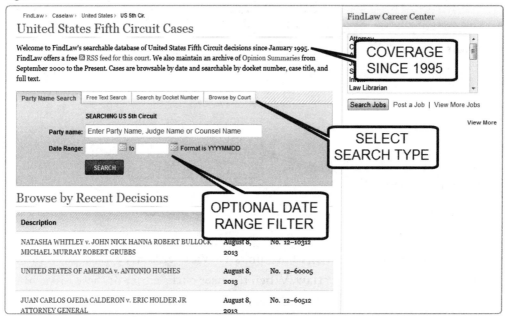

FindLaw only searches one circuit court at a time. If you need to search multiple circuits (for free), see the discussion of Google Scholar's ability to search all circuits together.

Individual State Online Case Law Databases in FindLaw

In contrast to the U.S. Supreme Court or the Circuit Courts of Appeals case law database search menus, which appear as soon as you click their links, it takes several more steps to find each state's FindLaw-created case law database search menus. After selecting the **Cases & Codes** tab on the upper-left side of **FindLaw's home page** at http://lp.findlaw.com (see Figure 6.10), follow these steps:

- Scroll down to **State Resources.**
- Select a state.

- Scroll down to **State Court Opinions**.
- Click on one of the links that have a FindLaw notation. An example looks like this: **Delaware Supreme Court Opinions – FindLaw cases for Supreme Court of Delaware** (see Figure 6.17).

Figure 6.17 FindLaw's State Case Law Database

While the state portion of FindLaw's **Opinion Summaries Archive** only covers six states (California, Delaware, Florida, Illinois, New York, and Texas) back to the year 2000, the **State Resources** page offers case law databases (labeled "FindLaw cases") for all fifty states dating back to 1997 (for most states). All the state databases can be searched or browsed the same way as FindLaw's other courts databases as explained earlier, except for California, which will be described later. Unfortunately, each state must be searched separately.

FindLaw's **State Resources** pages link to each state's official court site, with some offering a searchable case law database. Sometimes FindLaw's **State Resources** pages will also link to non-official sites and these sites might offer a searchable case law database.

THE PUBLIC LIBRARY OF LAW (PLOL)

SELECTED FEDERAL AND ALL STATES ONLINE CASE LAW DATABASE

PLoL (http://www.plol.org) is a free, full-text keyword-searchable database of cases provided by the pay database Fastcase (see Chapter 9 on Fastcase). PLoL only includes a limited number of courts and a limited range of dates. To search more courts and date ranges, PLoL includes a link to the paid content found at Fastcase (or see Chapter 3 regarding the free Fastcase mobile App). PLoL requires registration (including a telephone number) to view the full text of cases from the following courts:

- All fifty states' (and Guam's) appellate and supreme court cases from 1997 to present
- All U.S. Supreme Court cases from 1754 to present
- All federal Circuit Courts of Appeals cases from 1950 to present (except for the 11th Circuit, which provides cases from 1981 to present, and the Federal Circuit, which provides cases from 1982 to present)

The PLoL case law database does not include federal district cases, federal bankruptcy cases, or any non-case law legal materials. The tabs to the right of the **Case Law** tab (**Statutes, Regulations, Court Rules, Constitutions,** and **Legal Forms**) only link to the official government websites where you can search those materials.

To search case law, select the **Case Law** tab and enter a citation, docket number, party name, or keywords and phrases into the search box. This will search all jurisdictions for which PLoL has cases. Choose the **Advanced Options** link to limit your search by a date range (month/year), a specific state's case law, a specific federal circuit, or the U.S. Supreme Court. (You can leave the court search boxes blank to search all courts included in the PLoL database.) PLoL only allows researchers to select one jurisdiction or all jurisdictions. PLoL searches can include Boolean connectors (*AND, OR, NOT*), phrase searching, wildcard characters (the asterisk), and proximity connectors (*W #*).

THE FREE LAW REPORTER, 2011–DATE (FLR)

SELECTED FEDERAL AND ALL STATES ONLINE CASE LAW DATABASE

On April 4, 2011, The Center for Computer-Assisted Legal Instruction (CALI) launched **The Free Law Reporter** (**FLR**) at http://www.freelawreporter.org. FLR provides a free, keyword searchable database of all slip and final opinions (including "unpublished" opinions, orders, and motions) from the appellate courts of all fifty states, the U.S. Supreme Court, and the federal appellate courts (but not the federal district or bankruptcy courts). All courts must be searched together.

CALI explains FLR as an experiment that builds on **Report of Current Opinions** (**RECOP**), which is a project of **Public.Resource.org's** Carl Malamud. Click the **About** tab on the site's home page (http://www.freelawreporter.org) for the full explanation. RECOP provides weekly feeds to FLR, so the database is not as up-to-date as other free case law databases (which are often updated daily). Fastcase collaborates with Public.Resource.org with the weekly feed (http://bit.ly/hERkLM). Coverage begins with January 1, 2011, and continues forward, but we did find many earlier cases in our test searches. The database is powered by Apache Solr, which, according to the FLR Web site, "allows for sophisticated searching."

Unfortunately, there is no documentation at FLR or Apache Solr's site telling users how to search, but in our test searches we found that we were, indeed, able to perform sophisticated searching. It appears that Google type searches (keyword and phrase searching with Boolean connectors) will work. We were also able to use parentheses to create our searches, which is something you cannot do at Google.

Our search (shown in Figure 6.18) brought back 173 cases. To view an individual case, click on the case name. You can also download the FLR e-book volume in which your case resides, or you can download your search results as an e-book.

Figure 6.18   FLR's Search

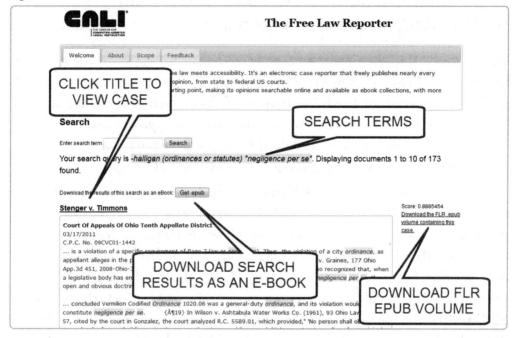

FINDACASE NETWORK

SELECTED FEDERAL AND ALL STATES ONLINE CASE LAW DATABASE

The pay case law database **VersusLaw** offers the free **FindACase Network** case law database (http://www.findacase.com). FindACase distinguishes itself from PLoL by offering free access to federal district court cases and by offering broader date coverage for most of the courts included in its database. The following courts are included in the FindACase database:

- **U.S. Supreme Court:** 1886 to present
- **Federal Circuit Courts of Appeals:** Date coverage varies, but some circuits go as far back as 1930.
- **Federal District Courts:** Date coverage varies, but some districts go as far back as 1930.
- **State and D.C. Appellate Courts:** Date coverage varies, but some states go as far back as 1910.

The home page of FindACase offers a **Simple** search, but we would suggest clicking the **Try an advanced search** link (found below the simple search box) to conduct a better search (http://findacase.com/research/advanced-search.aspx).

To search FindACase by jurisdiction or court, you first select a state and then choose the courts associated with that state. Begin by selecting one state. You may then select any combination of that state's appellate court cases, federal district court cases, federal circuit court cases, and U.S. Supreme Court cases. If you do not select any courts associated with the state you select, FindACase will search all applicable courts. Grouping by states means that you can't search all state court cases together or all federal court cases together.

For example, as illustrated on the advanced search menu in Figure 6.19, after we selected New York, we could search one or more of the following: New York Appellate Courts, U.S. District Courts of New York, Second U.S. Circuit Court of Appeals, or U.S. Supreme Court. To search an additional state, we would have to start this process over again by picking another state from the list, then selecting the available courts in that state, and so on.

Figure 6.19   FindACase's Advance Search

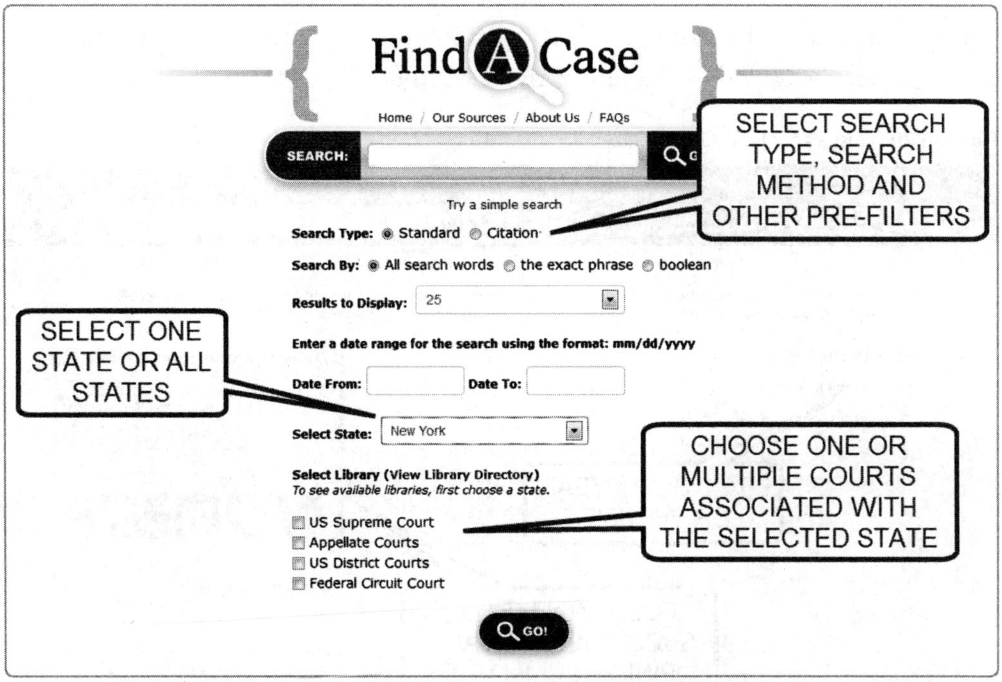

After selecting a state in which to search, FindACase provides two search types: **Standard** (keywords/phrases) or **Citation**. After choosing the **Standard** search, you would enter keywords/phrases into the search box and then select whether to search by **all search words, the exact phrase**, or **Boolean**. The site has a **FAQs** page (http://findacase.com/faq.aspx) that provides some tips on searching, but it does not provide great detail on search techniques. For example, there is no indication as to whether the *AND* Boolean connector or the plus sign (+) should be used to connect words. Our test searches indicate that the *AND* Boolean connector works but the plus sign does not. There is also no indication as to whether the various searches can be mixed and matched but our mixed phrase/Boolean search seemed to work. A date range can also be entered.

Although FindACase is free to search and viewing the full text of cases is free, there is a $7.95 fee per case to view footnotes, citations, and docket numbers.

JUSTIA

U.S. SUPREME COURT ONLINE CASE LAW DATABASE

Justia's U.S. Supreme Court Center database can be reached by either clicking on the **Supreme Court Center** link found near the bottom of the home page (http://www.justia.com) or by using this URL: http://supreme.justia.com. The database coverage reaches back to Volume 1 of the U.S. Reports (1791).

Figure 6.20   Justia's Supreme Court Center

To full-text search, enter keywords or phrases into the search box at the top right-hand side of the page (see Figure 6.20) and connect them with Boolean connectors. Justia's search protocols are the same as Google's. Even though it's not apparent, you can also enter a citation (e.g., *1 U.S. 1*) or a party name into the full-text search box. You can also browse by **Volume, Year,** or **keyword search** (see Figure 6.20).

Justia has traditionally allowed users to search by court, via a drop-down menu next to the search box. At the time we wrote this book, however, the menu had been removed. Although Justia told us they were in the process of revising their search feature, we do not know if the court-specific feature will return. If it does not return, you will need to search the entire site and then browse all results to locate the cases you want.

Justia also offers free subscriptions to case opinion summary newsletters for the U.S. Supreme Court and other U.S. appellate and state courts. You will need to create a Justia account and subscribe (http://law.justia.com/subscriptions) to select the free newsletters you wish to receive. You can also follow Justia on Google+ or "like" it on Facebook.

For databases that offer additional free U.S. Supreme Court resources, such as audio files of both the oral arguments and opinion announcements, see **Oyez** (http://www.oyez.org).

JUSTIA FEDERAL AND STATE COURTS' ONLINE CASE LAW DATABASE

Justia used to provide a search feature to search all federal and state cases together, but it, along with the court-specific search for the U.S. Supreme Court, is no longer on the website. We hope it will return by the time you read this book. You can still browse federal and state court cases, however, at http://law.justia.com/cases/. Here you can first select the court you want, then the year, and then browse by month.

Justia also provides a page for U.S. Federal Case Law at http://law.justia.com/cases/federal, and it is organized a bit differently than the main case law page. For the U.S. Courts of Appeals, browsing cases is done by series (e.g., F.2d) and then by volume or by circuit/year/month.

For the U.S. District Courts, browsing cases is done by state and then by choosing either the entire district (e.g., Alabama Federal District Court) or a specific district (e.g., the Middle District of the Alabama Federal District Court). Once the court is selected, a year (back to 2005 or earlier) must be selected and then a month. Dates of coverage vary by court. For example, the Fifth Circuit dates back to 1901, but Alaska District Court cases only go back to 2005. All cases on Justia are listed in reverse chronological order.

Justia also provides links to the official sites of all federal and state courts at http://law.justia.com/courts/. After choosing a federal or state court, you will then be taken to the official website for that court. Most of the court sites will have a link to opinions on the home page, either in a side bar, or in a row of tabs near the top of the screen. Each court's site is different, however, so to search or browse opinions you may have to look for the link.

ACCESSLAW

CALIFORNIA ONLINE CASE LAW DATABASE, 1934 TO PRESENT

In previous chapters, we have noted that the State Bar of California, unlike almost every other state bar, does not provide a free member-benefit, full-text case law research database such as Fastcase or Casemaker. (See Chapters 8 and 9 for a discussion of member-benefit databases.) Fortunately, for anyone who wishes to search California case law full-text for free and back to 1934, FindLaw offers **AccessLaw,** which is specific to California. Anyone can use this free resource, but you will need to create a free **FindLaw** account (http://linkon.in/csv4n0). (See also Chapter 4, to learn about the California case law database that is searchable back to 1850. It is provided by LexisNexis as part of its contract to publish **California's Official Reports** (http://www.lexisnexis.com/clients/CACourts).

After selecting the **Cases & Codes** tab on the upper left-hand side of FindLaw's home page at http://lp.findlaw.com (see Figure 6.10), follow these steps to locate the California Supreme Court and Court of Appeals Opinions:

- Scroll down to **State Resources** (see Figure 6.11).
- Select **California.**
- Click **California Supreme Court and Appellate Court Opinions - Find-Law California Supreme Court and Court of Appeals cases with citation, since 1934** (see Figure 6.21).

To use FindLaw's California Supreme Court and Court of Appeals Opinions database described below, you must be logged into your free FindLaw account. After you click FindLaw's **California Supreme Court and Court of Appeals Opinions** link, do not get misled by the **Opinion Summaries** link or any of the **Related Resources** links on the right-hand side of the page (http://www.findlaw.com/

cacases/index.html). Instead, you must scroll down the page to the **Powered By AccessLaw** database. Although it defaults to a **Citation Search**, a tab for an **Advanced Search** menu is also offered.

Figure 6.21 FindLaw's California Supreme Court and Court of Appeals Search

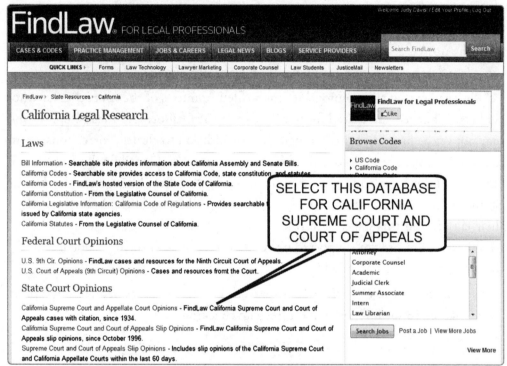

Cases can be searched by the following criteria:

- Party Name
- Full-Text by keywords and phrases
- Judge's Name
- Attorney Name
- Docket Number
- Cite Check (See Chapter 18 for details on the Cite-Check feature.)

Cases can also be browsed by date or volume if you scroll down the **Advanced Search** page.

Once you click on a case result, notice the links labeled **Do Another California Case Law Search** and **Cases Citing This Case.**

> **CAVEAT:** The **Do Another California Case Law Search** link does not always appear to work, however, and we have informed FindLaw, so hopefully there will be a fix by the time you read this.

At the bottom of the California Supreme and Appellate Court Cases page, FindLaw has posted a warning about relying on this database (and the same goes for most free databases, even ones found at official court sites):

"Please note that 'slip opinions' are the 'as filed' opinions of the court that have not yet been enhanced and edited for publication in the California Official Reports and may not yet be final as to the issuing court. In addition to clerical corrections, opinions on this page are subject to modification and rehearing until final, and Court of Appeal opinions are subject to a grant of review or depublication order by the Supreme Court. Opinions certified or ordered partially published are set forth in their entirety on this page. (See rules 976, 976.1, and 977, Cal. Rules of Court.) Modifications to previously posted opinions will appear as separate documents on the day modifications are filed."

As with any case law research, be sure to cite check your cases before filing a brief. (See Chapter 18 for information on free cite checking sites.)

CASETEXT

A "CROWDSOURCED" CASE LAW DATABASE

Recently, the phenomenon of "crowdsourced" case law databases have popped up at various websites. **Casetext** (https://casetext.com/) is a good example of a crowdsourced case law database. Taking a step back, let's define a crowdsourcing site. A crowdsourcing site, according to Wikipedia, is a site that obtains "[n]eeded services, ideas, or content by soliciting contributions from…an online community, rather than from traditional employees or suppliers. This process is often used to subdivide tedious work or to fund raise startup companies and charities, and it can also occur offline. It combines the efforts of numerous self-identified volunteers or part-time workers, where each contributor…adds a small portion to the greater result" (http://en.wikipedia.org/wiki/Crowdsourcing). Wikipedia is a good example of a crowdsourced site. It describes itself as, "[a] multilingual, web-based, free-content encyclopedia project… based on an openly editable model…written collaboratively by largely anonymous Internet volunteers who write without pay. Anyone with Internet access can write and make changes to Wikipedia articles...[if it is] verifiable against a published reliable source, thereby excluding editors' opinions and beliefs and unreviewed research" (http://en.wikipedia.org/wiki/Wikipedia:About).

The Casetext founders are two lawyers, Jake Heller and Joanna Huey, who created a database of case law and then allowed registered users to add the following to any case: (1) tags, (2) annotations/analysis, (3) replies to and comments on other users' annotations/analysis, (4) links to secondary sources (such as news or law review articles) that discuss the case, (5) briefs or transcripts, and (6) related cases (indicating whether their treatment of the case is positive, negative, or distinguishing). Casetext differs from Wikipedia in one major respect: Casetext encourages users to add their own analysis while Wikipedia excludes editors' opinions and beliefs.

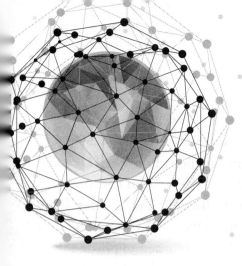

Chapter 7

FREE GOVERNMENTAL ONLINE CASE LAW DATABASES

This chapter will focus on three governmental websites that provide free online case law databases. We will also discuss a stand-alone, free case-law database for California Cases found at the California court's official site but supplied by LexisNexis. Free non-government-affiliated online case law databases aree discussed in Chapter 6. Other online case law databases, such as those that are available free only as a member benefit through certain bar associations, will be discussed in Chapters 8 and 9.

All of the free databases have some sort of limitation, such as limited ranges of dates, limited court coverage, no search option (just browsing), or limited documentation. Although government sources tend to have a high degree of reliability, we would recommend using member-benefit databases (Casemaker, Fastcase, or others) because they will usually offer more sophisticated searching. Regardless of which database you use, probably none of them are 100 percent reliable, so it's imperative that researchers cite check their cases.

FEDERAL DIGITAL SYSTEM (FDSYS) UNITED STATES COURTS OPINIONS COLLECTION

In 2009, the U.S. Government Printing Office (GPO) began migrating all of its government documents (which GPO refers to as Collections) from **GPO Access** to a new system: **GPO FDsys (Federal Digital System)** at http://www.findlaw.com/ cacases/index.html. Originally, U.S. court opinions were not included in FDsys, but in a 2011 beta test project, a limited number of courts' opinions from the U.S. appellate, district, and bankruptcy courts (back to April 2004) were added to a new FDsys Collection, the United States Courts Opinions Collection. The beta test project, operated jointly by the U.S. Government Printing Office (GPO) and the Administrative Office of the United States Courts (AOUSC), is meant to provide free public access to opinions and "the secure transfer of files to GPO from the AOUSC maintains the chain of custody, allowing GPO to authenticate the files with digital signatures." As of 2013, the beta test is still ongoing (see the ever grow-ing list at http://linkon.in/fdsyscourts). By the end of 2013, the project included sixty-five courts (nine appellate courts, twenty-one district courts, and thirty-five bankruptcy courts):

United States Courts of Appeals:

- Second, Fourth, Fifth, Seventh, Eighth, Ninth, Tenth, Eleventh and D.C. Circuits

United States District Courts:

- Twenty-one districts, including courts from twenty states and the District of Columbia

Bankruptcy Courts:

- Thirty-five courts from twenty-eight states and the District of Columbia

Court opinions are searched in the same way any other FDsys Collection is searched, except that some of the search fields are unique to court opinions, such as the party name and docket search fields. Figure 7.1 shows an **Advanced Search** (http://linkon.in/y2uMZC) in the United States Courts Opinions Collection.

Figure 7.1   U.S. Courts Opinions Collection Advanced Search

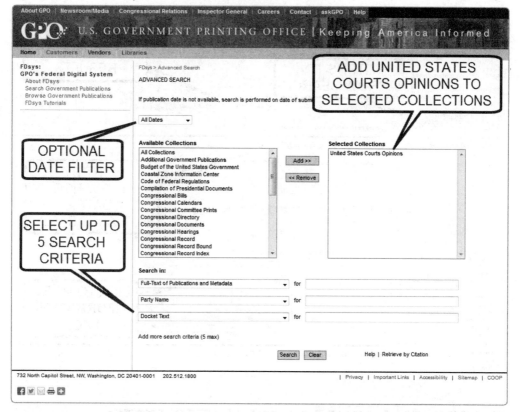

The user selects the collection to search (in this instance the United States Courts Opinions). The name of that collection is then added to the **Selected Collections** box on the right side of the screen. An example of search results are shown in Figure 7.2. Once an opinion is located, all associated opinions within the same case can be accessed from the opinion's **More Information** page.

The results can be:

- Sorted by **Relevance, Date** (New to Old or Old to New), or **Alphabetically** (Z to A or A to Z).

- Re-sorted (see the left-side column) by **Collection, Date Published, Government Author, Organization, Person, Location, Keyword, Court Type, Court Name, Circuit,** or **State.**

- Narrowed by clicking into the **Within Results** box to the right of the search box and then entering one or more keywords into the search box to re-run the new keywords within the original search results.

Figure 7.2 U.S. Courts Opinions Collection Advance Search Results

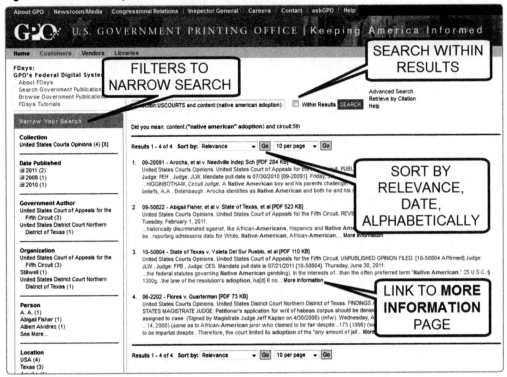

THE SUPREME COURT OF THE UNITED STATES

The **Supreme Court of the United States** provides a website (http://www.supremecourt.gov) that may be helpful for some legal researchers. This site may not always be the best choice for finding Supreme Court opinions, but because it does provide some useful resources and information (and because FDsys currently does not provide a searchable database of Supreme Court opinions on its site), we will briefly describe it here.

The Supreme Court website's home page (Figure 7.3) has a full-text keyword search box in the upper right corner. To search court opinions, you would click into the **All Documents** radio button. However, in addition to court opinions, you will retrieve other documents such as transcripts and dockets. (See the Dockets chapter to learn about limiting your search to Docket Files.) Opinions are typically available within five minutes of being released from the Bench, but older opinions go back only to the 1991 Term.

> See Chapters 7, 8, and 9 for other free Supreme Court web sites that have better search options and date coverage.

Thus, this site may be more useful for researching more recent Supreme Court opinions than older ones.

Figure 7.3 U.S. Supreme Court's Home Page

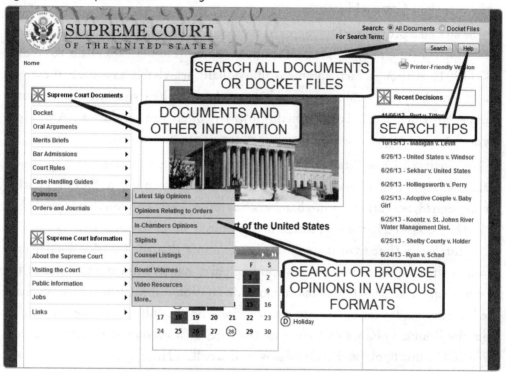

A **Help** button underneath the search box leads to a **Search Tips** page (http://www.supremecourt.gov/search_help.aspx) that explains the site's search function. The search function recognizes the Boolean operators *AND, OR, NEAR* (within fifty words) and *NOT* (to exclude a term). You can put exact phrases in quotation marks, and you can use parentheses to create more sophisticated searches. For example, searching for *(supreme NEAR court) AND (miranda NEAR warning)* would require *supreme* to appear near *court* and *miranda* to appear near *warning*, but it would not require that all four words appear near each other. An asterisk (*) acts as a wildcard for letters at the end of a word. So searching *justi** would search for *justice, justify, justification,* etc. Searches are not case-sensitive, even when words are put inside quotation marks.

Remember that your search terms can also include the name of a party, an attorney, or a judge.

You can browse **Recent Slip Opinions, Opinions Relating to Orders, In-Chambers Opinions,** and **Opinions of the Court** for terms back to 2008 at http://www.supremecourt.gov/opinions/opinions.aspx, in addition to other Court-related documents such as **Counsel Listings.**

The site also provides PDF copies of the bound United States Reports volumes (see http://www.supremecourt.gov/opinions/boundvolumes.aspx) back to volume 502 (1991). Although each volume is individually searchable as a PDF, these volumes, like the print versions, are really useful only when you know the volume number in which a case is published. However, when you conduct an **All Documents** keyword search, the bound volumes are also included.

The site has a **Case Citation Finder** (http://www.supremecourt.gov/opinions/casefinder.aspx) that allows you to enter terms into a search box to find the citation for any signed, *per curiam*, or in-chambers Supreme Court opinion that is published or will be published in the near future in the United States Reports—so it goes back much further in time than the rest of the site. Note that the Citation Finder only searches the citation information (including party names), not the full text of the opinion. Likewise, search results only include citation information. Once you have the full citation, however, you can use it to look up the full text of the case, either from the Bound Volumes collection on this site, or from one of the other sources discussed in this book, such as FindLaw or Cornell's LII.

To use the Case Citation Finder, enter any elements you know from the citation information. For example, you can enter the name of one party, the names of both parties, or the name of one party and the volume number of the United States Reports in which the case is found. The default connector for search terms is the Boolean *OR*, but you can also use *AND* as a Boolean connector and enclose phrases in quotation marks to make your query more specific. A drop-down menu allows you to sort your results by **Volume number, Petitioner,** or **Respondent** (see Figure 7.4).

Figure 7.4   U.S. Supreme Court's Case Citation Search Results

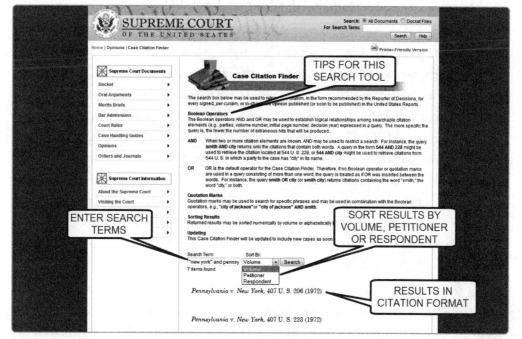

Additional Resources on the U.S. Supreme Court Website

The Supreme Court website provides additional resources that may be useful to some researchers. The **Courts' docket** (http://www.supremecourt.gov/docket/docket.aspx) is available for the current Term and the prior Term. (See Chapter 15, Dockets, to find out where you can obtain older Supreme Court dockets.) Users can search the docket by entering the Supreme Court docket number, a lower court docket number, or the name of the case. The docket also allows keyword searches.

The site also provides **Court Rules, Case Handling Guides,** and other information useful for litigating a case in the Supreme Court. Access these and other links from the sidebar on the left side of the home page (http://www.supremecourt.gov/default.aspx). Although the site's FAQ page states that briefs are available for the current Term (by clicking the **Merits Briefs** link in the left sidebar), the link actually goes to a page that directs the user to the **ABA Preview** website.

CALIFORNIA OFFICIAL REPORTS PUBLIC ACCESS

California is one of the only states that does not provide a member-benefit legal research database, such as Fastcase or Casemaker, to its state bar association members. (See Chapters 8 and 9 for a discussion of Casemaker and Fastcase, respectively.) But there is a resource for California lawyers who wish to research California case law for free back to 1850. It is the **California Official Reports Public Access Web site**, which is provided by LexisNexis as part of its contract to publish California's Official Reports (http://www.lexisnexis.com/clients/CACourts). At the time of this book's publication, California appears to be the only state with a case law database of this nature provided by LexisNexis. Check your state court's official site to find out if another vendor provides a similar free database for your state. See Chapter 5 to learn about FindLaw's free full-text California ACCESSLAW case law database, searchable back to 1834.

You do not need to be a member of the California State Bar to use the site, but you must agree to the terms and conditions of use by checking a box and clicking the **Begin Searching Opinions** link. Then the home page defaults to a **Search By Terms** page where the researcher uses natural language words or phrases to search for published or unpublished cases (see Figure 7.5). **California Appellate** and **Supreme Courts** can be searched together or separately and a date restriction can be added to the search. The **Search by Terms** page is very basic and does not accept Boolean connectors or truncation symbols. Researchers type their research issue into the search box using terms (keywords), phrases, lists, or a "natural language" sentence (e.g., *Where can I find cases about "negligence per se" and also products or goods?*). Although there is a warning that a search will only retrieve the twenty-five most relevant cases, test searches retrieved varying numbers of results higher than twenty-five and up to one hundred.

Figure 7.5   California Courts' Case Search

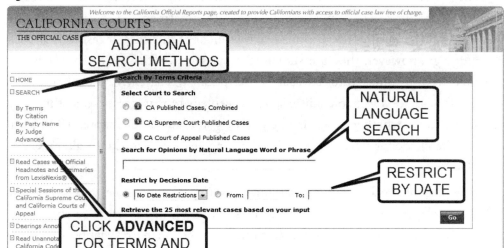

Figure 7.6 shows a search results page with one hundred results. It is displayed in the **Cite View,** which shows the citation and our search terms highlighted within partial sentences. This view can be switched to **Full, KWIC** (KWIC stands for *keywords in context,* which displays each case result with twenty-five words on either side of the keywords), or **Custom.** (For example, case results could be displayed with a citation only or with a citation and the counsel names only. There are over twenty custom display options.) Results can be **Sorted By** either **Relevance** or **Date.** The **Focus** search allows a researcher to enter one or more keywords or phrases to re-run the search within the current search results to narrow down the search further.

Figure 7.6   California Courts' Case Search Results

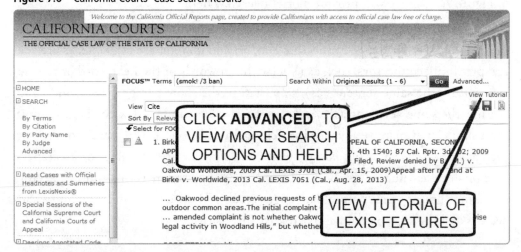

When a case is being viewed, colored "treatment" flags indicate how other cases have treated your case (e.g., positive, negative, etc., treatment). The green plus sign (see Figure 7.7) indicates there is positive treatment of this case. If researchers click the plus sign, however, they are shown this message: "ERROR: Shepard's is not available to you under your current subscription agreement." Nevertheless, the treatment flags are a valuable editorial enhancement to this database, as they let a researcher know whether a case is likely to be good law. (See Chapter 18 to learn how to cite check for free. For pay cite checking services, see **Casemaker's Case-Check+**.)

Many options are available to customize printing. For example, you can choose (1) the display format (e.g., full text or citation only), (2) whether to show your search terms in boldface, (3) whether to include the Shepard's symbols, and (4) select the line spacing, font type, and size options that you prefer. When you click the printer icon in the upper right side of the screen, a pop-up box will appear to allow you to select the various printing options.

On the left-hand column of the search page for both Terms (natural language) or **Terms and Connectors** (see Figure 7.5), there are additional search options: **By Citation** (official only), **By Party Name** (plaintiff or defendant or both), **By Judge**, and **Advanced**. The **Advanced** search link will take you to a **Search By Terms & Connectors** page that looks almost identical to the **Search by Terms** (natural language) screen. The only difference is that the search box, now labeled **Search for Opinions by Terms & Connectors**, will accept Boolean operators with your search terms.

Although LexisNexis has provided some helpful tips for **Terms and Connectors** searching, you must first run a search to view them (by clicking **Advanced** as shown in Figure 7.7), so we will provide a brief overview here.

The **Terms and Connectors** searching on this site functions similarly to the pay Lexis databases. The basic connectors *and, or,* and *and not* are available, as are several proximity connectors, such as *w/n* (within *n* words of the next word or phrase) *w/s* (within the same sentence as), *w/p* (within the same paragraph as), and *w/seg* (within the same segment as). *And not* can also be combined with the proximity connectors for even more advanced searching. In addition, several search commands, such as *atleast, allcaps, caps, nocaps, plural* and *singular* are available to researchers. And finally, the wildcard symbols (*!*) and (*) can be used in Terms and Connectors searching (but not in a natural language search). The Boolean and proximity connectors and the search commands are case insensitive.

Note: Although you are not required to enclose phrases in quotation marks in the **Terms and Connectors** searches (but you are in Terms (natural language) searches) our test searches show that it is a good idea to always put them in quotation marks, both in natural language and **Terms and Connectors** searching. Figure 7.7 shows the results of a Terms and Connectors search.

Figure 7.7   California Courts' Terms and Connectors Search Results

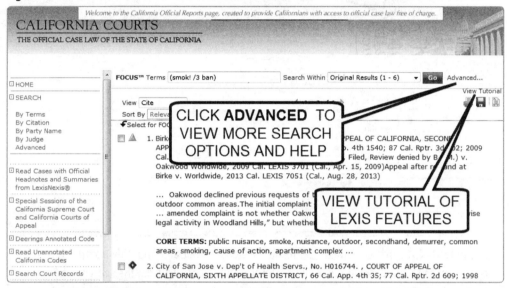

From the search results page, you can click the **Advanced** link to the right of the search box to go to a page that allows you to refine your search with **Focus** (search within results) and restrict it by date and document segment. After you click the **Advanced** link, the right side of that page displays a list of **Search Connectors** and explanations, as well as a **How Do I** section and a link to **Tutorials** (see Figure 7.8).

Figure 7.8   California Courts' Terms and Connectors Advanced Search

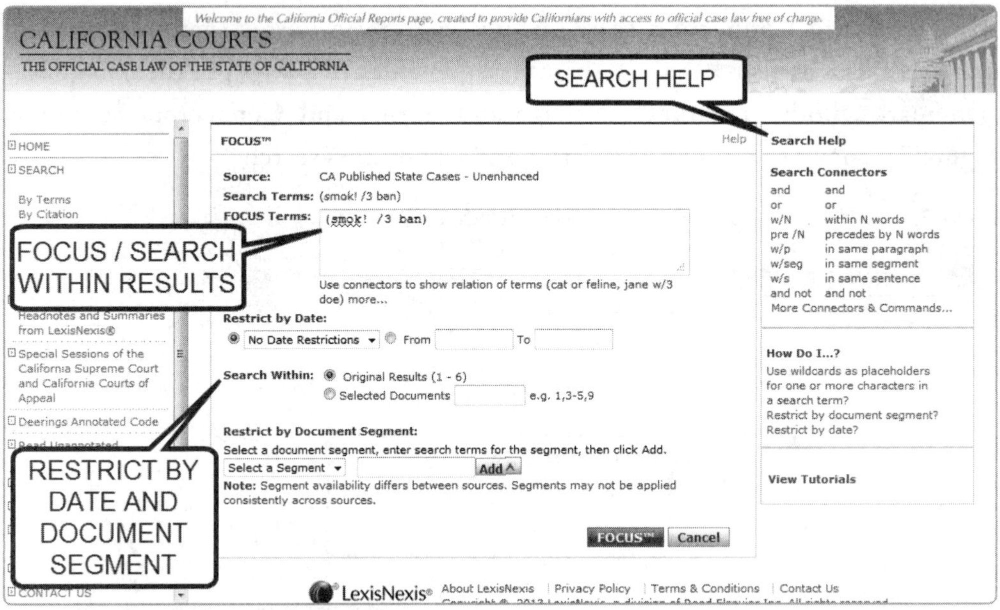

Important Note: The LexisNexis California database is updated monthly according to the court's website, but clicking the Lexis "i" (information) icon link from the search page leads to an information page that states that the update schedule is quarterly. For those who prefer using LexisNexis's California database, it's important to use another free (or pay) database to update your research to ensure you do not miss any new cases. To cut down on retrieving cases already retrieved from the Lexis search, the *Public Library of Law (PLoL)* is the better choice of any of the free databases (See Chapter 6), because it's the only one that allows for a combined keyword and month/year date range search. (Google Scholar's keyword search only offers a date range search by year, and FindLaw's California ACCES-SLAW keyword search doesn't offer a date range search at all.)

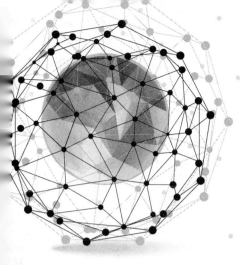

Part IV

BAR ASSOCIATION FREE MEMBER-BENEFIT DATABASES

Forty-seven state bar associations (plus some local bars and other legal professional associations) subscribe to legal research databases on behalf of all their members. In turn, they provide their members with free access as a member benefit. These legal research databases offer more sophisticated search options and broader date coverage than the free case law databases discussed in Chapters 6 and 7. Their legal research databases typically include state, D.C., and federal legal materials (such as case law, codes, etc.).

The state bar associations of California, Delaware, and Montana are the only states that do not yet offer this member benefit. Of the forty-seven state bar associations that do offer this member benefit, forty-six of them subscribe either to **Casemaker** or **Fastcase.** The forty-seventh state bar association, the Pennsylvania Bar Association (PBA), offers access to **InCite**, a customized LexisNexis database created for the PBA.

The Pennsylvania InCite database provides access to all Pennsylvania Supreme Court cases back to 1791, Superior Court cases back to 1895, and Commonwealth Court cases back to October 1970. However, InCite is quite limited in its date coverage for most cases outside of Pennsylvania. It only offers the five most current years of decisions for other state's cases, except New Jersey for which it goes back to the beginning years.

Because so many attorneys have access to Casemaker and Fastcase, we have decided to write a chapter about each one. Our goal is to serve as the "hidden" manual to these two databases. To access these member benefit databases, members will typically need to enter their bar association membership number and a password.

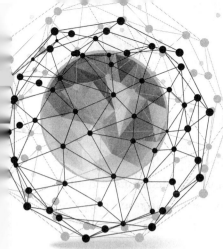

Chapter 8

AN INTRODUCTION TO CASEMAKER

Casemaker is an online legal research database that was originally launched by the Ohio State Bar Association in 1998. As of September 2013, a consortium of twenty-three state bar associations and one local bar subscribe to the database. Subscribers include: Alabama, Alaska, Colorado, Connecticut, Idaho, Indiana, Kansas, Kentucky, Maine, Massachusetts, Michigan, Mississippi, Nebraska, New Hampshire, North Dakota, Ohio, Rhode Island, Santa Clara County Bar Association, South Carolina, Texas, Utah, Vermont, Washington, and Wyoming (http://www.casemakerlegal.com/ProductsStateBarConsortium.aspx). If your bar association is part of the consortium, visit your bar's website and click on the link to Casemaker to access its materials.

All law students have free access to **Casemaker** (http://www.casemakerx.com/) and all subscribers have access to the mobile **Casemaker App** (see Chapter 3).

Although we have listed which associations offer Casemaker (Chapter 9 describes Fastcase), alliances seem to shift, so lawyers should visit their legal associations' website to learn if this member benefit is available. Most associations will place a prominent link to either Casemaker or Fastcase on the upper right-hand side of their website's home page, but some states hide the link. Also, many associations fail to place an explanation next to the link that it's a free legal research database for members. It's just something you have to know about, and now you do!

In 2011 and 2012, Casemaker made several changes: First, Casemaker introduced products that are not part of the free member-benefit plan but can be subscribed to separately by consortium members (http://www.casemakerlegal.com/BuyNow.aspx). The products include **CaseCheck+**, a citation service that includes negative history, **CiteCheck**, an automated cite checking software for legal briefs, and **CasemakerDigest**, a daily summary of state appellate decisions and all federal circuits. Second, Casemaker launched a subscription service to non-consortium members.

SEARCHING CASEMAKER

The Navigation Bar

The Navigation Bar appears on every page of Casemaker and includes the following tabs (see Figure 8.1):

1. **Home** (to return to the home page)
2. **Client** (to assign a client and matter number to each search)
3. **My Folders** (to retrieve saved documents that you have dragged into Casemaker folders)
4. **History** (to review all of your past searches; you can choose to delete all of them or keep just one week or one month; this is the same as My Recent Searches)
5. **Videos** (to watch a tutorial—for example how to create folders—or learn about a product, such as CaseCheck+)
6. **Help** (to read the User Guide). A new **Live Chat** feature was added while we were writing this book. It allows you to instant message with Casemaker customer support. The feature is not shown in Figure 8.1 but can be found at the top right of the page when logged into Casemaker.
7. **Webinar** (to register for a free live Webinar)

Figure 8.1   Casemaker Navigation Bar

Figure 8.2 Casemaker's Home Page

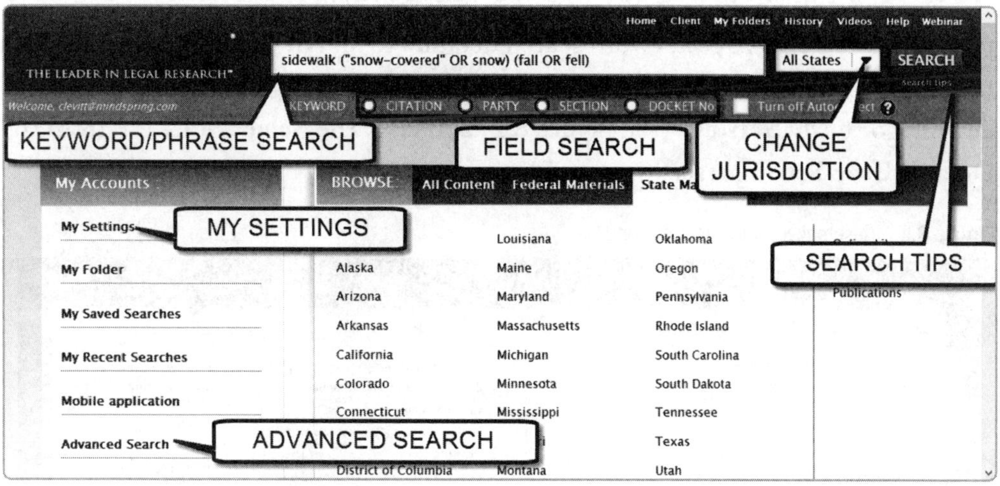

The Default Search: All States, Keyword/Phrase, and All Books

To begin a search, enter your keyword(s)/phrase(s) into the search box located at the top of Casemaker's home page (see Figure 8.2). The default search is a keyword/phrase search through **All States** and through all "Books" (see Figure 8.3). *Books* is Casemaker's label for each distinct type of legal material found within its database. For example, California case law is considered a Book; New York case law is considered another Book, and California codes is yet another book, and so on. Casemaker also labels groups of Books as a "Library."

Figure 8.3 Casemaker's Default Search

If you wish to have a narrower search, you can change the default searches as described in the next few sections.

How to Override the All States Jurisdiction Default

Although the home page keyword search defaults to an **All States** search, there are two ways to change the default jurisdiction. To permanently change the **All States** default, go to **My Settings** (see Figure 8.2) and click the **Select State** tab from the **Default User Settings** (see Figure 8.3).

Figure 8.4   Casemaker's Jurisdiction Menu

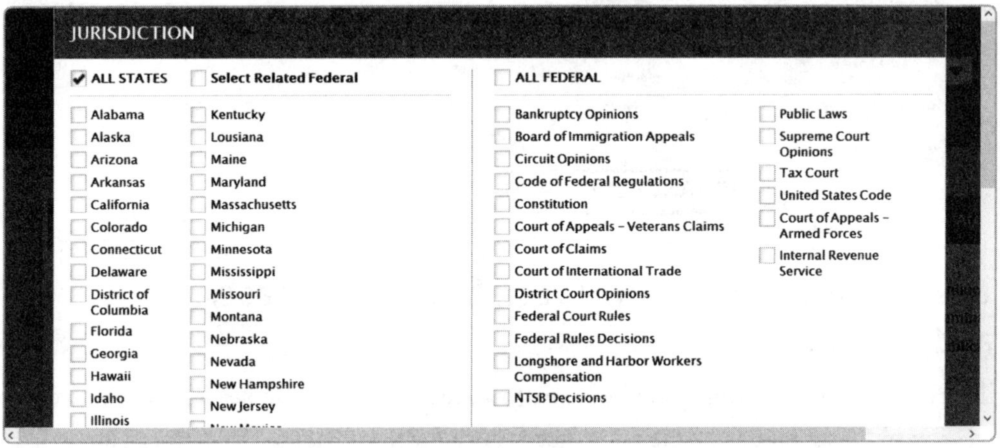

Then, select your new default jurisdiction from the **Jurisdiction** menu (see Figure 8.4). You can choose to search using almost any of the following combinations:

- **All States** only
- **All States** and **Select Related Federal**
- **All States** and **Select Related Federal,** and one or more (but not all) from the **All Federal** list (If you try to combine **All States, Select Related Federal,** and **All Federal** you will get an error message)
- **All Federal** only
- **All States** and **All Federal**
- **All States** and one or more from the **All Federal** list
- **All Federal** and one or more from the **All States** list

Once you select your jurisdictions, scroll down and click **OK**.

If you choose **All States** or **All Federal**, or just one state, your choice will be reflected in the jurisdiction box, but if you make a combination selection, such as **All States** and **Internal Revenue Service**, only **All States** will be reflected in the jurisdiction box, but rest assured, the search *will* be performed through both of your choices.

To change jurisdictions on an *ad hoc* basis, click the down-arrow to the right of **All States** (see Figure 8.3) to pop up a **Jurisdiction** menu (see Figure 8.4) and select one or more jurisdictions the same way you did in the **My Settings** example above. Once you select your jurisdictions, scroll down and click **Save** and then **Close**.

Be aware that when you change your jurisdiction on an *ad hoc* basis, it will change back to the default after your search is completed.

How to Change the "All Books" Default Setting

To change the all Books default, visit **My Settings** and click the **Select Data Type** tab from the **Default User Settings** (see Figure 8.3). You can then choose which Book(s) will be your default.

How to Override Keyword/Phrase Default Searching Using Field Searching

As noted earlier, while the **Keyword** search is the default, you can opt to search by Field (see Figure 8.2) by clicking into one of the Field radio buttons (**Citation**, **Section**, **Docket No.**, or **Party**) located on the horizontal bar below the search box. After clicking into one of the radio button, enter your search into the same search box where keywords/phrases are entered (see Figure 8.2). The following are some sample Field searches:

> **Citation:** *64 N.E.2d 25*
>
> **Section:** *2 U.S.C. 1*
>
> **Docket No.:** *CV8-936*
>
> **Party:** To locate the case *Vincent v. Voight*, enter *Vincent Voight*

At the end of the field radio buttons, notice the **Turn Off Autocorrect** checkbox (see Figure 8.2). If you leave **Autocorrect** on, Casemaker will autocorrect a case or statute citation. For example, if you typed *3ne2nd5* into the **Citation** search, this would be autocorrected to the proper citation format: *3 N.E. 2nd 5*. We would advise leaving it on.

Case Law Advanced Search (Field Search)

From the home page, Casemaker provides an **Advanced Search** for case law. When the **Advanced Search** link is selected from the bottom of the left-hand column of the home page (see Figure 8.2), an **Advanced Search** menu will pop up (see Figure 8.5) where you can enter information into one or more fields to better pinpoint results. You can search by the following fields: **Cite**, **Case Name**, **Docket Number**, **Court**, **Attorney**, **Judge**, **Panel**, and **Decided Date**.

Figure 8.5   Casemaker's Advanced Search for Case Law

These field search boxes cannot be combined with keyword searching from this search page. Later in the chapter we will discuss where they can be combined with keywords.

The **Advanced Search** defaults to **All states** (unless you have permanently changed the default jurisdiction using **My Settings**). As noted earlier, you can change jurisdictions on an *ad hoc* basis.

Advanced searches can be useful for many reasons: You can mix and match the Advanced Search fields when you only know bits and pieces about a case, such as one of the parties' names, the date, and the court. You can also produce a list of all reported cases involving a specific opposing attorney (or an attorney you are considering hiring or a judge you are appearing before) to learn about what types of cases they deal with and what the outcomes were. Searching by party name can be useful to learn how litigious someone is or to learn who typically represents them. Remember, this only works with reported cases. For pending cases or unreported cases, you will need to conduct docket searching (see Chapter 15).

To use the **Court** field, you must enter the full name of the court. Casemaker is in the process of creating a list of court names. Casemaker has sent us some preliminary information about the upcoming list: "The list will be under Help at the top left of the page, and since it will be a very long list, we will probably split it up by state. We will add something like "See list of courts under help tab" in the Court block under the **Advanced Search**, and we will also try to have a drop down for the court names that they can choose from."

Browsing or Searching by "Library" and "Book"

You can also search or browse Libraries or Books by clicking the **All Content, Federal Materials**, or **State Materials** tabs found next to the word **Browse** on the horizontal bar on the home page (see Figure 8.6).

Figure 8.6 Browsing Casemaker

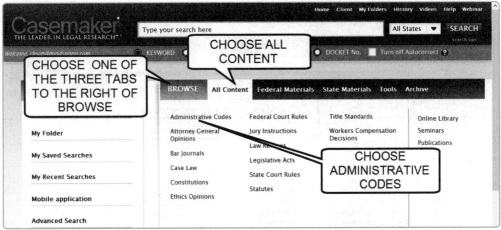

All Content

The **All Content** tab contains the following Libraries organized by type of material and then by state.

- **Administrative Codes**
- **Attorney General Opinions**
- **Bar Journals**
- **Case Law**
- **Constitutions**
- **Ethics Opinions**

- **Federal Court Rules**
- **Jury Instructions**
- **Law Reviews**
- **Legislative Acts**
- **State Court Rules**
- **Statutes**
- **Title Standards**
- **Workers Compensation Decisions**

If you choose one Library from **All Content**, such as **Administrative Codes**, as shown in the Figure 8.7, you are given two choices. The first choice is to search the entire **Administrative Codes** Library (all the listed states' Administrative Codes) together by entering your search terms in the top search box. The second choice is to search one Book (a specific state's **Administrative Code**) by selecting that state.

Figure 8.7   Casemaker's Options for Searching a Library

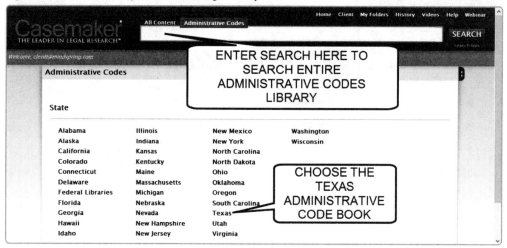

1. If you select just one state, you are then given more choices (shown in Figure 8.8): Choose a Field to search (**Keyword**, **Title**, **Chapter**, or **Section**) or choose the **Combined Search**.

2. Enter your search into the top search box (but if you chose the **Combined Search**, you are then offered a search form to search any combination of the four fields, as shown in Figure 8.9).

3. Browse the Code by selecting any of the Titles from the Table of Contents.

4. Important: Click **View Currency** to learn how current each Book is.

Figure 8.8 Casemaker's Options for Searching One Book

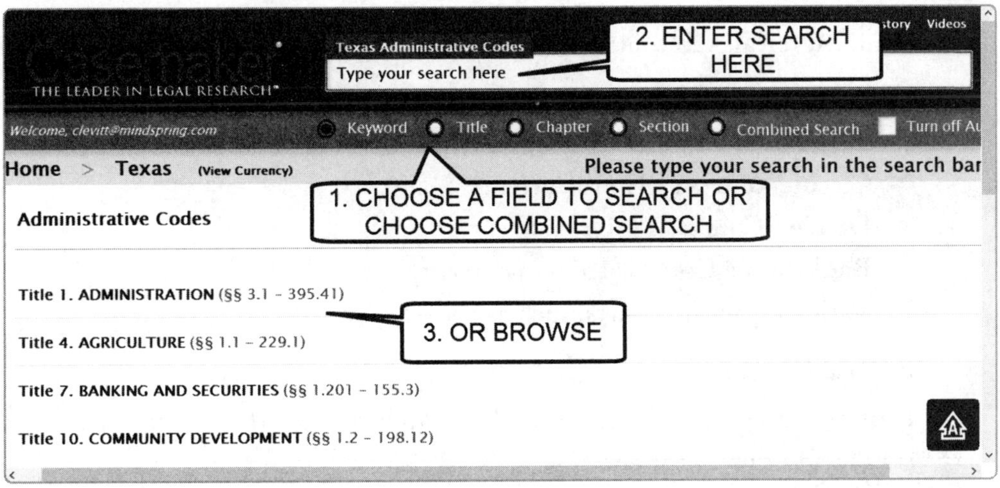

Figure 8.9 Casemaker's Options for a Combined Search

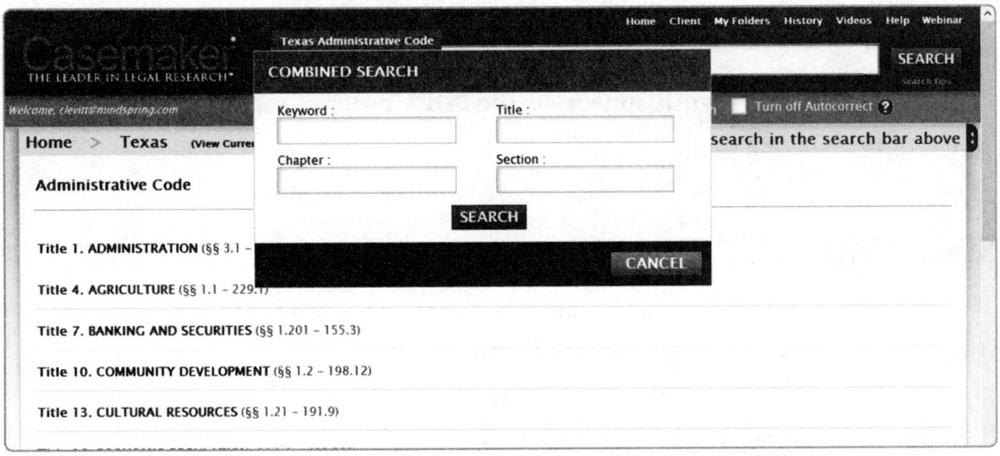

The Field choices and browsing choices will differ with each state depending on the type of material and jurisdiction. For example, in Figure 8.9, the fields for the Texas Administrative Code are **Keyword, Title, Chapter,** and **Section** or **Combined Search** but for Texas case law the fields are **Keyword, Citation, Docket,** and **Panel** (judges) or **Combined Search.** The fields for the Alaska Administrative Code are only **Keyword** and **Combined Search.**

Once the options for the combined search are entered, the **Combined Search** form shown in Figure 8.9 appears.

This is one of the places we alluded to earlier where you can combine a keyword search with other fields by selecting the **Combined Search** (as shown in Figure 8.9).

Federal Materials

The **Federal Materials** tab contains twenty federal Books, such as:

- **Opinions** from the:
  - **Supreme Court** (1754 to current)
  - **Circuit Courts** (1930 to current)
  - **District Courts** (1930 to current)
  - **Bankruptcy Courts** (1979 to current)
  - Various specialty courts, such as the **Tax Court**

- **Federal Court Rules**
- **United States Code** (Users can also search the last three years of session laws in addition to the code.)
- **Code of Regulations** (CFR)
- **Public Laws**
- **Constitution**

The search options work similar to the **All Contents** search above—you can search or browse any Book.

State Materials

The type and number of Books found in the **State Materials** will vary from state to state because not every state's Library is created equal. Some states offer additional materials. Nevertheless, all members of the consortium have access to all fifty states' full Libraries (as well as the entire Federal Library). Each state's Library includes at least the following basic Books:

- **Case Law**
- **Statutes** (or Codes)
- **Constitution**
- **State Court Rules**
- **Session Laws**

In the Alaska example (see Figure 8.10), there are so many Books that we couldn't get them into just one screenshot. So, add to this list: Ethics Opinions, Fairbanks Code of Ordinances, Juneau Code of Ordinances, Jury Instructions, The Kenai Peninsula Borough Code, Local Federal Court Rules, Municipal Codes, Session Laws, Seward City Code, Statutes, and Workers Compensation Decisions.

Figure 8.10 Casemaker's State Books for Alaska

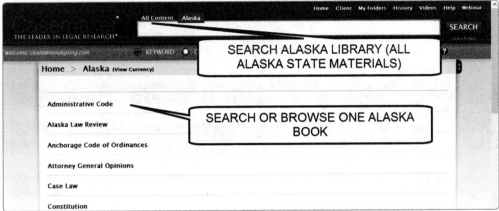

The **State Materials** search options work the same way as we described in the **All Contents** search above—you can search a state's entire Library together or you can click just one of the state's Books and search or browse it separately.

How to Construct a Keyword Search Using Boolean and Proximity Connectors

Those who used prior versions of Casemaker will be happy to know that the new version offers an easier search experience because the proximity and Boolean connectors are similar to Lexis's and Westlaw's. If you click **Search Tips**, which is located on every Casemaker page just below the Search button (see Figure 8.2), the chart displayed in Figure 8.11 will pop up to remind you how to construct your search.

Figure 8.11 Casemaker's Proximity and Boolean Connector Search Tips

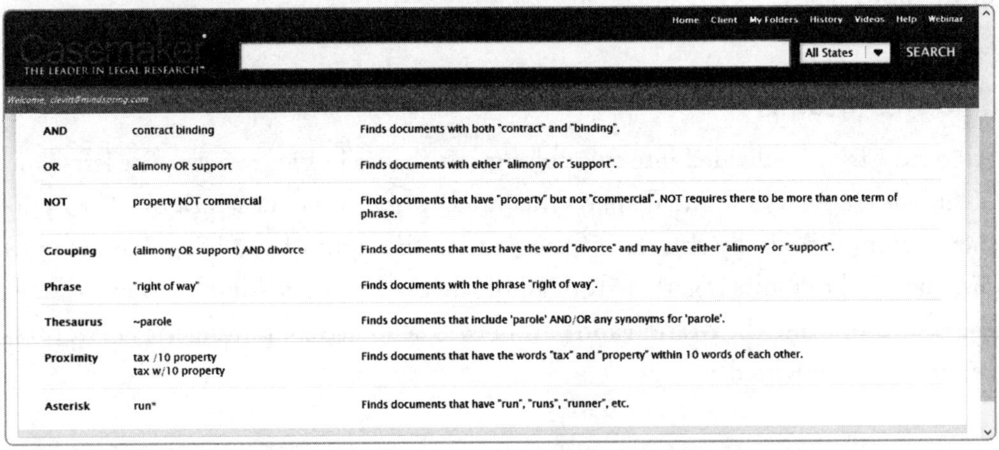

AND	contract binding	Finds documents with both "contract" and "binding".
OR	alimony OR support	Finds documents with either "alimony" or "support".
NOT	property NOT commercial	Finds documents that have "property" but not "commercial". NOT requires there to be more than one term of phrase.
Grouping	(alimony OR support) AND divorce	Finds documents that must have the word "divorce" and may have either "alimony" or "support".
Phrase	"right of way"	Finds documents with the phrase "right of way".
Thesaurus	~parole	Finds documents that include 'parole' AND/OR any synonyms for 'parole'.
Proximity	tax /10 property tax w/10 property	Finds documents that have the words "tax" and "property" within 10 words of each other.
Asterisk	run*	Finds documents that have "run", "runs", "runner", etc.

In our search, as shown in Figure 8.12, we selected **All States** (and all Libraries) and the words/phrases:

sidewalk /10 ("snow-covered" OR snow*) (fall* OR fell).

Figure 8.12   Casemaker's Keyword Search

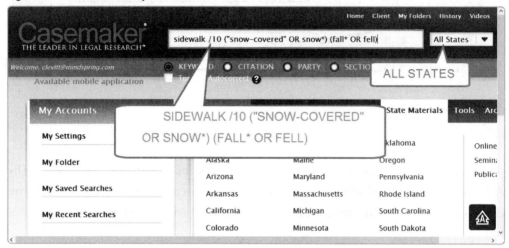

This instructs Casemaker that we are searching for the word *sidewalk* within ten words of the phrase *snow-covered* or any word that begins with the word *snow* (e.g., *snowing, snowed,* etc.) and any word that begins with *fall* (e.g., *falling*) or the word *fell.* You do not have to add the *AND* Boolean connector between words or phrases. It is the default when you leave a space between words or phrases. The backslash (/) and a number to the right of the backslash (without any space) indicates how many words you want between the words (or phrases). In this example we want anywhere from no words to ten words between the word *sidewalk* and the phrase *snow-covered* or the word *snow.*

The Results List

All results lists are divided into two columns as shown in Figure 8.13. The left-hand column is an **Overview** and displays the number of results in each Book. The right-hand column (basically the rest of the page to the right of the left-hand column) displays all the results together from all of the Books in one long list that includes the keyword(s) and the citation and part of each sentence containing the keyword(s) (which are highlighted).

Figure 8.13 Casemaker's All States Search Results

You can click **Save Search** (see Figure 8.13) to save this search and return to it later (by clicking **My Saved Searches** from **My Accounts** on the left-side column as shown in Figure 8.12). This allows you to re-run the search without having to type it in again.

Notice the last choice in the left-hand column of Figure 8.13 is **CaseKnowledge.** This refers to online books that contain your keywords and which you can lease via Casemaker for one year. Be sure to read the book title and description carefully prior to purchasing. In this sample Texas search, the book was a Colorado treatise which probably wouldn't be helpful for Texas practitioners.

Selecting a Book from the Results List

You can click on just one of the Books from the left-hand column (see Figure 8.13), such as **Cases**, to create a list of only case results.

Once you choose a book, such as **Cases** (see Figure 8.14), we can now **Search Within Results** (add more keywords or phrases to your original search to narrow it down) or view results from just one state (click **Show All** to show all states that have results). We can also now add Field searching (see the left-hand column beginning with **Courts**) to our keyword search.

Figure 8.14   Casemaker's Search Within a "Book"

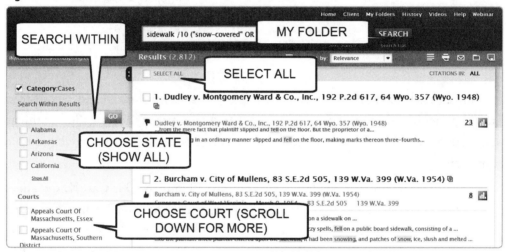

Earlier we noted that although you cannot combine a field and keyword search on the **Advanced Search** page, there were other places where you could. The Results list is one of those places.

Each Book offers Fields that are unique to that Book. For instance, if you select **Administrative Code**, you would only be offered a **Section** and **Title** Field, but if you select **Cases** from the **Overview** results list (see left column of Figure 8.13), you can narrow your results by a specific field such as **Courts** (shown in Figure 8.14). If you scrolled down past **Courts**, you would also see the following Fields listed:

- **Cite**
- **Docket Number**
- **Case Name**
- **Judge**
- **Attorney**
- **Decided Date**

There are other features and functions offered to you once you select a Book (see Figure 8.15):

Figure 8.15   Casemaker Icons on the Results List

1. **View details:** Click this icon to show a citation-only list without your keywords highlighted within partial sentences.
2. **Print** the list
3. **E-mail** the list
4. **Save to Folders:** You must first create a Folder—select **My Folder** (see Figure 8.14) and enter a name for the folder . Then select one or more documents or **Select All** (see Figure 8.14) before you select the Save To Folders icon. You also could drag one document at a time into the folder. Folders are only available to you when you are logged into Casemaker.
5. **Download:** This allows you to download the list or full-text documents to your hard drive so you can retrieve the list or documents when you are not logged into Casemaker.
6. **Sort by** drop-down menu (allows you to re-sort results by **Relevance, Date,** or **Most Cited**)

Figure 8.16   Casemaker Icons for a Selected Document

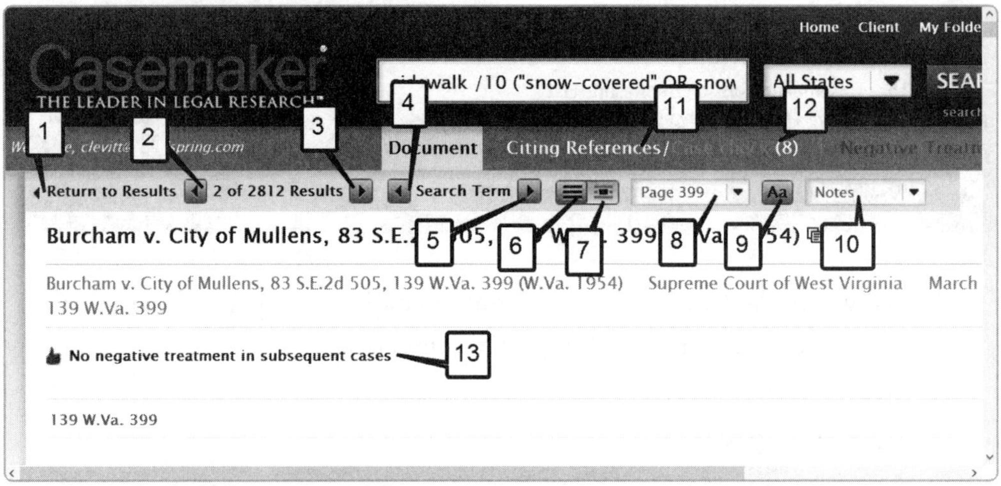

Selecting a Document from the Results List

Once you select a specific document from the Results list, you will be offered some of the same features as when you select a Book (see Figure 8.15). In addition, you are offered the following features and functions (see Figure 8.16):

1. Return to Results list
2. Next Result
3. Prior Result
4. Search Term (choose the back arrow to highlight the prior search term)
5. Search Term (choose the forward arrow to highlight the next search term)
6. Display the full document
7. Display paragraphs with hits
8. Jump to a specific page
9. Increase or decrease font size
10. Notes – Add, Show, or Hide: You can add a note to any document you are viewing by clicking the down arrow to the right of the word **Notes**. A drop-down list will appear at which point you can select **Add Notes**. A blank note screen will appear. Write your note and click **Save**. If you save the document to a Folder, the note will remain automatically (look for it at the end of the document). You can opt to hide or show the note when you are viewing or printing the document (see Figure 8.18 later in the chapter).

You can also choose whether to include the note when you e-mail or download the document (choose **Notes** under the **Attach** option).

11. Citing References/Case check

12. Number of other cases that have cited this case

13. Editorial treatment

Case Check

Every Casemaker subscriber has free access to **Case check**. If a case has been cited to, you will see a **Citing References/Case check** notation just below the search box (see number 11 in Figure 8.16). When you click **Case check**, you will then see a list of citing cases. There is no editorial treatment to inform you how your case was treated by the citing cases unless your bar has included **CaseCheck+** in its member benefit subscription. If your Bar has not included **CaseCheck+**, you can pay to add it.

As of October 2013, Indiana, Nebraska, Ohio, and Washington include **Case-Check+** as part of members' benefits. Be sure to check your bar's benefits.

You can see that our subscription does include **CaseCheck+** because there is editorial treatment as shown by the green thumbs up and the notation, **No negative treatment in subsequent cases,** shown in call-out box 13 in Figure 8.16.

In this example, eight other cases (see call-out box 12 in Figure 8.16) have cited to your case. You can click on any citing case to review it and Casemaker will take you directly to the page where your case is cited with the citation in red text. This makes it easy for you to quickly learn how your case was treated by the citing case. If you want to return to your original search's Results list, click the browser's back button.

> **CITATOR CAVEAT: Case check** and **CaseCheck+** are not as reliable as BCite (Bloomberg Law), Shepard's (Lexis and Lexis Advance), and KeyCite (Westlaw and WestlawNext).

Even though **CaseCheck+** includes signals to indicate negative history, you still have to read each of the citing cases to learn how they treated your case. Additionally, **Case check** and **CaseCheck+** do not display positive history, while BCite, Shepard's, and KeyCite do.

We have found cases where Casemaker indicates negative history for a case but Fastcase does not, and we have found the opposite. (Fastcase uses algorithms to find negative history, and Casemaker uses human editors. They probably each need to do both.)

Unpublished cases are included in both the citator and case law databases of Casemaker, Bloomberg Law, Lexis, Lexis Advance, Westlaw, and WestlawNext. However, unpublished cases, while included in the case law database of Casemaker, are **not** included in **Case check** and **CaseCheck+**.

To combat these reliability issues, you will need to run a search using the party names or their citation as keywords to learn if your case(s) have been affirmed, reversed, or overruled. See Chapter 15 for details on how to run this type of search.

Annotated Statutes

A **Citing References** feature is coming soon. When viewing a statute, you will see a **Cite Ref** tab in the gray bar above your results. If you click on that tab, you will see the case citation(s) and a few sentences from the case(s) where the statute is referenced.

PERSONALIZING YOUR SEARCH EXPERIENCE AT CASEMAKER

Using the choices listed under **My Accounts** (on the left column of the home page; see Figure 8.2), researchers are able to personalize their search experience in the following ways:

- **My Settings** (e.g., You can change the **All States** default to the jurisdiction(s) of your choice or change the **All Data Type** default to the Books of your choice)
- **My Folder** (to retrieve saved documents that you have placed into Case-maker folders, to create new folders, or to move or re-name folders)
- **My Saved Searches** (to retrieve, delete, or re-name saved searches)
- **My Recent Searches** (Actually, all of your searches are retained, not just recent, unless you have chosen to delete all of them or you have chosen to keep just one week or one month; this is the same as **History**.)
- **Mobile application** (to register for a free mobile app to access your Case-maker account from your BlackBerry, iPhone, or Droid mobile device)

PRINTING

If you are viewing a results list (see Figure 8.13), and want to print either the whole list or the full text of every document in the list, you would click into the **Select All** box. If you want to print a partial list or the full text of selected documents, you would click into the check-box of one or more documents. After you make your selection, you click the printer icon (see call-out box 2 in Figure 8.15).

A pop-up window appears (see Figure 8.17) where you select a button to print the **List of items** (e.g., citations) or **Documents** (full-text). You can also decide whether you want your search words highlighted (**Term Highlighting**) and whether you want to attach a cover sheet (and you would then type your cover sheet text into the space provided).

If you want to print while you are viewing a document instead of a Results list, you will see a different pop-up (see Figure 8.18).

Figure 8.17 Results List Printing Options **Figure 8.18** Document Printing Options

You can choose to: print single or dual columns, highlight terms, include a list of citing references in your printed copy, attach any notes to the document if you created any (notes are usually displayed at the end of your document but if you also selected **Citing References**, they would appear before those), attach a cover sheet, and select a format (PDF, Word, Word Perfect, or HTML).

OTHER FEE-BASED SERVICES/PRODUCTS

If your state bar is not part of the Casemaker consortium, you can subscribe to the Casemaker legal research database or any of its other standalone products (**Cite-Check, CaseCheck+,** and **CasemakerDigest**) on your own. Select your state from the drop-down menu at http://www.casemakerlegal.com/BuyNow.aspx to learn about pricing. If your state bar is part of the Casemaker consortium, you won't see a price for Casemaker, only for CiteCheck, CaseCheck+, and CasemakerDigest. Casemaker consortium users can also subscribe to the standalone products by clicking the **Try CaseCheck+** link found on the home page of their state bar Casemaker page. However, if you are in a voluntary bar state and are not a member of your state's bar, you are told to contact your state bar (because you might consider joining your bar, if the cost is less than an individual Casemaker subscription).

As of October 2013, Indiana, Nebraska, Ohio, and Washington include all three products as part of members' benefits. Be sure to check your bar's benefits.

The first stand-alone product, **CasemakerDigest** (which some states, such as Texas and the states noted above, offer free as a member benefit), summarizes new cases within forty-eight hours of being decided. (Note: Casemaker adds new cases to its main database as soon as a case is released by the courts; it's only the Case-makerDigest that has a forty-eight hour delay.) You can receive the entire CasemakerDigest as an RSS feed or as an e-mail alert. The CasemakerDigest e-mail alert can be customized with filters. You can filter by one or more of the fifty-seven practice areas, by courts, by judges, or by one keyword.

The second stand-alone product, **CiteCheck**, is an automated cite checking software for legal briefs. The software extracts the case citations from your (or the opposition's) brief and then creates a list showing the subsequent negative treatment of each case.

The third stand-alone product is a citation service, **CaseCheck+**, which provides editorial treatment (see call-out box 13 in Figure 8.16) to alert researchers to subsequent negative treatment of any case they're currently viewing. CaseCheck+ uses a green thumbs-up icon (see call-out box 13 in Figure 8.16) to indicate there has been no negative treatment and a red thumbs-down icon to indicate there has been negative treatment.

Figure 8.19 provides an example of a CaseCheck+ review of a Texas appellate court decision. It shows the full-text of the lower court's opinion, *Lottman v. Cuilla*, 279 S.W. 519 (Tex.Civ.App.1925) and also makes a note of **Citing References** (2).

This indicates that two cases cited to the lower court's opinion. The red thumbs-down icon indicates negative treatment of the lower court's *Lottman* opinion. The text to the right of the red thumbs-down icon, **Reversed**, informs you that the negative treatment was a reversal and provides the case name and citation—288 S.W. 123 (Tex.Com.App. 1926), 675-4570, Lottman v. Cuilla—to the higher court's reversal.

Figure 8.19   CaseCheck+ Review: Lower Court Opinion

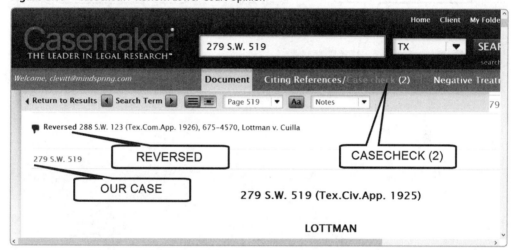

If you click on the case citation, it will bring you to a page where you will need to click on the case citation again to read the higher court's reversal of your case. Then, you will be taken to the first page on which Lottman, **279 S.W. 519**, is cited to in the higher court's opinion (see Figure 8.20). However, you may either have to scroll down to find the word **Reversed** or you can use the **Find** function to find the exact page where the higher court actually reversed the lower court. To deploy the **Find** function, if you have a PC, hold down the **Control** and **F** keys. If you have an Apple computer, hold down the **Command** and **F** keys. A **Find** box will pop up where you can enter the word **Reversed** and be taken to the correct page with the word **Reversed** highlighted. (Casemaker displays the citation to the lower court's opinion in red text.)

Figure 8.20   CaseCheck+ Review: Higher Court Reversal

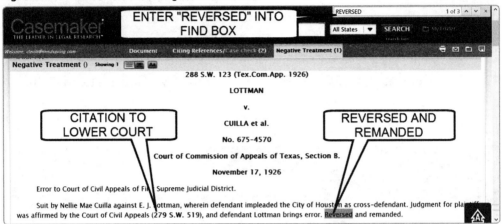

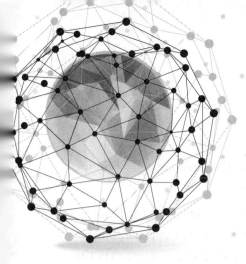

Chapter 9

AN INTRODUCTION TO FASTCASE

As noted in the introduction to Part IV, forty-seven state and local bars plus other legal professional associations subscribe to legal research databases (which include case law and other legal materials) on behalf of all members and provide free access to their members as a member benefit. To access these member-benefit databases, members will typically need to enter their bar association membership number and a password. These legal research databases typically offer more material than the free case law databases discussed in Chapters 6 and 7 and also offer more sophisticated search options and broader date coverage.

As of January 2014, twenty-four state-level bar associations (as well as fourteen local and specialty bar associations, libraries, and other entities) subscribe to Fastcase's free case law, statutory, and regulatory research database and offer it for free as a benefit to their members. The twenty-four state bar associations subscribing to Fastcase are: Arizona, Arkansas, D.C., Florida, Georgia, Hawaii, Illinois, Iowa, Louisiana, Maryland, Minnesota, Missouri, Nevada, New Jersey, New Mexico, New York, North Carolina, Oklahoma, Oregon, South Dakota, Tennessee, Wisconsin, Virginia, and West Virginia.

The fourteen local and specialty bar associations, libraries, and other entities subscribing to Fastcase are: American Immigration Lawyers Association, Cincinnati Law Library, Cleveland Metropolitan Bar Association, Georgetown University Law Center, Jenkins Law Library (Members), Kern County Bar Association, Law Reader, Los Angeles Law Library, Marquette Law School, National Association of

Consumer Bankruptcy Attorneys, NY Criminal and Civil Courts Bar Association, San Fernando Valley Bar Association, Social Law Library, and TrialSmith.

Unlike Casemaker, not all bar associations offer the entire Fastcase collection for free to members, and this is detailed later in the chapter.

For mobile device users (even non-subscribers), there is a free app for Fastcase (see Chapter 3). Approximately 100,000 individuals use the free app while more than 600,000 people (retail and bar subscribers combined) access Fastcase via the Web using their computer.

Although we have listed which associations offer Fastcase, alliances seem to shift, so lawyers should visit their legal associations' website to learn if this member benefit is available. Most associations will place a prominent link to either Casemaker or Fastcase on the upper right-hand side of their website's home page, but some states hide the link. Also, many associations fail to place an explanation next to the link that it's a free legal research database for members. It's just something you have to know about, and now you do! To see if any of the associations to which you belong have contracted with Fastcase on your behalf, visit their website or visit the list of subscribing entities at http://www.fastcase.com/barmembers.

As noted in the prior chapter, because so many attorneys have access to Casemaker and Fastcase, we have decided to write a chapter about each one. Our goal is to serve as the "hidden" manual to these two databases.

Fastcase began as a full-text state and federal case law–only database. The site later integrated the U.S. Code and the codes of forty-five states plus D.C. (Fastcase explains that Arkansas, Mississippi, Ohio, Pennsylvania, and Wyoming are missing from its database because those states' copyright laws prevent Fastcase from integrating their codes into its database. Instead, Fastcase provides links to those five states' official government websites.) Fastcase also now includes other materials such as regulations, attorney general opinions, constitutions, and court rules, but not all are integrated into Fastcase's database. For some, Fastcase simply provides a link to the official site where you can search the materials. You can review Fastcase's list showing which materials are integrated and which require you to link to an official site (http://www.fastcase.com/whatisfastcase/coverage).

CASE LAW OFFERINGS

If you have access to the entire Fastcase collection (called the Fastcase National Premium plan) you can research all state Supreme Court and Courts of Appeals from 1950 (or earlier*) to the present and all Federal courts**.

> ***NOTE:** About half of the states' case-law databases date back to 1950, while the other half date back to the 1800s. For example, case law from the New York Court of Appeals dates back to 1885 while case law from the California courts date back only to 1950. Use this URL for a list of coverage dates: http://www.fastcase.com/whatisfastcase/coverage/.
>
> ****NOTE:** Some bars have opted to offer their members the "Fastcase Federal Appellate Plan," which includes all the courts listed above except for the Federal District and Bankruptcy Courts, while other bars offer just their own state's federal and state courts for free (which is what the Florida Bar does, for instance). Attorneys who need access to all the courts can upgrade to the Fastcase National Premium for an additional $195 annual fee paid to Fastcase.

The following Federal courts are part of the Fastcase National Premium plan:

- **United States Supreme Court,** 1754 to present
- **Federal Circuit Courts of Appeals,** 1924 to present
- **Federal District Courts,** 1912 to present**
- **Federal Bankruptcy Courts,** 1979 to present**
- Various specialized federal courts (dates vary):
    - **Board of Tax Appeals** (vols. 1–47)
    - **Tax Court Memorandum Decisions** (vols. 1–59)
    - **U.S. Customs Court** (vols. 1–70)
    - **Board of Immigration Appeals** (1996 to present)

The Federal District and Bankruptcy Courts are included as a free member benefit for all bar associations participating in Casemaker and are also available free at Google Scholar.

BEGINNING A SEARCH

The following information is shown on the welcome page (see Figure 9.1):

- **Quick Caselaw Search**: Enter your search here to search case law.

- **All Jurisdictions**: You can search the case law of all jurisdictions by clicking into the **All Jurisdictions** radio button. Alternatively, you can choose to search the jurisdiction(s) you last searched (displayed to the right of the **All Jurisdictions** radio button).

- **Switch to Advanced Caselaw Search**: We will explain this in the next section.

- **Last 10 searches**: Fastcase automatically saves your last ten searches and displays them on your Welcome page. Click any one of them to re-run the search without having to type it into the search box.

- **Start a New Search**: To search other legal materials beyond case law, such as **Statutes** or **Regulations**, select it from the column on the left.

- **Help**: Fastcase offers all kinds of help and customer service, from its **User Guide** and **Tutorials**, where you can watch on-demand videos or sign up for live webinars, to **Live Chat** or **E-mail**.

Figure 9.1   Fastcase Welcome Page

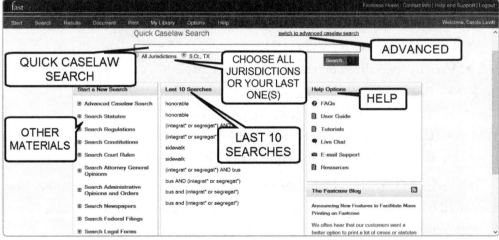

Choosing the Advanced Caselaw Search

To search case law in one or multiple jurisdictions simultaneously (instead of all), users must select the **Switch to Advanced Caselaw Search** link (see Figure 9.1). Unfortunately, there is no way to create a unified search of cases and all other legal material (e.g., statutes, regulations, etc.) at Fastcase. This contrasts with Casemaker, which allows you to search all legal materials in a unified search. However, Fastcase does provide an "all"-state statutes (we've put "all" in quotation marks because the statutes of Arkansas, Mississippi, Ohio, Pennsylvania, and Wyoming are missing as we've previously explained).

Selecting Your Caselaw Search Type

After you select **Advanced Caselaw Search**, the top part of the screen displays:

- Three **Search Type** options: Click into one of the three radio buttons located above the search box – **Keyword Search (Boolean)**, **Natural Language**, or **Citation Lookup**.
- The search box: Enter your search here (see Figure 9.2).
- **Show Search Tips**: We advise that you check this box (as shown in Figure 9.2) so you can readily see the correct search **Syntax** (how to construct a search, such as how to use Boolean and proximity connectors if you have selected **Keyword Search (Boolean)**. Depending on which search type you selected, the **Syntax** search tips will be different. Most attorneys will be familiar with Fastcase's Boolean and proximity search syntax if they are Bloomberg Law, Casemaker, Google, Lexis, Lexis Advance, Westlaw, or WestlawNext searchers (although there are some slight variations). Fastcase's search menu and syntax are quite user friendly, but we would prefer if Fastcase also offered distinct search fields for judge, attorney, or party names. Fastcase does offer a date field.

Figure 9.2   Fastcase Advanced Caselaw Search

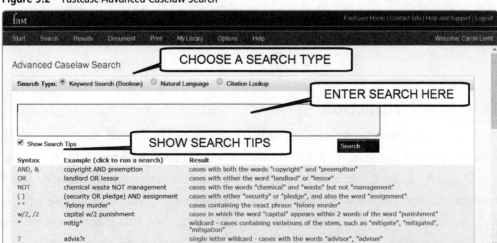

Creating an Advanced Caselaw Search

Figure 9.3 shows that we have chosen to conduct a **Keyword Search (Boolean).**
The Syntax for that search type is displayed above the search box so we know exactly
how to construct our search. We are searching for cases about integration or segre-
gation and bus. We enter our search terms into the search box like this:

(integrat* OR segregat*) AND bus

Figure 9.3   Fastcase Boolean Keyword Search

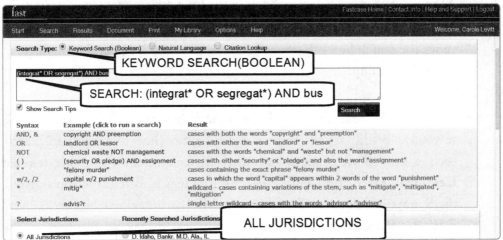

Using the asterisk after the first two words instructs Fastcase that we are looking
for any word that begins with the root *integrat* or the root *segregat* so our results for
integrat* will include *integrate, integrating, integration,* etc. (with similar results for
the word *segregat**). We use the parentheses to indicate that we want cases that have
either the root word *integrat* OR segregat** (or both) and the word *bus.* We are
searching for cases in **All Jurisdictions** (indicated above). There are other jurisdiction choices discussed below and shown in Figure 9.4.

Selecting Jurisdictions

As you scroll down the screen, you will see jurisdictional menus (see Figure 9.4).
Notice that you can search by **All Jurisdictions, All Federal Appellate, All State,
All District,** or **All Bankruptcy Courts.** (You can only select one of them; to select
multiple jurisdictions, use the **Individual Jurisdictions**). Note: You may see different choices if your bar association doesn't subscribe to the full Fastcase collection.

As an efficiency tool, you will also see a list of jurisdictions that you recently searched (you can only select one of them).

Figure 9.4 Fastcase Jurisdictions

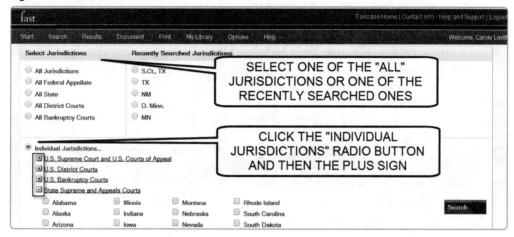

If you don't want to search all courts (e.g., **All State Courts**), but would prefer to search one or more state courts, click into the **Individual Jurisdictions** radio button. You are then offered a menu of four groups of courts to select from. By clicking the plus sign to the left any of these courts, such as **State Supreme and Appellate Courts,** you can then choose to search one or more of these state courts. Although not shown in Figure 9.4, there is a **Select All** radio button at the bottom if you wanted to search all and a **Clear All** radio button. You can continue to click the plus signs for the other groups of courts and mix and match any courts that you would like to search together. For instance, you could search the Illinois state courts and the Iowa Bankruptcy courts together or all of the U.S. District Courts and U.S. Bankruptcy Courts together, and so on.

Other Search Options

After choosing your courts (see Figure 9.4), there are other search options (see Figure 9.5).

- Enter a **Start Date** and **End Date**
- Limit **Authority Check** to show only cases that cite your case within your search results or expand **Authority Check** to the entire Fastcase database or choose both (See the section Red Flags, Bad Law Bot, and Authority Check later in the chapter.)

- Choose the maximum number of results per page (10, 20, 50, or 100)
- Choose from six useful sorting features: **Relevance***, **Case Name** (alphabetically), **Decision Date, Court Hierarchy, Cited Generally** (cases are sorted from most cited to least cited in the entire database), or **Cited Within** (cases are sorted from most cited to least cited only within your search results). The **Relevance, Case Name**, and **Decision Date** sorting choices can also be made after your results list is displayed (see Figure 9.6).

Figure 9.5   Fastcase Additional Search Options

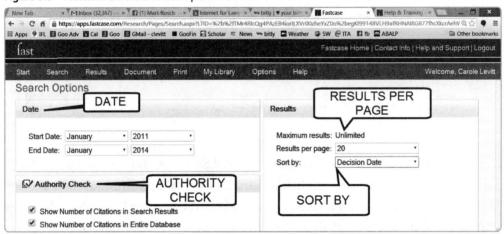

*Fastcase explains "Relevance" this way: "The purpose of the Fastcase Relevance score is to tell you which documents on your list of search results are more likely to contain a substantive discussion of the search terms you entered. The higher the percentage, the more likely that the document contains a substantive discussion of the topic."

Results List

Figure 9.6 shows the anatomy of a **Results** list:

Figure 9.6 Fastcase Results List

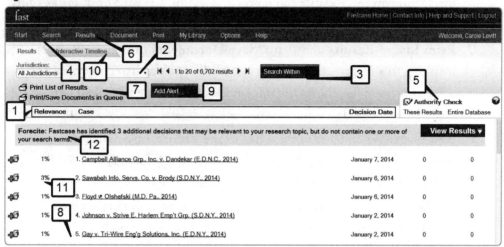

1. Re-sort the way the results are displayed by clicking the column headers labeled: **Relevance, Case,** or **Decision Date**. If you choose to re-sort by **Decision Date**, the most current case to the oldest case will display. However, if you click **Decision Date** a second time, the oldest case to the most current will display.

2. Re-sort by **Jurisdiction**: Use the drop-down menu labeled **Jurisdiction** to display the results of just one jurisdiction (e.g., if you chose **All Federal Appellate** cases, you could then limit the Results list to only your Circuit).

3. **Search Within**: This allows you to search within your results to narrow them down. (You can achieve the same results by using the **Modify** choice to add more search terms as discussed in the next bullet point.)

4. **Modify Search**: Clicking on the **Search** tab located on the navigation bar and then clicking **Modify Search** displays your original search so that you can modify your search terms, dates, jurisdiction, and so on. If you began your original search in case law, the modified search will be re-run there. If you want to search somewhere other than case law, use the same **Search** tab on the navigation bar and select **Search Regulations** (or **Search Statutes**, etc.) to switch from case law to **Regulations**. Note: Your original search terms are deleted, so you will need to re-enter them or create a new search.

5. Sort **Authority Check** by **These Results** or **Entire Database** (described later in the chapter).

6. Choose the type and amount of information displayed on the **Results** list by clicking on the **Results** tab on the navigation bar to: **Show Titles Only**, **Show First Paragraph**, or **Show Most Relevant Paragraph**.

7. **Print List of Results** and **Print/Save Documents in Queue**: Before invoking this feature, first choose one of the options listed in point 6 above so your printed list shows the information you need (described later in the chapter).

8. **Red Flags**: When you see a red flag to the left of a case name, this alerts you that there is negative history about the case. (There are no red flags in this Figure, but they are described later in the chapter.)

9. **Add Alert**: When you click the **Add Alert** button, you are saving your search and asking Fastcase to continuously run your search for you. Then, whenever new documents that match your search terms are added to Fastcase's database, Fastcase will alert you by e-mail. To cancel your alert, go to **Options** > **Manage Alerts**.

10. **Interactive Timeline**: For those who prefer a visual representation of their results, there is also an **Interactive Timeline** and a citation summary described later in the chapter.

11. **Relevance percentages** (described later in the chapter)

12. **Forecite:** If Fastcase identifies decisions that do not contain one or more of your search terms, but it ascertains that a particular decision may nonetheless be relevant to your research topic, you will be alerted by **Forecite** which is placed in a yellow shaded box above the list of cases.

Navigating within a Case and to Another Case

After clicking on one of the case results, the full text of the case appears. Notice there is a red flag at the top of the screen. This indicates negative history. You may also notice that **People Who Care** is highlighted. That is because we did a **Search Within** search (discussed earlier) to add those words to our search after the fact. The results list is displayed in the left-hand column in case you want to jump to a different case.

Figure 9.7   Fastcase Anatomy of a Case

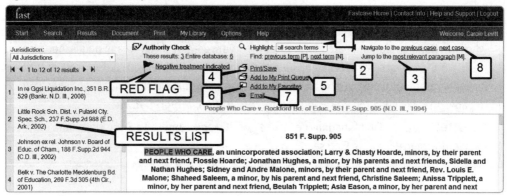

You have the choice of scrolling through the case to read it in its entirety with all search terms highlighted, or you can:

1. Go directly to the pages where a specific search term can be found by choosing one of them from the drop-down menu labeled **all search terms** (to the right of **Highlight**).

2. After you select a search term, click **previous term** or **next term**.

3. **Jump to the most relevant paragraph**

4. **Print/Save** (described later in the chapter)

5. **Add to My Print Queue** (to print later; also described later in the chapter)

6. **Add to My Favorites** (which saves the case in your Fastcase **My Library** for quick retrieval of the case during your current session or next time you log onto Fastcase and click **My Library**)

7. **E-mail** the case to yourself or anyone else

8. **Navigate to the next case or previous case**

If you want to select text in a case (or statute, etc.) to copy it into a document, a small menu pops up with the option to **Copy text** or **Copy with Citation**. The **Copy with Citation** is a handy option because it saves you the time of copying and pasting the citation into your document.

All U.S. Supreme Court cases released after February 2011 and all state supreme court cases released after February 2011 include case summaries from Justia.

> **CAVEAT:** When we highlighted our search term *bus*, we were taken to pages that included the word *bus* but also words where *bus* was just part of a word (e.g., *Columbus*). Also, when we highlighted our search term *integrat** we were not taken to any pages, because there were no pages that included the exact word *integrat**. Unfortunately, you do not have the option of typing in a search term, such as *integrat*, which would have taken you to pages that included the words *integrate*, *integration*, *integrated*, etc.
>
> **SOLUTION:** Use the Find function (**control F** for PCs and **command F** for Macs) and enter the word *integrat* into the Find search box.

Red Flags, Bad Law Bot, and Authority Check

If there is red flag (see Figures 9.7 and 9.8), this indicates negative treatment of your case. Fastcase uses algorithms to find this negative history and calls it their "Bad Law Bot." The **Authority Check** notation on the right side of the **Results** list (see Figure 9.8) will show you how many cases have cited to each case within **These results** (3 in our example search) and in the **Entire Database** (6 in our example search). Clicking the number to the right of **These Results** or **Entire Database** will take you to the same place: the **Authority Check Report**. From this report, you will be able to read the citing cases. If there is no red flag, then the **Authority Check** cases cite to your case, but not in a negative manner.

Figure 9.8 Fastcase Authority Check

Figure 9.9 shows the **Authority Check Report** for the *People Who Care* case in Figure 9.8.

Figure 9.9 Fastcase Authority Check Report

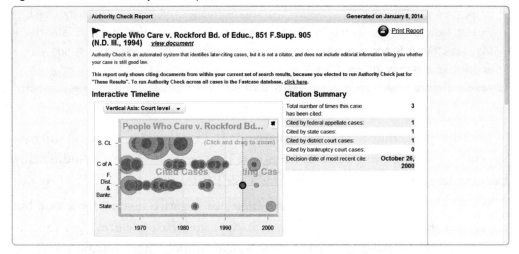

Figure 9.10 shows the rest of the **Authority Check Report**, showing the negative case first (the **Bad Law Bot**) and the other citing cases beneath that.

Figure 9.10 Fastcase Authority Check Report, Continued

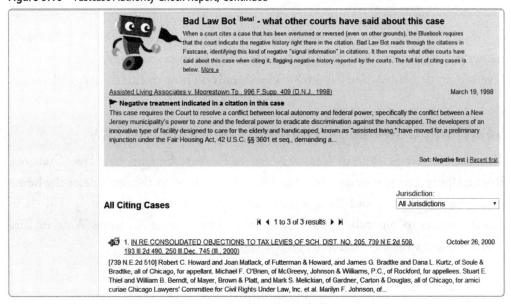

> **CITATOR CAVEAT:** Fastcase's authority is not as reliable as BCite (Bloomberg Law), Shepard's (Lexis and Lexis Advance), and KeyCite (Westlaw and WestlawNext). According to Fastcase, "We do not hold Authority Check out as a complete replacement for services such as Shepard's or KeyCite... (http://www.fastcase.com/faq/)." And, on the *Authority Check Report*, Fastcase states: "Authority Check is an automated system that identifies later-citing cases, but it is not a citator, and does not include editorial information telling you whether your case is still good law."

Even though Authority includes signals to indicate negative history, you still have to read each of the citing cases to learn how they treated your case. Additionally, Fastcase does not display positive history, while BCite, Shepard's, and KeyCite do.

We have found cases where Fastcase indicates negative history for a case but Casemaker does not and we have found the opposite. (Fastcase uses algorithms to find negative history, and Casemaker uses human editors. They probably each need to do both.)

Unpublished cases are included in both the citator and case law databases of Fastcase, Bloomberg Law, Lexis, Lexis Advance, Westlaw, and WestlawNext. However, unpublished cases, while included in the case law database of Fastcase, are *not* included in Authority.

To combat these reliability issues, you will need to run a search using the party names or their citation as keywords to learn if your case(s) have been affirmed, reversed, or overruled. See Chapter 18 for details on how to run this type of search.

Searching Other Legal Materials beyond Case Law

To search a specific type of legal material at Fastcase beyond case law (**Statutes**, **Regulations**, etc.) you must select one from the column on the left side of the home page (see Figure 9.1) and then search each type of material separately. This is in sharp contrast to Bloomberg Law, Casemaker, Lexis, Lexis Advance, Westlaw, and WestlawNext where all materials can be searched simultaneously.

Annotated Statutes

Fastcase has begun an annotated statutes project, which is now up to thirty-seven states (plus the U.S. Code). They will continue to add annotations to other states' statutes.

Transactional Search Options: Newspaper Archive, Legal Forms, and Federal Filings

Fastcase also provides access to a newspaper archive, legal forms, and federal filings through various business partners. Fastcase refers to these as transactional search options because you will pay per transaction.

- **Search Newspapers:** You can search newspaper articles from more than 4,000 newspapers at Newsbank.com for free, view summary results for free, and then download, for a fee, the full text of the articles that you want.

- **Search Legal Forms:** You can search U.S. Legal Forms for free, view results for free, read the model documents (watermarked) for free, and then download, for a fee, model legal documents.

- **Search Federal Filings:** You can search Justia's federal dockets database for free but to view the full docket and retrieve any of the pleadings, you will have to have a subscription to PACER and pay the transactional amount.

Before paying for newspaper articles or legal forms, be sure to visit your public library's website to learn if there are any comparable resources that you can remotely access for free (using your library card number).

PRINTING

To print only your Results list, click **Print List of Results** (see Figure 9.6, number 7). Your printer's dialog box will appear and you can choose where to print the document (e.g., to your local printer, etc.) or you can save it as a PDF.

If you saved documents while using the Fastcase App on your mobile device, you will be able to print them later when you log into Fastcase on your computer. See Chapter 3 for details about the app.

To print a single document that you are viewing, click the **Print/Save** link (see Figure 9.7, number 4). Then, a **Print Document** screen will appear. However, we advise that you instead click the **Add to My Print Queue**, to print all documents later (see Figure 9.7, number 5). Another way to add documents to your queue is by selecting one or more **Print Queue** icons from your **Results** list, which is located in the first column and looks like a printer with a plus sign (see Figure 9.8). Once selected, the plus sign becomes a minus sign. When you are done adding documents to your Queue, choose **Print** from the navigation Bar and then choose **View Print Queue.** The **Print Documents** screen, shown in Figure 9.11, will appear.

Figure 9.11   Fastcase Print Documents Screen

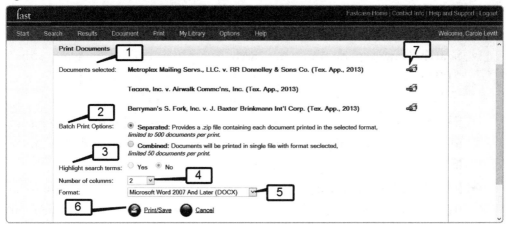

1. The documents you selected to print will be listed.

2. Choose your **Batch Print Options**: If you choose **Separated**, each document will be placed into a separate file with a separate file name, but all documents will be placed into one zip file (for up to 500 documents per print). If you choose **Combined**, your documents will be printed to one single file with one single file name (for up to 50 documents per print).

3. Choose **Yes** to **Highlight search terms** in your printed document (or **No** to not highlight).

4. Select **Number of columns** (1 or 2) from the drop-down menu.

5. Make your **Format** selection (e.g., **.PDF, .DOC, .DOCX, .RTF**) from the drop-down menu.

6. When you click **Print/Save** again, your documents will be downloaded to your computer. You can also click **Cancel.**

7. The printer with a minus sign icon (in the right hand column) is the **Remove from print queue** icon. Click that to remove a document.

Enterprise Cloud Print Plug-in

In 2011, Fastcase created a cloud print plug-in (for Internet Explorer, Outlook, Word, Firefox, and Adobe Reader) for law firms who had an enterprise-wide Fastcase contract. When enterprise users are viewing a website, blog, or Word document that includes case citations, or even a web-based pay database (such as Bloomberg Law, Lexis, Lexis Advance, Westlaw, and WestlawNext, etc.), they can click the **Print all cases cited on this page** button (from the plug-in) to list all of the cases and then click the **Generate Document** button (from the plug-in), to save or print the cases from Fastcase instead of from the website or document they are searching. This could save a firm print charges imposed by those vendors. Depending on the firm's contract with those other vendors, this could be a large cost-savings. Besides saving money, this plug-in could also save enterprise users time because they can avoid cutting and pasting citations from a blog post, for example, to find the cases online to read them. With just two clicks, the Fastcase plug-in finds the cases and allows users to save or print them.

INDIVIDUAL SUBSCRIPTIONS TO FASTCASE

If your bar association does not offer free access to Fastcase (or another database), you can purchase an individual **Fastcase** subscription (https://www.fastcase.com/subscription/) at the following costs:

- **National Premium**: $95 per month or $995 annually
- **National Appellate**: $65 per month or $695 annually

If you are uncertain about Fastcase, try their twenty-four hour free trial subscription. You will need to contact Fastcase to learn about enterprise pricing.

If you don't mind searching Fastcase on your mobile device, there is a free (even to non-subscribers) mobile Fastcase App. See Chapter 3 to learn about the free mobile app.

SYNCING

If you mark a case as a **Favorite** when researching from your computer, your favorites will automatically be synced to your iPhone, iPad, and Android Fastcase App. If you **Save** a document when you are researching from the Fastcase App, that document will be synced to your computer, and you will be able to print it.

NEW DEVELOPMENT

On July 9, 2013, William S. Hein & Co. and Fastcase announced a new partnership. HeinOnline subscribers will soon be able to hyperlink to Fastcase's federal and state case law anytime a case is mentioned in a publication hosted at HeinOnline (primarily law journals and historical state statutory materials). In addition, HeinOnline subscribers will be able to access Fastcase's citation tool (Authority Check) and Bad Law Bot. And, on the flip-side, Fastcase will integrate HeinOnline's Law Journal Library (over 1,800 titles back to their first volumes), its Session Laws Library, its State Attorney General Reports and Opinions, and its Historical Archive of State Statutes and other historical state statutory materials, into Fastcase search results. However, Fastcase users will only be able to view HeinOnline's list of results and its abstracts for free. To access the full articles, Fastcase subscribers would also have to subscribe to HeinOnline. Bar associations will also have the option to add the Hein material to their member benefit plan.

Part V

RESEARCHING LEGISLATION

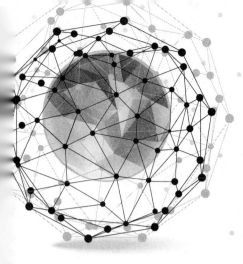

Chapter 10

FEDERAL STATUTORY RESEARCH

A great deal of detailed federal statutory information is available online through free websites. We've arranged this chapter by first discussing where to find and research the U.S. Constitution found at two sites: **FDsys** at http://www.gpo.gov/fdsys and Cornell Law School's **LII** site at http://www.law.cornell.edu/constitution) and the Declaration of Independence (found at the Library of Congress's **Primary Documents in American History** page at http://linkon.in/Iz30I7). Then we will explain where to find and research the United States Code at three sites: **FDsys** (http://linkon.in/y2uMZC), Cornell's **Legal Information Institute** (http://www.law.cornell.edu/uscode/text), and the Office of the Law Revision Counsel's **United States Code Online** (http://uscode.house.gov/browse.xhtml).

This Chapter will focus on finding and using sites that track the federal legislative process, from newly introduced and recently signed bills to bills that never made it out of committee and more.

UNITED STATES CONSTITUTION AND DECLARATION OF INDEPENDENCE

The U.S. Constitution is a featured collection on the home page of **FDsys** (http://www.gpo.gov/fdsys). In the right-hand column under Browse is a link titled Constitution of the United States of America: Analysis and Interpretation link (see Figure 10.1).

Figure 10.1   FDsys Home Page

This link will take you to a page of **Additional Government Publications**. On this page are links to PDFs of the 1992, 2002, 2012, and 2013 editions of the Constitution, along with seven supplements. If they are not displayed, click the plus sign to the left of the link to the Constitution, and they will appear (see Figure 10.2). The supplements are cumulative, so you only need to read the most current one.

Figure 10.2   FDsys Additional Publications

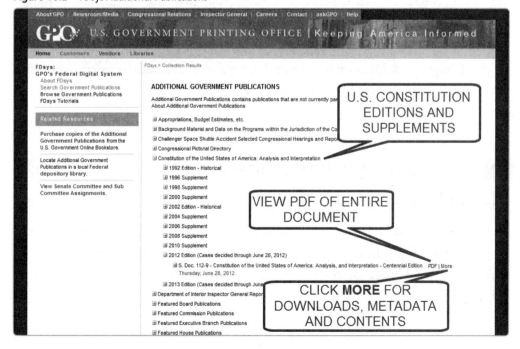

To keyword search the PDF of the Constitution, use the Find function (**Control F** if you are a PC user or **Command F** if you have an Apple device). To keyword search all editions and supplements of the Constitution together, first select Advanced Search from the home page (see Figure 10.3), then follow these steps, outlined in the next Figure:

1. Choose the Additional Government Publications Collection from the **Available Collections** menu.

2. Click the **Add** button to add this Collection to Selected Collections (on the right side of the page).

3. Then select **Publication Name** (from the search criteria's **Search in** drop-down menu).

4. From the **Select Value** drop-down menu, choose **Constitution of the United States of America: Analysis and Interpretation**.

Figure 10.3   FDsys Steps for Searching the Constitution

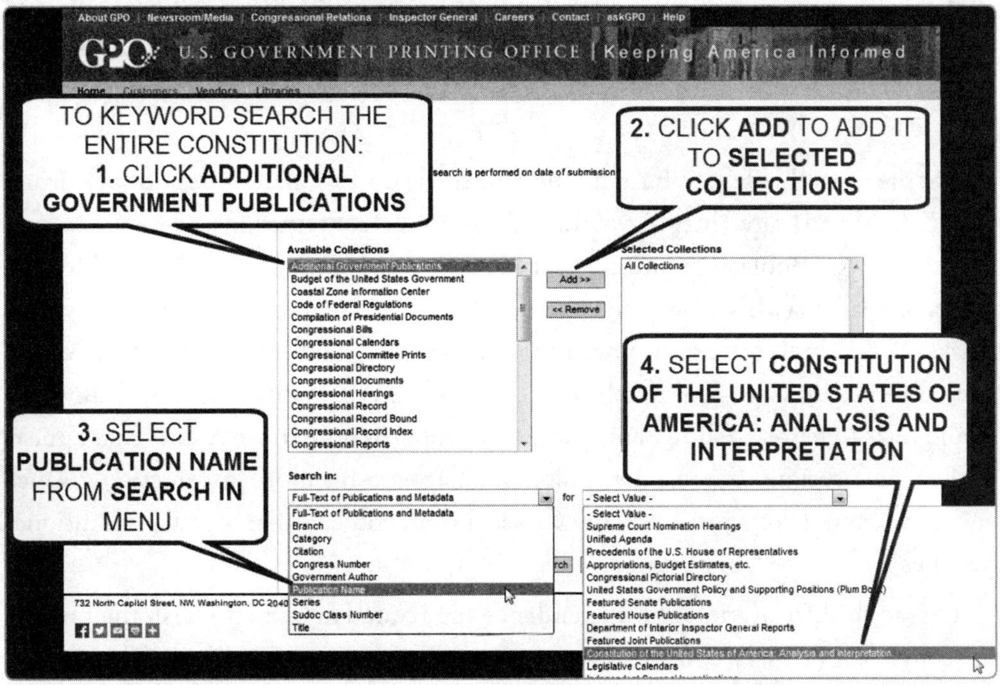

Now your screen should look similar to the one in Figure 10.4. Click the **Add more search criteria** link (near the bottom of the page) and choose **Full-Text of Publications and Metadata**. Finally, enter your keywords in the search box at the bottom right side of the page (see Figure 10.4). See Chapter 5 to learn about general FDsys search protocols that apply to all Collections.

Figure 10.4   FDsys Steps for Searching the Constitution, Continued

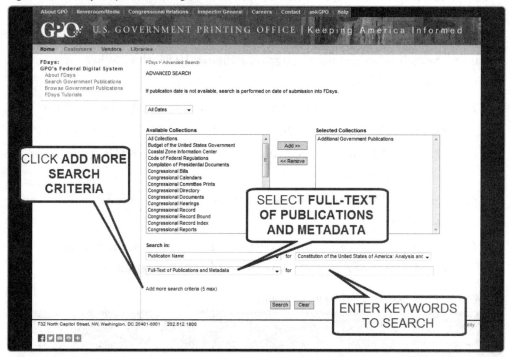

Another searchable database of the Constitution can also be found at Cornell Law School's LII site (http://www.law.cornell.edu/constitution). Cornell's search engine uses the Boolean connectors *AND, OR,* and *NOT.* The user can perform a wildcard search with an asterisk (*), and phrases are searched by using quotation marks. LII's search feature has been updated recently and now searches the entire site, rather than individual databases. To search the Constitution specifically, you would have to first search the entire site, then filter to only those results that appear in the Constitution. (See the discussion in Chapter 5 for more information.) Once you have filtered your results to the Constitution, you can then conduct additional searches within the Constitution.

To read the Declaration of Independence and related documents, visit the Library of Congress's Primary Documents in American History page (http://linkon.in/Iz30I7). To keyword search the Declaration, use your browser's Find function (**Control+F** or **Command+F**).

UNITED STATES CODE (U.S.C.)

THREE SITES COMPARED

Three helpful websites offer free online, searchable versions of the United States Code. Two of them—**FDsys** (http://linkon.in/y2uMZC) and the **House of Representatives' Office of the Law Revision Counsel (OLRC) United States Code Online** (http://uscode.house.gov/browse.xhtml)—provide other legislative material as well (which we will discuss in Chapter 13). The third site, **Cornell Law School's LII** site (http://www.law.cornell.edu/uscode/text), lacks much of the legislative material that the two preceding sites contain, but it is still quite useful. (In addition to the U.S. Code and Constitution, Cornell also provides links to World legal materials—both foreign and international—at http://www.law.cornell.edu/world/ and to state statutes by topic at http://www.law.cornell.edu/wex/state_statutes.)

Although the former OLRC beta site is now the "official" website for the United States Code Online, only the OLRC's print version of the U.S.C. is the "official" version (published every six years). All three websites use the online OLRC version of the U.S.C. to create their online searchable databases. Although it may seem redundant to have three databases, each is unique in terms of its search and updating features and dates of coverage. Thus, deciding which database to search will change from time to time, depending on your needs.

If a researcher wants to use the most up-to-date U.S.C., the OLRC United States Code Online version is a better choice over FDsys and Cornell. The United States Code Online site states that it updates the U.S.C. throughout a congressional session on an ongoing basis instead of delaying the update process until the end of the session. FDsys and Cornell do not make any representations about their currency. OLRC's currency information is found by selecting the **Currency and Updating** tab in the left-hand column of any page on the OLRC site. (Currency and Updating are discussed later in the book.)

For those who want to conduct a retrospective U.S.C. search, the OLRC site or FDsys are the best choices because they date back to the 1994 edition. Cornell only has the current version of the U.S.C.

For those who prefer to jump back and forth between sections (offering the look and feel of browsing a book), the OLRC or Cornell versions will work best.

Sometimes a researcher only knows the popular name of an act—e.g., the Racketeer Influenced and Corrupt Organizations Act (RICO)—rather than the citation or other information. The best choices for those who prefer to browse through lists of popular names would be **Cornell's Table of Popular Names** feature (http://www.law.cornell.edu/topn/0; see Figure 10.5) or the **OLRC's Popular Name Tool** (http://uscode.house.gov/popularnames/popularnames.htm). For those who prefer to keyword search popular names, the best choice would be FDsys, which offers a Short Title search criteria option of its U.S.C. Collection from the Advanced Search page (see Chapter 7).

Figure 10.5   LII Table of Popular Names

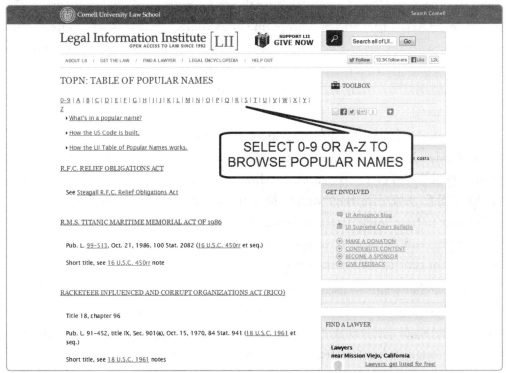

THE OLRC UNITED STATES CODE ONLINE

The newly updated **ORLC United States Code Online** has many helpful search features. The home page (http://uscode.house.gov/browse.xhtml) offers boxes to search the U.S.C. by keyword as well as by title and section number (see Figure 10.6). Underneath the search boxes is a table of contents with links to browse the Code.

You can perform a citation search by using the **Jump To** boxes on the home page (see Figure 10.6). To do this, leave the keyword search box empty and fill in the title and section number that you want to retrieve. Even if you only know the section number but not the title, you can enter just that number in the Section box to retrieve any section with that number found within the Code. (Note that you cannot do the reverse; searching for just a title number without a section number will retrieve no results.)

Figure 10.6   OLRC United States Code Search

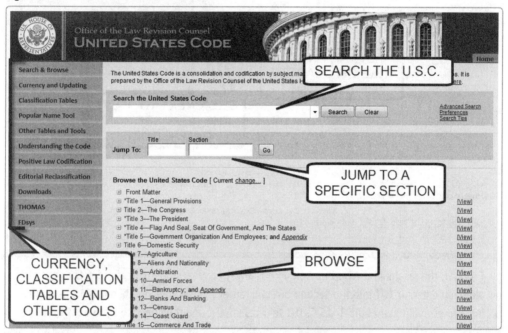

Your search results will appear in a pop-up box (unlike keyword searches, where the results appear on a regular page of the site). If your search retrieved more than one section, you can browse through the different sections by using the arrow tools at the top of the screen, as shown in Figure 10.7. Note that the forward and backward arrows serve a different function than the Next and Previous links underneath them. The arrows allow you to browse through your search results (1 U.S.C. 101, 2 U.S.C. 101, etc.). **Next** and **Previous** jump to the next section in the code (1 U.S.C. 101, 1 U.S.C. 102, etc.). You can use these links, along with the Title number and Chapter number links to browse the code.

Figure 10.7   OLRC Search Results

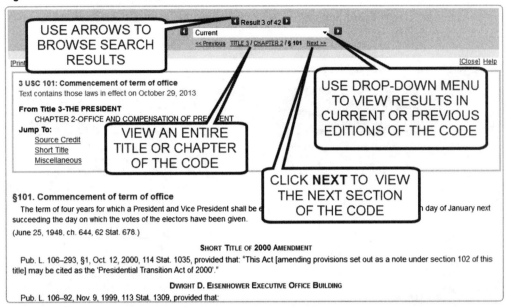

> **CAVEAT:** the results in the pop-up box do not always appear in numerical order. For example, although entering *101* into the Section box will retrieve all sections numbered 101, the browsing arrows might jump from 1 U.S.C. 101 to 4 U.S.C. 101, and then back to 3 U.S.C. 101, etc.

A sidebar on the left side of the screen provides links to **Currency and Updating** information, **Classification Tables**, the **Popular Name Tool**, and **Other Tables and Tools**, as well as resources to help understand various aspects of the Code and the functions of the Office. A **Downloads** link leads to a page with downloadable files for the most current updates or "release points" of the United States Code. At the bottom of the sidebar are links to **FDsys** and to **THOMAS.** (The THOMAS link now goes to Congress.gov, which is discussed later in this book.)

OLRC United States Code Online also provides a handy **Advanced Search Options** page at http://uscode.house.gov/advancedSearch.xhtml (see Figure 10.8). Among other options, you can choose which version of the U.S.C. to search back to 1994, which title(s) or section(s) to search within, which fields to search, including text, citation, heading, future amendments, and more. Links in the upper right corner of the page allow the user to specify **Preferences** such as the number of search results per page, the search results view (context or citation), and the sorting order (code number or relevance).

Figure 10.8   OLRC United States Code Advanced Search

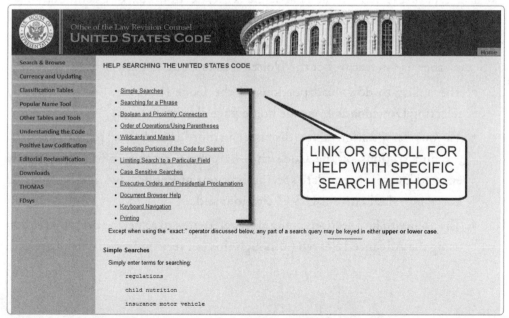

The OLRC **Help Searching the United States Code** page (http://uscode.house. gov/static/help.html) explains specific searching and browsing options available on this site (see Figure 10.9).

Figure 10.9   OLRC United States Code Search Help

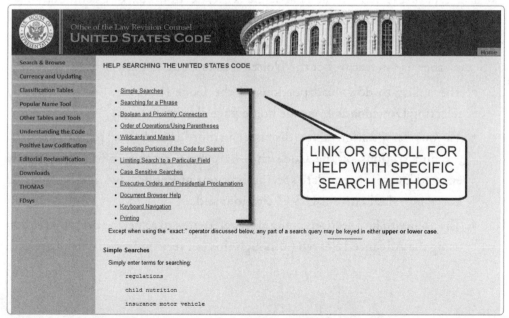

The United States Code Online can be searched by Simple Searches, which search the entire text of the code for the best match containing all your search terms. Phrases may be searched by enclosing them in quotation marks.

The help page also describes the operation of the site's search engine and includes tips for the use of Boolean connectors, wildcards, and order of operations. Boolean connectors—*AND, OR, NOT*—and proximity connectors—*NEAR/* (e.g., alien NEAR/3 homeland) *ADJ* (adjacent; e.g., alien ADJ homeland), *BEFORE/* (e.g., alien BEFORE/6 homeland)—may be employed to refine the search. (The *AND* operator by default has precedence over *OR*, but you can override the default order by using parentheses.)

The United States Code Online offers two types of wildcard searches; one uses question marks and the other uses an asterisk. Each question mark wildcard symbol represents one character. For example, typing *int??city* into the search box indicates a search for any word that begins with *int*, is followed by any two characters, and then ends with *city*. The search results might include the words *intercity* or *intracity*, or both words. An asterisk wildcard indicates an unlimited number of characters. For example, a search for *child** would return search results that include *child*, *child's*, *children*, *childish*, and so on. Other helpful hints explain case-sensitive searches, locating executive orders and presidential proclamations, document browser help, and special keyboard navigation functions.

If researchers do not want to conduct a keyword search of the entire U.S.C., they can also keyword search within a particular Title, Section, etc., or a combination of any of the available criteria. For example, in Figure 10.10, the number 42 was entered into the Title search box, restricting that search to Title 42 only.

Some other useful features of the United States Code Online include:

- The ability to download portions of the Code (by Title, Section, etc.) by selecting **Downloads** from the home page side bar;
- Various classification tables (discussed in more detail below) to help researchers find sections of the Code that have been recently affected by newly enacted laws or to translate specific citations of Public Laws and Statutes At Large into their current U.S.C. citation; and
- The ability to find sections containing references to a specific title and section using the **Advanced Search** (although this is a very imprecise type of search).

Figure 10.10 OLRC Advanced Search Example

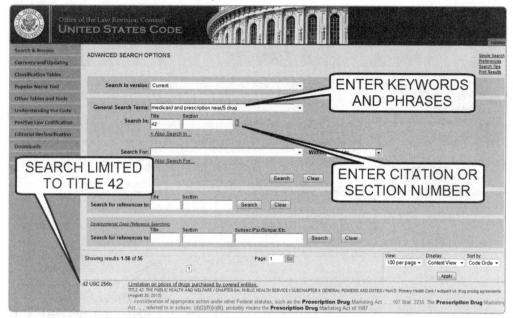

Updating the OLRC United States Code Online

Although a previous resource known as USCprelim used to provide preliminary release updates, the OLRC no longer provides this resource. The OLRC's Currency and Updating page (see left-hand column in Figure 10.10 or use this URL: http:// uscode.house.gov/currency/currency.shtml) now states that "If the section has been affected by any laws enacted after [the currency] date, those laws will appear in a list of 'Pending Updates.' If there are no pending updates listed, the section is current as shown." According to the OLRC United States Code Online's Currency and Updating page, (http://uscode.house.gov/currency/currency.shtml), as of August 28, 2013, for example, all Titles in the United States Code Online (http://uscode. house.gov/) are current through Pub. L. 113-31. The currency information on this page is updated as the code is updated. One can also consult the U.S.C. classification tables (see Figure 10.11) to be sure of the latest laws that affect the Code.

Figure 10.11   U.S.C. Classification Tables

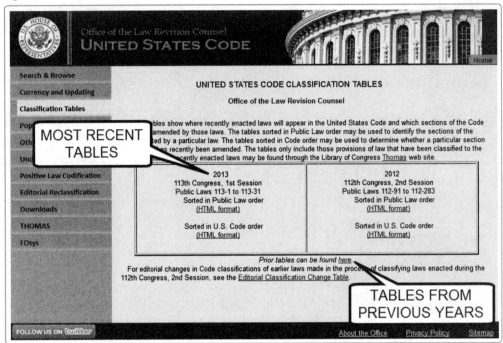

Near the top-left corner of every section of the OLRC version of the U.S.C. is a date and a statement that the text contains those laws in effect as of the date shown (see Figure 10.12). If the section has been affected by any laws enacted after that date, those laws will appear in a list of "Pending Updates." If there are no pending updates listed, the section is current as shown.

Figure 10.12   OLRC Currency Date

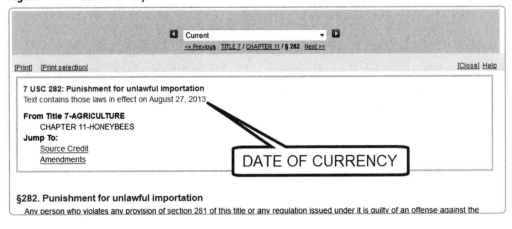

When present, the list of pending updates provides the public law numbers of each law affecting the section in some way—either the text of the section, a statutory note set out under the section, or a table of contents preceding the section. Following the list of pending updates is a **View Details** link that provides more specific information about how each new law has affected the section.

The **Classification Tables** (http://linkon.in/Hmnmnx, shown in Figure 10.11) can also be used to find the latest laws affecting the Code. The Classification Tables indicate which sections of the Code have been affected by recently enacted laws. They show where the newly enacted laws and amendments will eventually appear in the U.S.C. The user can view the tables either in Public Law order or in U.S. Code order. The text of public laws listed as Pending Updates or appearing in the Classification Tables can be found in a number of sources, such as the Government Printing Office's FDSys (Federal Digital System) or Congress.gov.

THE CORNELL LII U.S.C. DATABASE

Cornell LII (http://www.law.cornell.edu/uscode/text) has made some improvements thanks to its recent site redesign.[7] The link to the **Table of Popular Names** has returned to the main page of the U.S.C. database (see Figure 10.13), along with a link to the **Parallel Table of Authorities**. Part of the redesign included removing the ability to search specific databases, including the U.S.C., however.

Figure 10.13   LII Quick Search by Citation

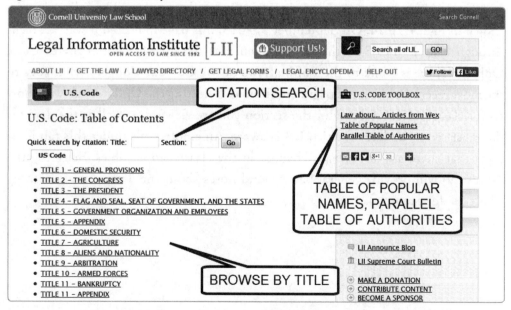

---

7   LII is in the process of further redesigning their search to be more user-friendly. These instructions are accurate as of March 2014, but the site may be changing in the near future.

Figure 10.13 shows how a researcher can browse a numerical list of Titles or perform a Quick search by citation (by Title and Section). In the redesigned version, the Keyword search of specific databases has been eliminated, unfortunately. It is possible to search the entire site and then filter to a specific database such as the U.S. Code (see following section). You can also search the U.S. Code, as well as specific titles, at OLRC United States Code Online site, as described earlier.

How to Keyword/Phrase Search Cornell LII

Cornell LII (http://www.law.cornell.edu/) does not offer as sophisticated Boolean and proximity searching as the OLRC and FDsys sites do. To keyword search Cornell's databases, use the Boolean connectors *AND, OR, NOT* (*AND* is the default, so there is no need to type it in—simply leave spaces between words). Phrase searching is allowed (surround phrases by quotation marks). After you search, you can use the list of filters that appear to the left of the search results to choose the database for which you want to view documents. See Chapter 5 for additional information.

How to Navigate through Cornell LII's U.S.C. Results

After you select a Title to browse (or after you have conducted a keyword/phrase search and filtered your results to the U.S. Code), the result will look like the one shown in Figure 10.14. On September 9, 2013, this page indicated it was "Current through Pub. L. 113-31" (the same currency as the OLRC United States Code Online). There is a link to the **Public Laws of the Current Congress** that goes to the most recent Public Laws pages on Thomas. Selecting the **Updates** tab will show recent classification updates for the section you are viewing, as well as the date for the most recent update of which LII is aware. An empty table under this tab indicates that there are no relevant changes in the classification tables. Selecting the **Notes** tab will provide general background notes about the Title you are reading (Title 14, for example).

Figure 10.14   LII U.S.C. Sample with Updates Pending

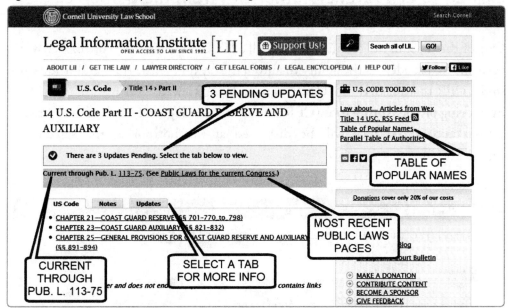

Updating the Cornell LII U.S.C. Database

After you click the **Updates** tab (see Figure 10.14), the Sections that have Updates Pending will be displayed (see Figure 10.15). If you want to read the change, then click on the **Public Law** link or the **Statutes at Large** link.

Figure 10.15   LII Updates

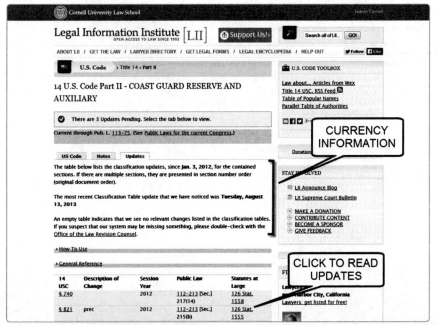

Linking to CFR Parallel Authorities from the Cornell LII U.S.C. Database

One of the most useful features of Cornell LII's U.S.C. database (http://www.law.cornell.edu/uscode/) is the ability to automatically link to the rules and regulations in the CFR that relate to the U.S.C. section being viewed. This feature is activated by clicking on the **Authorities (CFR)** tab noted (see Figure 10.16). If there are any related authorities, they will be displayed at the bottom of the screen (see Figure 10.16).

Figure 10.16   LII CFR Authorities

Figure 10.17 shows links to several CFR Authorities relating to the U.S.C. section that we were researching. You can double-check the currency by visiting the e-CFR database.

Figure 10.17 LII CFR Example

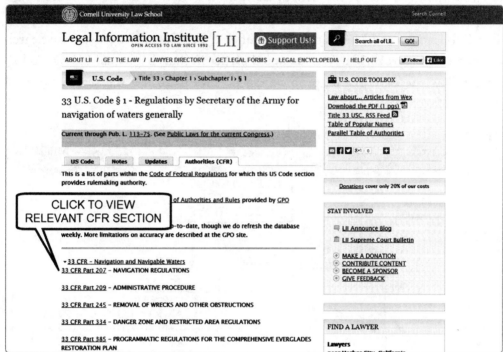

Note that the U.S. Code title and section numbers and the CFR parallel authority title and section numbers do not always match up as in the above Figure, but they are, nevertheless, related. Sometimes you will see a completely different Title number.

THE FDSYS UNITED STATES CODE DATABASE

FDsys allows the user to keyword search or browse the United State Code. As noted earlier, the main difference between various FDsys Collections is their Search Criteria, so when you choose the **U.S.C. Collection** from the **Advanced Search** page (http://linkon.in/y2uMZC) and click the downward arrow to the right of Full-Text Publications and Metadata, you are offered U.S.C. Collection-specific Search Criteria (see Figure10.18). Also, as noted earlier in this chapter, all FDsys Collections follow the same search protocol, so be sure to review the search protocol discussed in Chapter 5.

Figure 10.18   FDsys U.S.C. Collection-Specific Search Criteria

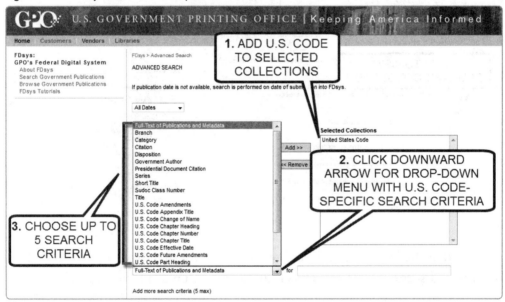

Down in the middle of our search results page (see Figure 10.18), there are links to several versions of the full text of U.S.C. sections dealing with our search (*water pollution*) and a link to **Show only recent editions** (if we don't want the older versions of the Code displayed in our results). We can refine our search by clicking on links in the left-hand column, such as **Government Author, Organization,** and **Date Published.** By clicking the **See more** link in the **Dates Published** section, you can see results back to 1994.

Figure 10.19 FDsys Search Results

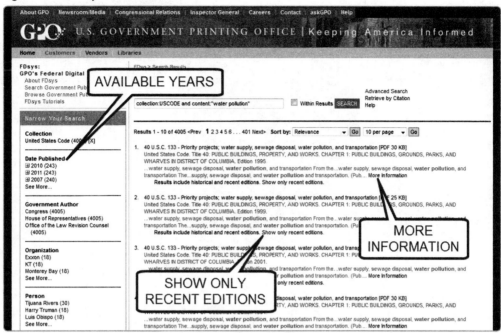

Clicking the **More information** link found with each result (see Figure 10.19) displays **Metadata** (see Figure 10.20). Metadata refers to information about the document. For example, the Metadata informs us that this Title of the U.S.C. (33) is not positive law, that the section's Public Law number is Pub. L. 92-500, §2, its date is October 18, 1972, and its Statutes at Large citation is 86 Stat. 828.

Figure 10.20 FDsys Search Result Metadata

Chapter 11

FEDERAL LEGISLATIVE AND CONGRESSIONAL MATERIALS

Searchable databases of federal legislative and congressional materials (other than the U.S. Code), such as public laws, bills, resolutions, hearings, congressional reports, and committee reports can be found at four governmental sites, which we will describe individually in the upcoming sections. (For non-federal legislative research (state, local, territorial, and tribal law, see Chapter 13.)

Legislative and congressional materials are valuable to researchers for the following reasons:

- To track a current bill as it is proceeding through the legislative process
- To discern the legislative intent of a bill
- To conduct research about the history of a bill that was never passed (and, thus, would not be contained in a Public Law database or the U.S.C.)
- To read a public law in its entirety (instead of trying to piece it together once it has been scattered throughout various sections of the U.S.C.)

CONGRESS.GOV

UNITED STATES LEGISLATIVE INFORMATION

In 2012, the Library of Congress introduced a new Web site called **Congress.gov** (http://beta.congress.gov/), which presents the Library of Congress's congressional information system in a modern and user-friendly format. By the end of 2014, Congress.gov will completely replace **THOMAS.gov**, the site that had provided the federal government's legislative information since 1995.

While most of the URLs for **THOMAS.gov** and **THOMAS.loc.gov** automatically redirect to http://beta.congress.gov/, some do not because not all information has been transferred to Congress.gov. For instance, as of January 2014, nominations, treaties, House and Senate Executive communications, legislation from the 101st and 102nd Congresses (1989–1992), and the Congressional Record from the 101st to 103rd Congresses (1989–1994) still hadn't been transferred from Thomas to Congress.gov. Users can compare the information available on the two sites by visiting the *Coverage Dates for Legislative Information* page at http://beta.congress. gov/help/coverage-dates. Until all the information at Thomas gets transferred to Congress.gov, use http://thomas.loc.gov/home/thomas.php.

Because Congress.gov will be the ongoing site, we will discuss it first. During the transition period, the URL is http://beta.congress.gov/ but it will eventually be switched (and will automatically redirect to) Congress.gov. Congress.gov contains the sections listed below (most will be discussed in greater detail in this chapter):

1. **Legislation** (http://beta.congress.gov/legislation) is available from the 103rd Congress (1994) to the present.

2. **The Congressional Record** (http://beta.congress.gov/congressional-record) is available from the 104th Congress (1995) to the present.

3. **Members** (http://beta.congress.gov/members) Congress member profiles are provided for all members since 1973 and selected members from 1947-1972.

4. **Committees** (http://beta.congress.gov/committees). Information is available for all House and Senate committees for the current Congress, with links to specific Committee pages.

5. **The Legislative Process** (http://beta.congress.gov/legislative-process) provides basic information on the legislative process and is a good resource for the general public.

6. **Committee Reports** (http://beta.congress.gov/congressional-reports) are available from 1995 to the present.

Links to the first five sections outlined above are available from tabs across the top of any page on the Congress.gov site (see Figure 11.1). You can keyword search all but the fourth and fifth sections outlined above directly from the Congress.gov home page.

Figure 11.1 Congress.gov Home Page

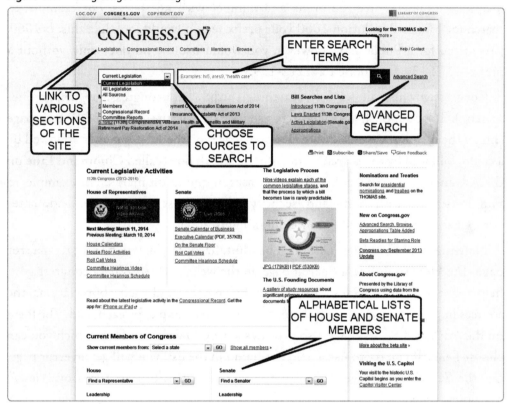

Searching Congress.gov for Legislative Information

All the legislative materials in Congress.gov use the same search method, which we will now describe. From the home page (see Figure 11.1), choose which source to search from a drop-down menu to the left of the search box. Sources include **Current Legislation, All Legislation, All Sources, Members of Congress, the Congressional Record,** and **Committee Reports.** After you have selected a source, enter your search terms into the box and click the magnifying glass icon.

In addition to searching with keywords and phrases (enclosed in quotation marks), you can also link them together with the Boolean connectors *AND* and *OR*. Researchers can run more sophisticated searches, such as field and prefix searches, as described below.

Prefix searching can be used to search by bill, resolution, and amendment numbers, each of which includes an alphabetical prefix and a number, such as *hr* for House Bills or *sjres* for Senate Joint Resolutions. To search for one of these documents by number, enter the prefix and number with no spaces. For example, to search for House Resolution 1060 your prefix search would look like this: *hr1060*. (To search for a Public Law, however, you would use the number only, without a prefix—*112-139*, for Public Law 112-139.)

Congress.gov also allows field searching (http://beta.congress.gov/help/refine-search/). To accomplish a field search, use the form on the **Advanced Search** page (http://beta.congress.gov/advanced-search), or type the field qualifier, followed by a colon, followed by the search term, into the search box (called **Command Line** on the **Advanced Search** page), and put phrases in quotation marks. For example, to find legislation with homeland security in the most recent title field, enter *latestTitle:"homeland security"*, as we did in Figure 11.1.

Note that the "*T*" in *latestTitle* must be capitalized, or you will be sent to an error page. The **How to Refine a Search** page on the website (http://beta.congress.gov/help/refine-search) provides a list of searchable fields and their abbreviations, the sources in which you can search them, and a search example for each field. The form on the Advanced Search page also provides a dropdown menu from which you can choose fields. If you try to use a field not found in the list, you will get an error page. See the **Search Tips** page (http://beta.congress.gov/help/search-tips-overview/) for more details.

Once you have run a search (e.g., a Current Legislation search for "endangered species" as shown in Figure 11.2), you can **Refine by** in two ways. The first refinement option is to use "facets," which represent particular data fields, such as Legislation or Congress shown in the Refine By sidebar on the left side of the results page. Use them to filter the search results to retrieve only items that contain that facet and specific value. In Figure 11.2, the original search for *"endangered species"* has been refined so that the results include only the Legislation (selected from the sidebar's **Limit Your Search** section), Congress facets, and the value 113 (materials from the 113th Congress selected from the sidebar's Congress section).

Figure 11.2 Refining Search Results at Congress.gov

A number appears beside each facet that indicates how many results match that facet value.

Although the help page says that you cannot select multiple values (e.g., in Figure 11.2, note the values 112 and 113) for facets (e.g., see the Congress facet in Figure 11.2) in your search results, our test searches indicate that it is possible. A list of the main facets on Congress.gov is available on the **How to Refine a Search** page at http://beta.congress.gov/help/refine-search/.

The second search refinement available on Congress.gov is **Search within Results**. From any search page, you can check the **Search within Results** box next to the search box (see Figure 11.3), clear your original search terms, and type in additional search terms. All search terms, including the new ones, will appear at the top of the new list of search results.

Figure 11.3   Search Within Results at Congress.gov

To remove a term or refinement, click the gray or blue shaded link for it that appears underneath the search box, as shown in Figure 11.3. If you added a refinement by clicking it in the left sidebar, clicking it again will remove it.

Navigating Search Results on Congress.gov

The search results list gives brief information about each item. You can sort the list by **Relevancy, Date of Introduction, Latest Action, Number,** and **Title** (alphabetically). Use the drop-down menu just above the search results, and click **Go** once you have made your sorting selection (see Figure 11.4). You can use another drop-down menu near the right side of the page to display 25, 50, 100, 250, or 500 results per page.

Figure 11.4 Congress.gov Search Results Navigation

The item type (appears in a pink box with red letters (e.g., **Bill, Resolution**, and **Congressional Record Article**, shown in Figure 11.4), just above the blue link (e.g., *H.Res.220* shown in Figure 11.4) for the item. Different information appears below the item link, depending on the type of document it is. The names of bills and resolutions are in boldface type. Below that (shown in the *H.R.5923* example in Figure 11.4) is a link to the sponsor of the legislation (*Rep. Hastings*), along with a link for information on any co-sponsors. Underneath that is the Latest Action taken (*Introduced*). Finally, a graphic **Tracker** indicates where the item is in the legislative process (*6/14/12 Referred to…*).

Resolutions have similar features to bills, including the Tracker timeline. Congressional Record Articles have a link (for HTML and PDF) to the page in the Congressional Record where the article appears.

Viewing Legislation Pages on Congress.gov

Click an item link to view the full content for each item. Figure 11.5 shows the landing page for a law. Pages for other legislation types have features similar to the ones described here.

Figure 11.5 Landing Page for a Law at Congress.gov

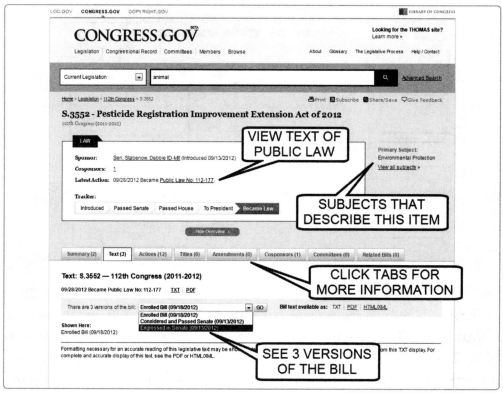

The top part of the item information page repeats the brief information that appeared in the item results list. The bottom of the page is arranged into tabs to help researchers quickly find key information about the document. The tabs for a law include a **Summary of the law, the full Text, Actions taken, Titles, Amendments, Cosponsors, Committees,** and **Related Bills.** Each tab shows the number of items available for that category. If you select **Text (3)** as shown in Figure 11.5, you can read various versions of the bill. You will most likely be interested in the Enrolled Bill because it is the "Final official copy of a measure as passed in identical form by both chambers and then printed on parchment for presentation to the President." This definition (and many others) can be found in Congress.gov's Glossary (discussed in the next section).

Another useful feature on the page includes subject information, as assigned by legislative analysts. The researcher can click the **View all subjects link** to see all subjects assigned to the legislation. From there, you can click a link for the primary subject to retrieve other legislation in the same subject category (see Figure 11.6).

Figure 11.6   Viewing Subjects Assigned to the Legislation

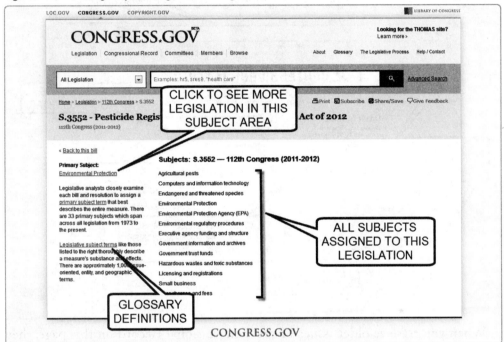

CONGRESS.GOV

Certain legislative terms used on Congress.gov include links to definitions in a Glossary. (See **primary subject term** and **Legislative subject terms** in Figure 11.6.) However, when there is no link for a word that you need defined, visit Congress. gov's **Glossary** (http://beta.congress.gov/help/legislative-glossary).

The Congressional Record on Congress.gov

Congress.gov has several additional features that are worth mentioning here. For example, in addition to keyword searching the Congressional Record from the home page as described earlier, you can also keyword search it at its own landing page, found at http://beta.congress.gov/congressional-record. The default display for the Congressional Record page is the most recent issue available, but you can retrieve any other issue back to 1995 by date (a drop-down menu next to the Date search box allows you to select a date from the calendar without typing it) or by a combination of year and page number (see Figure 11.7). Information about the Congressional Record App (for the iPhone and the iPad) is available on this page.

Figure 11.7   Congressional Record at Congress.gov

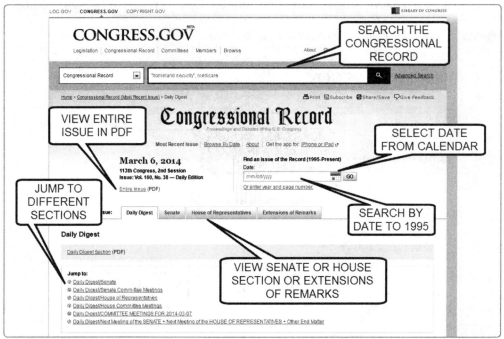

When you retrieve older issues of the Congressional Record on this page, they appear in the same format as the most current issue, illustrated in Figure 11.7, along with the same links and tabs. You can also view the complete issue in PDF by clicking the **Entire Issue link** under the date (in red).

Committee Information on Congress.gov

The **Committees of the U.S. Congress** page (http://beta.congress.gov/committees) provides information about Committees in general, as well as links to individual pages for all current congressional committees. The individual committee pages include an Overview section that lists legislation the committee has considered recently, as well as links to meeting schedules, live video for House committees, and the official committee website. Below the **Overview** is a results list of legislation and reports associated with the committee. The researcher can sort and refine these items similarly to a regular search on Congress.gov (see Figure 11.8).

Figure 11.8   Committee Information at Congress.gov

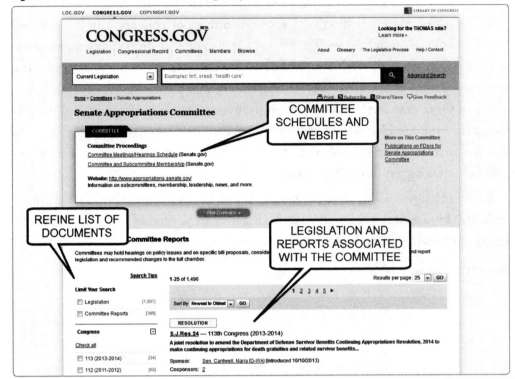

Committee Reports on Congress.gov

Committee reports are keyword searchable from the home page of Congress.gov and from their separate landing page at http://beta.congress.gov/congressional-reports. Alternatively, you can retrieve a report by a combined **Report Type** (**House** or **Senate**) and **Number** (citation) search using the **Find a Report** lookup tool (see Figure 11.9).

Figure 11.9   Committee Reports at Congress.gov

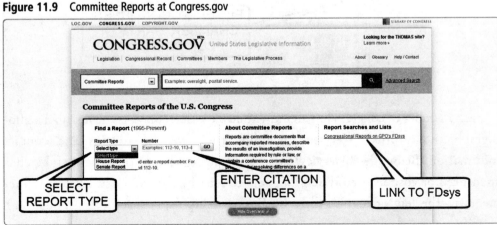

Finding Members of Congress on Congress.gov

Like the other categories discussed above, members of congress can be searched from the home page of the site. The home page also offers a drop-down menu at the bottom of the page that allows users to view members of congress by state. The Members of the U.S. Congress landing page (http://beta.congress.gov/members) offers an **Overview** section with two drop-down menus with A–Z lists of current members (one for **House** and one for **Senate**). The **Overview** also has links to member directories and member guides for accessing additional information about members of congress (see Figure 11.10).

Below the Overview section is a results list of all current members, listed alphabetically (House first and then Senate). This list can be filtered by **state, Congress, House or Senate, party,** or **Members currently serving**.

Figure 11.10   Members of Congress on Congress.gov

Each member of congress has an individual page that contains the member's photograph and a brief Overview, including their website address and contact information. Below the Overview is a list of all legislation that the member has sponsored or cosponsored. Users can sort the list by date and use a list of refinements in the left sidebar to filter by **Sponsorship** (sponsored or cosponsored),

Congress, Chamber, Legislation Type, Subject, Status (current legislation only), and **Committee.**

Learn about the Legislative Process on Congress.gov

Congress.gov includes a section called **The Legislative Process** (http://beta. congress.gov/legislative-process) that provides educational videos to help the general public and students understand the legislative process. The videos are short (mostly under five minutes) and include a written transcript of the narration. A **Diagram of the Legislative Process** is also provided (underneath the list of videos) in PJG and PDF formats.

LIBRARY OF CONGRESS'S THOMAS LEGISLATIVE AND CONGRESSIONAL MATERIALS

As noted earlier, the Library of Congress's twenty-year old THOMAS site will be replaced by Congress.gov at the end of 2014. The only way to reach the THOMAS site is to use this URL: http://thomas.loc.gov/home/thomas.php or the ones noted below. All general Thomas URLs (such as thomas.loc.gov and www.thomas.gov) will redirect you to Congress.gov.

Figure 11.11   THOMAS Home Page

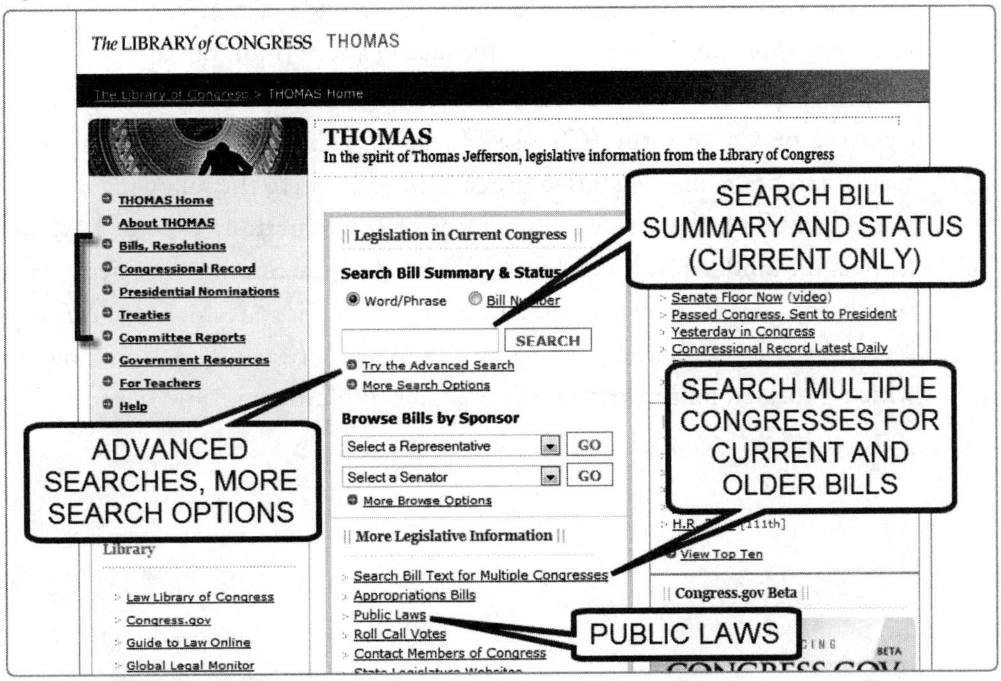

As of January 2014, THOMAS offers various databases, such as:

- **Bill Summary and Status** (BSS) at http://thomas.loc.gov/home/thomas. php: When searching the BSS database from the home page (see the middle column of Figure 11.11), you are limited to searching current bills only. To search further back in time (back to 1973), you will need to use the **Advanced Search** page, explained later in this section). You can select to search BSS by **Bill Number** (you must precede the bill number by *h.r.* or *s.*, etc.), **Word/ Phrase,** or **Browse Bills by Sponsor.**

  Although you can keyword and phrase search the BSS, it does not search the full text of the bill. It is only searching through: sponsor(s); cosponsor(s); official, short, and popular titles; floor/executive actions; detailed legislative history; Congressional Record page references; bill summary; committee information; amendment information; and subjects (indexing terms assigned to each bill).

- **The BSS Advanced Search.** This option at http://thomas.loc.gov/home/ LegislativeData.php (shown in Figure 11.12) allows you to search only one Congress at a time, back to 1973 (93rd Congress), except for amendment data, which only goes back to the 95th Congress (1977). You still cannot search full text. **Your Words/Phrases** can be limited to **Exact Match Only** or expanded to **Include Variants,** such as plurals. It is not necessary to use quotation marks to indicate a phrase. For example, a user can enter *think tank*, not *"think tank,"* to retrieve information about think tanks.

  As Figure 11.12 shows, you can also search by one or more of the following: **Sponsor or Co-sponsor** (Choose House or Senate Members), **Committee(s),** and **Stage in Legislative Process,** in addition to the following that are not displayed on the image below: **Date of Introduction, Type of Legislation,** and **Standard Subject Term** (a link below the Standard Subject Term search box goes to an explanation of Standard Subject Terms). You can also search by bill number (by changing the **Word/Phrase** drop-down menu, which is located on the first search box, to **Bill Number**).

Figure 11.12   THOMAS Bill Summary and Status Advanced Search

- **The Bill Text database** (see Figure 11.13). In contrast to the BSS, this database does search the full text of the bill, but only back to 1989 instead of 1973. You can search through one Congress at http://linkon.in/billtextone-congress or multiple Congresses at http://linkon.in/billtextmulticongress. Searches can be limited to: (1) Which Bills? **All Bills, Bills with Floor Action,** or **Enrolled Bills** (meaning it has been sent to the President); (2) From Where? **Both House and Senate, House Bills Only,** or **Senate Bills Only;** and (3) When? All, **First Session, Second Session,** or by date range for single Congress searches only.

Figure 11.13   THOMAS Bill Text Database

- **Browse Bills and Resolutions** (http://linkon.in/browsebyonecongress). Here you can browse by **Bill Number** (numerically), **Popular and Short Titles, Public Laws, Private Laws, Vetoed Bills, Sponsor Summaries, Subject Terms,** and **CBO Cost Estimates**, but only by one congress at a time. If you select Bill Number, you will need to then choose whether to browse the **Bills, Joint Resolutions, Concurrent Resolutions,** or **Resolutions of either the Senate or the House.**

- **Congressional Record.** You can link to the Record from THOMAS's home page (see the left-hand column of Figure 11.11 or use this URL: http://linkon.in/Hyzgds). The Record goes back to 1989 and is searchable by **Keywords, Phrases, Date Received or Session, Member of Congress**, and **Section of Congressional Record** (e.g., **Senate, House,** or **Daily Digest**).

- **Committee Reports.** You can link to the Reports from THOMAS's home page (see the left-hand column of Figure 11.11 or use this URL: http://thomas.loc.gov/home/LegislativeData.php?&n=Reports). Reports go back to 1995 and are searchable by **Keywords and Phrases, Report Number, Committees,** or **Date Available Online.** The Reports can also be browsed by selecting **House, Senate, Conference,** or **Joint.**

- **Public Laws.** You can link to the Public Laws from THOMAS's home page (see the middle column of Figure 11.11 or use this URL: http://linkon.in/ HoTZam). Public Laws cannot be keyword searched. Instead, the only option is to browse the Public Laws in numeric order. However, the database goes back to 1973, which is much farther back in time than the FDsys's Public and Private Laws database.

FDSYS LEGISLATIVE/CONGRESSIONAL MATERIALS (COLLECTIONS)

Each of FDsys's **Legislative/Congressional Collections** can be searched from the FDsys **Advanced Search** page (http://linkon.in/y2uMZC) by selecting the specific Collection from the Available Collections menu. More ways to search legislative/ congressional materials became available when the legislative/congressional materials migrated from GPO Access to FDsys; you can now select criteria such as **Full-text of publications and metadata, Branch, Citation,** or **Sudoc Class Number** from the **Search** in the drop-down menu. Those needing to retrieve a document by its citation can visit the **Retrieve by Citation** page (http://linkon.in/ Ij0nj3) and choose a collection from the **Collections** drop-down menu. For those who prefer to browse, visit the **Browse Government Publications** page (http:// linkon.in/HyFAsc) and browse through various legislative/congressional materials by **Collection** (e.g., Congressional Calendars), **Congressional Committee** (e.g., Energy & Natural Resources), **Date** (time frames ranging from the past 24 hours to the past year), or **Government Author** (e.g., Impeachment Trial Committee).

FDsys's search protocol is the same throughout all of its Collections; therefore, you should review this information before you search FDsys's legislative/congressional Collections, which we will discuss below.

FDsys's Public and Private Laws Collection goes back to 1995. For earlier years, see Congress.gov's **Legislation** section (which goes back to 1993) or THOMAS's **Public Laws and Private Laws**, which go back to 1989 (as noted on the first few pages of this chapter, by the end of 2014, THOMAS will be completely replaced by Congress.gov). FDsys's Public and Private Laws Collection can also be used to update the text of a U.S.C. section (if it was later amended) or to learn if it has been repealed. For example, after reading the text of 22 U.S.C. 6208 at the OLRC United States Code Online, visit **FDsys's Advanced Search** page (http://www.gpo.gov/ fdsys/search/advanced/advsearchpage.action), select the **Public and Private Laws Collection** from the Available Collections list, and click **Add** so it will appear in the

Selected Collections box. Next, select **United States Code Citation criterion** from the **Search in** drop-down menu and enter the U.S.C. citation (see Figure 11.14). Be sure to place periods in between each letter, as in Figure 11.15; "USC" without periods will not work. Our search for 22 U.S.C. 6208, which was enacted in 1994, revealed six results, with the first result (Public Law 111–202) showing a 2010 amendment (see Figure 11.15).

Figure 11.14   FDsys Public and Private Laws Search

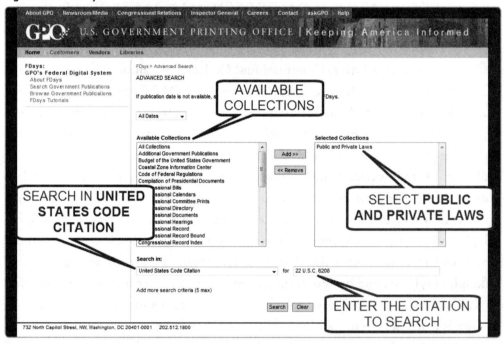

Figure 11.15   FDsys Public and Private Laws Search Results

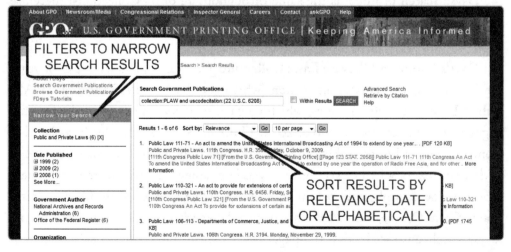

- **Congressional Bills** can be keyword searched back to 1993 by choosing **Congressional Bills** from the **Available Collections** list at FDsys's **Advanced Search** page (http://www.gpo.gov/fdsys/search/advanced/advsearchpage.action) and clicking **Add**. The next step is to click the **Search in** pop-up, where you will find nineteen different criteria to search by. To limit Bills to a specific Congress or multiple Congresses, choose the **Congress Number** criterion from the **Search in** list and click into the **Select Value** box to choose a Congress number. You can search by up to five criteria, so you could select five different Congresses to search or you could select one Congress and add up to four other criteria to search by, such as Bill Number. To search Bills by sponsor, you would select the **Sponsors and Co-sponsors criterion**. However, you would need to type in the sponsor's name. We prefer Congress.gov for this type of search because we can go directly to the member's landing page to see a list of legislation he or she sponsored.

- **History of Bills** offers fifteen different criteria by which to search. While this Collection is not available at the **Retrieve by Citation** page, a **Bill Number Citation** search criterion is one of the fourteen criteria that can be searched by choosing **History of Bills** from the **Available Collections** located on the **Advanced Search** page (http://www.gpo.gov/fdsys/search/advanced/advsearchpage.action). If you don't know in which Congress a specific bill number was introduced, you can search all Congresses (back to 1983) by selecting the **Bill Number Citation** from the Search in list and entering the bill number (e.g., enter *s. 9* to search for the history of every Senate Bill number 9 in every Congress back to 1983; for house bills, you would enter *h.r.1*, for example).

- **Congressional Reports** (also referred to as Committee Reports) offers twenty-two different criteria by which to search by choosing **Congressional Reports from the Advanced Search page's Available Collections** (http://www.gpo.gov/fdsys/search/advanced/advsearchpage.action). Dates of coverage go back to 1995.

- **Conference Reports** are not listed as a separate Collection, but can be searched by choosing the **Conference Reports** search criterion within the **Congressional Reports Collection** at FDsys's **Advanced Search** page (http://www.gpo.gov/fdsys/search/advanced/advsearchpage.action). Coverage goes back to 1995.

If you use Congress.gov's **Glossary,** as mentioned earlier in this chapter, it defines *Conference Reports* as "The document presenting an agreement reached by a joint temporary committee (a conference committee) appointed to negotiate a compromise between the House and Senate.")

- The **Congressional Record** can be searched by thirty-four different criteria back to 1994 by choosing it from the **Advanced Search** page's (http://www. gpo.gov/fdsys/search/advanced/advsearchpage.action) **Available Collections.**

- **Statutes at Large** (back to 1951) can be searched by twenty-two different criteria by selecting it from the **Advanced Search** page's **Available Collections** (http://www.gpo.gov/fdsys/search/advanced/advsearchpage.action).

HOUSE AND SENATE WEBSITES

For more information on the legislative process in general (or even just to find your Senator or Representative), use the **United States Senate** website at http://www. senate.gov and the **United States House of Representatives** website at http://www.house.gov.

Chapter 12

FEDERAL EXECUTIVE AND ADMINISTRATIVE LAW

The executive branch of the federal government is responsible for enforcing the laws of the land. This branch includes the president, the vice president, the cabinet, and various agencies. Agencies help execute policy by creating regulations based on laws. This chapter will explain several resources to help you locate and research executive (also known as administrative) law.

FDsys is useful as a starting point to conduct research about the executive branch of the federal government because FDsys allows you to access all the executive branch's Collections (http://linkon.in/y2uMZC) in one place, from regulations found in FDsys's Federal Register (FR) to presidential materials found in FDsys's Compilation of Presidential Documents. In the next pages, we will also discuss the Code of Federal Regulations (CFR), the publication into which the FR is codified annually. Then, we will also take a look at the White House site. Finally, we will discuss government agencies and how to locate and use them in your research.

THE FEDERAL REGISTER

The **Federal Register** (FR) is the official daily publication (printed Monday through Friday) of proposed and final rules, notices of federal agencies and organizations, and executive orders and other presidential documents. To browse the FDsys FR database by **year, month, date,** or **agency,** visit http://linkon.in/HvAoj9.

Figure 12.1   Federal Register

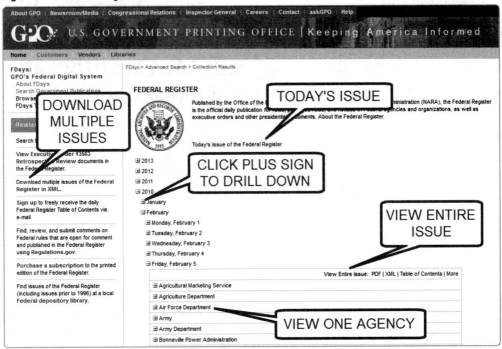

Links to the current day's issue of the FR and to issues from 1994 (volume 59) to the present are displayed on the home page (see Figure 12.1). Once a specific issue is chosen, you can view the **Entire Issue** in **PDF** or **XML** or just view the **Table of Contents.** You can also select to view information from just one agency.

To receive a daily e-mail alert of the FR Table of Contents, see http://linkon.in/ GMnUTU or see **Justia's Regulation Tracker.**

In the left-hand column of the home page, a link to download multiple issues (from 2000 to current) in XML is available. According to a story in the Washington Post (http://wapo.st/3PoN7F), "The technology (XML) will allow users, including Web site designers, to quickly gather data and manipulate the information with tools such as mapping software, word clouds, spreadsheets and e-mail alert systems...."

To search by keywords and other criteria, visit the **Advanced Search** page (http:// linkon.in/y2uMZC), enter a date (or leave the default date as **All Dates** in the **Publications Date** drop-down menu), choose the **Federal Register** from the **Available Collections** list, then choose how to search (by choosing criteria such as **Citation, Action,** etc. from the **Search in** drop-down menu), and finally, enter keywords or citations into the search box. Because all FDsys Collections follow the same search protocol, be sure to review the search protocol discussed elsewhere in this book.

Although you can search the FR Collection back to 1994, you can only **Retrieve by Citation** (http://linkon.in/wWzFn4) back to 1995 because page numbers do not appear in the 1994 FR database, except in the Table of Contents and the List of CFR Sections Affected (LSA).

THE CODE OF FEDERAL REGULATIONS

The **Code of Federal Regulations** (CFR) represents the annual codification of the general and permanent rules and regulations first published in the FR by the departments and agencies of the federal government. The CFR is divided into fifty Titles—distinct areas that are subject to federal regulation (e.g., Title 1 is Energy and Title 26 is Internal Revenue). One-quarter of the CFR Titles are updated at a time, on a rolling quarterly basis, until the full CFR has been updated each year. Presidential documents and executive orders are compiled annually (from the FR) into Title 3 of the CFR.

The CFR database at FDsys can be searched by first selecting the **Code of Federal Regulations** from the **Collections** menu on the **Advanced Search** page (http://linkon.in/y2uMZC) as shown in Figure 12.2.

Figure 12.2 Code of Federal Regulations Advanced Search

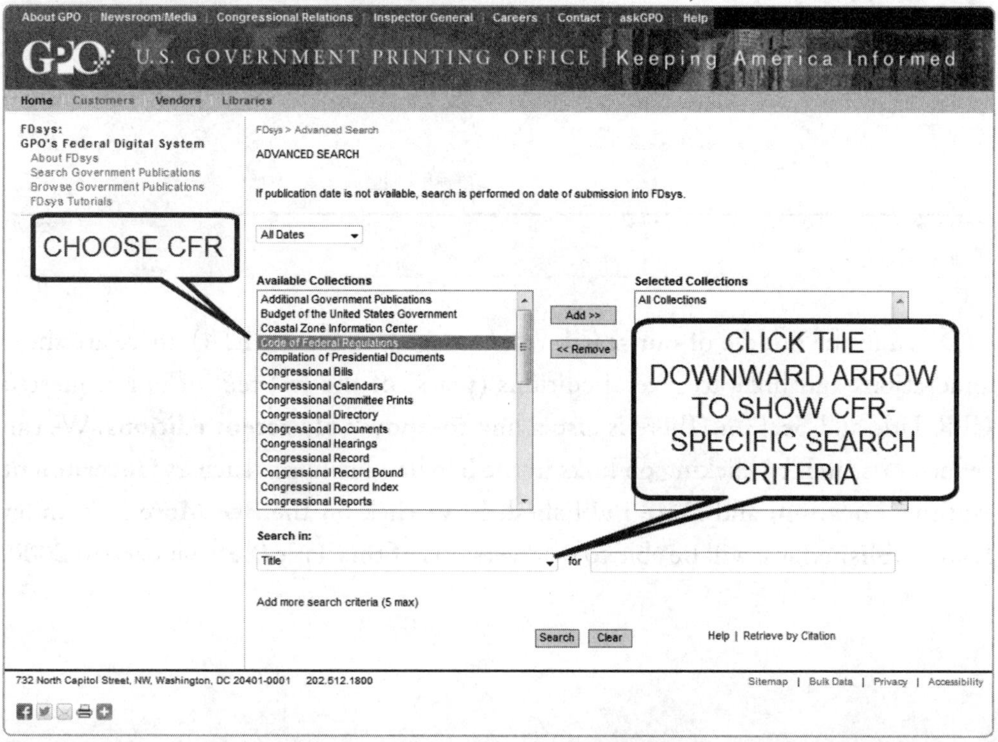

After you choose the **Collection,** the search criteria appropriate to that Collection will be available by clicking on the downward arrow on the right-hand side of the **Search in** drop-down menu. In Figure 12.3, we have chosen to search by the **CFR Title Number** criteria and **CFR Section Number** criteria. This search is different from a Retrieve by Citation search. A **Retrieve by Citation** limits you to one year while our search allows us to search through all years (from 1996 to the most current print version). **Retrieve by Citation** searches are discussed later in the chapter.

Figure 12.3   Code of Federal Regulations Search Criteria

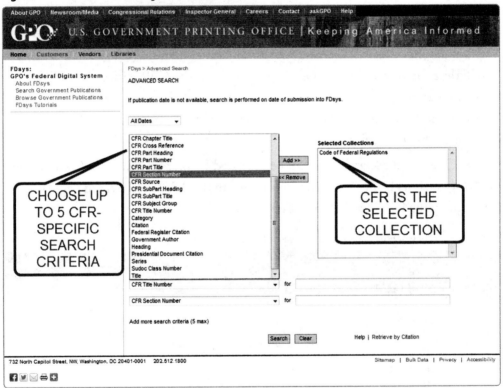

Down in the middle of our search results page (see Figure 12.4), there are short annotations and links to several editions (years) of the full text of our requested CFR Title and Section. There is also a link to **Show only recent editions.** We can refine our search by clicking on links in the left-hand column, such as **Government Author, Location,** and **Date Published.** If we click on the **See More** link under **Date Published,** we will be able to read versions of this Title/Section back to 2000.

Figure 12.4 Code of Federal Regulations Search Results

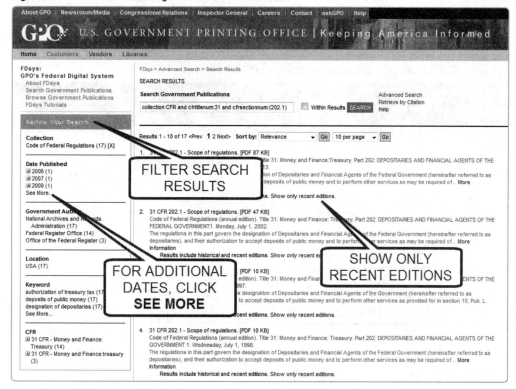

A keyword search can be performed from the **Advanced Search** page at http://linkon.in/y2uMZC (see Figure 12.2) by choosing **Full-text of Publications and Metadata** from the **Search in** drop-down menu and then entering keywords into the search box to the right. Instructions on FDsys's keyword search protocol are discussed elsewhere in this book. The CFR also can be browsed at http://linkon.in/x1xCe6 by: (1) selecting a year; (2) clicking the plus signs to drill down to a specific **Title, Part, Chapter,** or **Section**; and (3) choosing to view the document in **PDF** or **XML.** The PDF will look just like the print document while XML will be just the plain text of the document.

THE E-CFR

Although the **e-CFR** website (http://www.ecfr.gov) displays the branding of GPO Access, it has always run on a separate platform and was never actually a part of GPO Access. Therefore, e-CFR (see Figure 12.5) will not be taken offline, even though GPO Access has been taken offline and replaced by FDsys. However, it is still not deemed to be the "official" CFR and is described as an "editorial compilation of CFR material and Federal Register amendments produced by the National Archives and Records Administration's Office of the Federal Register (OFR) and the Government Printing Office" (http://www.ecfr.gov).

Figure 12.5   Electronic Code of Federal Regulations (e-FCR)

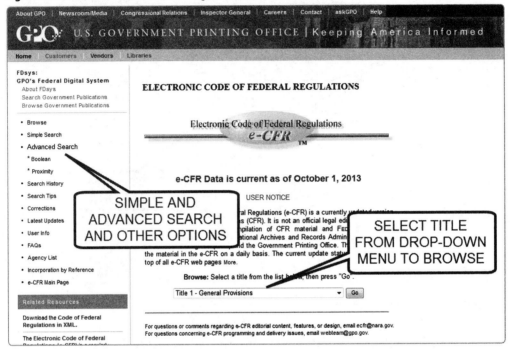

While the FDsys CFR database discussed in the previous section is updated only annually, the e-CFR is updated every day which is why we tend to use it more than the FDsys version. As amendments become effective, the Office of the Federal Register adds the changes to the current CFR database so you can view the full text of the updated CFR in one place instead of having to run a search in both the CFR and FR (or in both the CFR and LSA, discussed later in the chapter).

You can browse the e-CFR database numerically by **Title**, or you can keyword search the database using the **Simple Search** option or the **Advanced Search** option (in the left-hand column). The Simple Search option allows you to search the entire CFR (current) or just one CFR Title (current). You can search for your term anywhere within the text or within a specific region, such as a Part or a SubPart. The Advanced Search option offers you a Boolean and a Proximity search. Detailed **Search Tips** can be found at http://tinyurl.com/ecfrsearchtips.

SEARCHING THE LIST OF CFR SECTIONS AFFECTED (LSA) AND THE LIST OF CFR PARTS AFFECTED

The **List of CFR Sections Affected** (LSA) is a list of new revisions to the CFR, such as proposed, new, and amended federal regulations that have been published in the FR since the most recent revision date of a specific CFR Title. The LSA is issued monthly, but each LSA issue is cumulative.

To browse the LSA from 1997 forward by date, visit http://linkon.in/z1yFFa (see Figure 12.6) and select a year listed beneath Monthly LSA, select a month, and then click on the **PDF** or **Text link** of any Title to view the list of CFR parts and section numbers of that Title that have been affected. There will be a description of how it has been affected (e.g., amended, removed, or revised) and the FR page number will be listed where the change(s) can be found. You would need to then visit the **FR Collection** (discussed elsewhere in this book) to retrieve the text of the change.

Figure 12.6 Browse the List of CFR Sections Affected

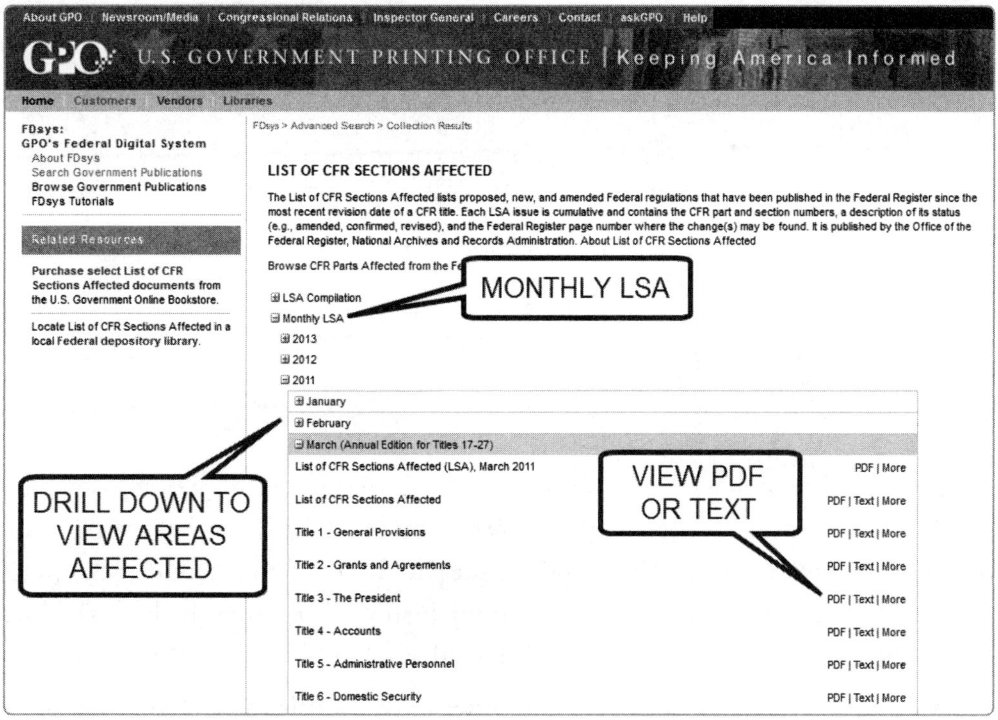

To browse the LSA by Title from 1986-2000, visit http://linkon.in/xeV05Q. Each CFR Title is listed individually and will include a list of changes from 1986-2000. Choosing Title 4, for example, will return a list beginning with the year 1986 (and ending with 2000) and any chapters of Title 4 that were affected during each of those years. There will be a notation of how they were affected (amended, revised, or removed), and the volume and page number of the FR where the change occurred will be included. You would need to then visit the FR Collection to retrieve the text of the change (see Figure 12.7).

Figure 12.7   Search the List of CFR Sections Affected (LSA)

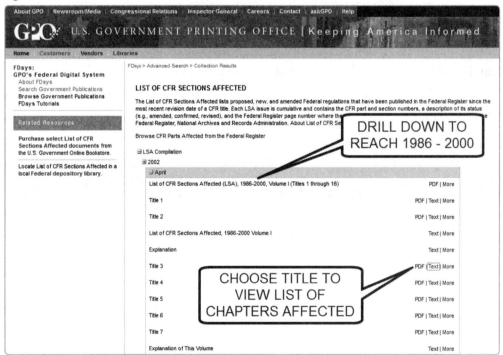

You might wonder why you would use the LSA instead of simply using the e-CFR (which incorporates all FR changes into the e-CFR database on a daily basis). The answer is this: There are searches at the LSA that cannot be accomplished at the e-CFR site, such as conducting historical research (by browsing the 1986–2000 LSA Compilation or searching older volumes back to 1997).

To search the LSA by keywords and other criteria, visit the **Advanced Search** page (http://linkon.in/y2uMZC), and enter a date (or leave the default date as **All Dates** in the **Publications Date** drop-down menu). Then choose **List of CFR Sections Affected** from the **Available Collections** list, choose which part of the

Collection to search (from the Search in drop-down menu at the bottom of the page), and enter keywords (or other criteria, such as **Branch**, **Citation**, or **Title**).

Although the LSA is not listed on the Retrieve by Citation search at http://linkon.in/Ij0nj3, you can conduct a Citation search of the LSA from the **Advanced Search** page (http://linkon.in/y2uMZC) by choosing the **List of CFR Sections Affected** from the **Available Collections** list, then choosing **Citation** from the **Search in** drop-down menu, and entering the citation in this format: *LSA, January, 2012, Title 1*. To learn the correct LSA citation format and to see a list of other Field operators (including Citation) unique to the LSA Collection, see the **Field Operators** page of the **Help** section at http://linkon.in/HvLIjA.

FDsys also allows users to browse **CFR Parts Affected** from the Federal Register (http://linkon.in/wUAkbv) to find final and proposed rules that affect the CFR (and that are published in the FR). To do so, select one of the following from the drop-down menu: **Last 24 Hours, Latest Week, Latest Month**, or **Choose Date Range** (see Figure 12.8). Then choose the **Title of interest** and then the **Part**. Clicking the **PDF** or **Text link** will bring back the full text of the rule (unlike the List of CFR Sections Affected where you have to take another step and visit the FR Collection to retrieve the text of the change to the rule).

Figure 12.8   Browse CFR Parts Affected

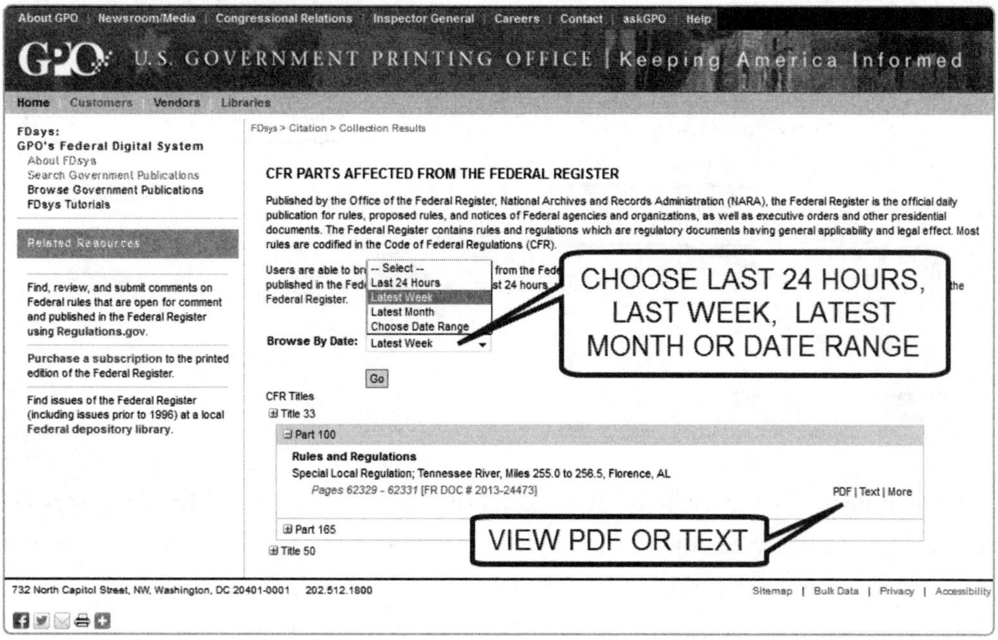

U.S. REGULATION TRACKER

Justia's free **U.S. Regulation Tracker** allows researchers to search and track regulations of specific federal agencies (back to 2005) through the Federal Register by **Department or Agency, Regulations Filed** (i.e., date), by **Full Text**, or by a combination of these search options (see Figure 12.9). The full-text search is powered by Google, so it can be searched by keywords and phrases (and the Boolean connectors Google allows, which are described elsewhere in this book). Results can be sorted by date or by relevance. Search results can also be limited to **Rules** (final), **Proposed Rules**, and so on. From the home page you can also select the option to **Browse by Government Agency** or **Browse by Date**. To use the Tracker, select **More Federal Regulations** from Justia's home page, or visit http://regulations.justia.com.

Figure 12.9   Justia's U.S. Regulation Tracker

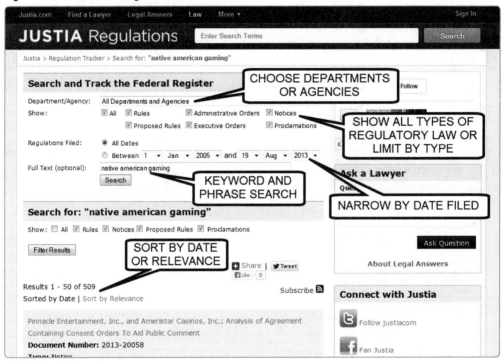

Researchers can subscribe to news feeds (e.g., RSS and others) for daily regulation alert updates. The Federal Register's own alert service (for the Table of Contents only) is also available and described elsewhere in this book.

FDSYS AND PRESIDENTIAL MATERIALS

FDsys offers several Collections relating to the President, including the **Compilation of Presidential Documents**, which is comprised of the **Daily Compilation** (January 2, 2009, to date) and its predecessor, the **Weekly Compilation** (1993 through its change to a daily on January 20, 2009). The Compilations include Presidential statements, messages, remarks, executive orders, State of the Union Addresses, and so on, released by the White House Press Secretary. At FDsys, the Weekly and the Daily Compilation can be browsed (http://linkon.in/GDBkV3; see Figure 12.10) and also **Advanced Searched** (http://linkon.in/y2uMZC).

Figure 12.10   FDsys Compilation of Presidential Materials

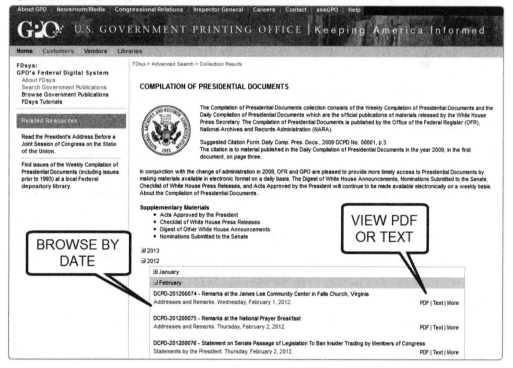

The **Public Papers of the Presidents of the United States Collection** (Presidential writings, addresses, and remarks of a public nature) can be browsed at FDsys back to 1991 (http://linkon.in/HxAy9L) and searched by choosing it from the menu at http://linkon.in/y2uMZC.

You can also conduct a **Retrieve by Citation** search for the Public Papers of the Presidents of the United States and the Weekly and Daily Compilations on FDsys's **Retrieve by Citation** page (http://www.gpo.gov/fdsys/search/showcitation.action).

To search the Public Papers of the Presidents of the United States or the Compilation of Presidential Documents by keywords and other criteria, visit the **Advanced Search** page (http://linkon.in/y2uMZC). Enter a date (or leave the default date as **All Dates** in the **Publications Date** menu), choose one or both of the Presidential Collections (noted above) from the **Available Collections** list, choose which part of the Collection to search (from the **Search in** drop-down menu), and enter keywords or other criteria, such as **Branch, President, Citation,** or **Title.**

There does not seem to be a separate **State of the Union Addresses Collection** at FDsys, but they can be searched at the **Advanced Search** page (http://linkon.in/y2uMZC). Select the **Compilation of Presidential Documents**, choose **Title** from the **Search** in drop-down menu, and then search the phrase *State of the Union.* If you wanted to narrow down your search to a specific year, you could also add a date. Instructions on FDsys's keyword search protocol are discussed elsewhere in this book.

THE WHITE HOUSE

The White House's site is at http://www.whitehouse.gov. There you can take a virtual tour of the White House, get biographical information about current and past presidents and vice presidents (and first ladies), e-mail the current ones, read press briefings, and more. You can even view the President's speeches on YouTube (http://www.youtube.com/whitehouse) and follow the White House (along with nearly 3 million other followers) on Twitter (http://www.twitter.com/whitehouse) or a host of other social media sites. All documents on the White House site are searchable by keyword.

FEDERAL AGENCIES

The executive branch also includes numerous federal agencies whose websites can be useful for legal research. Their sites can include a wide range of information, from directories of staff, rules, regulations, and reports to administrative decisions, laws, and forms. Sometimes it is easier to pinpoint a rule, regulation, or law at an agency's website instead of searching through the CFR, FR, or U.S. Code. For an example of an agency website, see the U.S. Department of Labor site shown in Figure 12.11 (http://www.dol.gov).

Figure 12.11   Federal Agency Website: Department of Labor

UNITED STATES GOVERNMENT MANUAL

The first resource we would recommend for locating agency websites is the **United States Government Manual**, the official handbook of the federal government (http://www.usgovernmentmanual.gov). The manual provides information about executive branch agencies and staff; legislative, judicial, and quasi-official agencies; international organizations in which the United States participates; boards; commissions; and committees. The manual is available at two sites, both of which provide the full text of the manual and links to the various agencies. The first site is the **United States Government Manual** site (http://www.usgovernmentmanual. gov), which is jointly administered by the Office of the Federal Register (OFR) and GPO, and the second site is part of **FDsys** (http://linkon.in/yM4kJK). At the United States Government Manual site, you will find only the current manual. The manual can be browsed by category or searched by keywords.

To find archived versions of the manual (from 1995–2010) and also the current version, you will need to visit FDsys, where the manual can be browsed by year (http://linkon.in/yM4kJK). When using the browsing feature, the entire year's manual can be downloaded as a PDF or just a specific section can be viewed as a PDF or XML text file (see Figure 12.12).

Figure 12.12   United States Government Manual

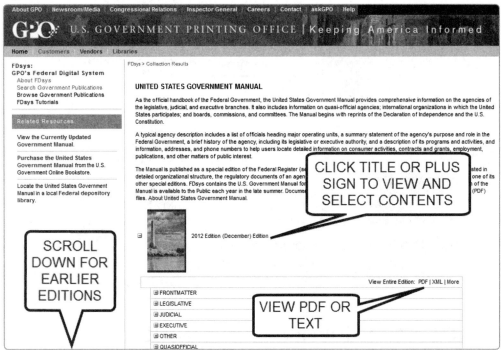

The manual can also be searched at FDsys by **Keyword, Citation,** etc., by choosing **Government Manual** from the **Available Collections** drop-down menu on the **Advanced Search** page (http://linkon.in/y2uMZC). More details on how to search FDsys are provided elsewhere in this book.

USA.GOV

USA.gov (http://www.usa.gov) is the second government site useful for locating agencies. In addition to linking to federal agencies, USA.gov provides links to Local, State, and Tribal agencies. At its **Government Departments and Agencies** page (http://www.usa.gov/Agencies.shtml), you can use the search box to keyword search by agency name. You can also follow the link to **USA.gov's A–Z Index of U.S. Government Departments and Agencies** (http://linkon.in/wuMtMP) where you can browse an alphabetical list of all federal government departments and agencies by name. Under the **Federal Government** heading, you can choose links for the **Executive, Legislative,** or **Judicial** branches, or you can browse by jurisdiction by selecting a link for **State Government, Local Governments,** or **Tribal Governments** (see Figure 12.13).

Figure 12.13   Government Departments and Agencies at USA.gov

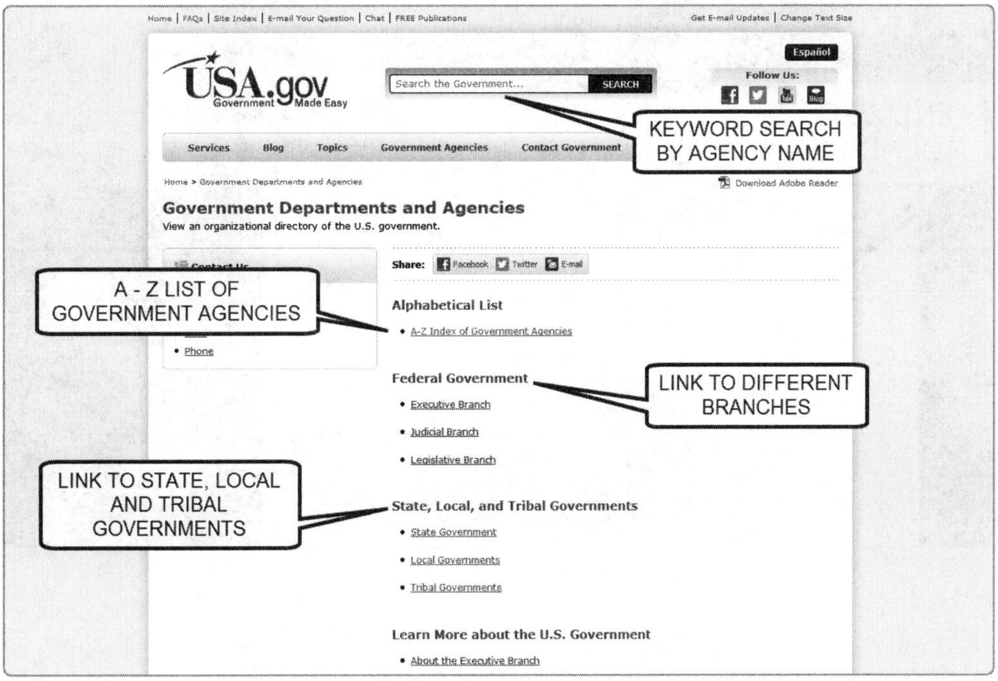

LOUISIANA STATE UNIVERSITY LIBRARIES FEDERAL AGENCIES DIRECTORY

The **Louisiana State University Libraries Federal Agencies Directory** (http://www.lib.lsu.edu/gov/index.html) can also be useful for locating federal agencies' websites. The directory includes Boards, Commissions, and Committees, as well as Executive, Independent, Judicial, Legislative, and Quasi-Official agencies (see Figure 12.14). On the right-hand side of the page (which this site refers to as the tool box), you can browse an alphabetical list of all agencies by clicking **Expand All** or you can keyword search the directory (if you are unsure of the exact agency name).

Figure 12.14   LSU Federal Agencies Directory

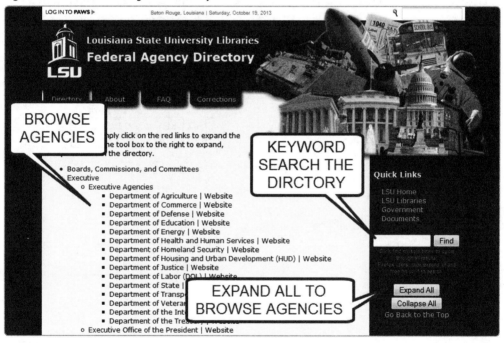

STATE AND LOCAL GOVERNMENT ON THE NET

Another resource that can be useful for finding administrative law, not only for state and local governments, but for territorial and tribal governments as well, is the **State and Local Government on the Net** site (http://www.statelocalgov.net), which we will discuss more extensively in Chapter 13. From the site's home page, click on the **Select State** drop-down menu on the left, choose a state, territory, or tribal government, and click the **Go** button. Then scroll down to the **Executive Branch** heading (which will list agencies) or scroll down to the **Boards and Commissions** heading (see Figure 12.15). Browse through the list to link to the appropriate entity's website. For links to local executive branches and agencies, use the **Local Govt** drop-down menu on the left side of the page.

Figure 12.15 State and Local Administrative Law

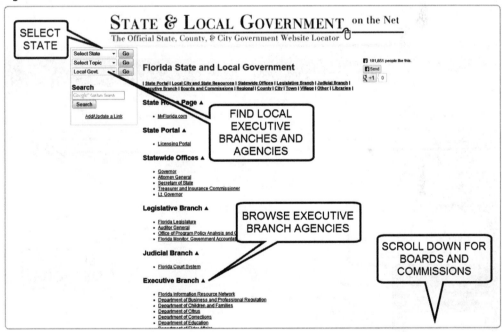

FOREIGN COUNTRIES' EXECUTIVE BRANCHES

To access information about foreign countries' executive branches, see Chapter 14.

FINDING DEFUNCT FEDERAL AGENCIES' AND COMMISSIONS' WEBSITES

If you ever find that you need to research a government agency that no longer exists, you many still be able to conduct your research by using a website called the **CyberCemetery** (http://govinfo.library.unt.edu/default.htm), which is the product of a partnership between the University of North Texas Libraries and the GPO. It provides permanent public access to defunct federal government agencies' and commissions' websites and publications.

You can search or browse the site. The **Search the CyberCemetery** page (http://govinfo.library.unt.edu/search.htm) allows keyword searching and also accepts quotation marks for phrase searching, the asterisk (*) wildcard symbol, and the plus or minus sign (+, -) which requires or excludes a term from the search, respectively. The search page explains each of these features (see Figure 12.16).

Figure 12.16   CyberCemetery

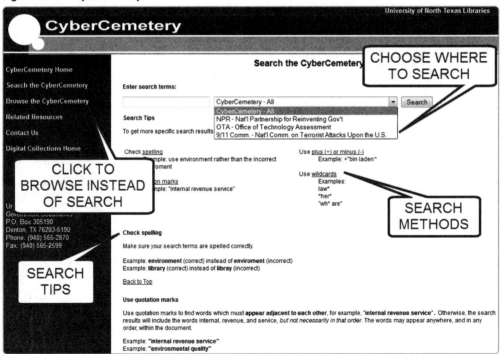

A drop-down menu to the right of the search box lets you choose to search within one of the following:

- All of CyberCemetery
- NPR (the National Partnership for Reinventing Government)
- OTA (the Office of Technology Assessment)
- The 9/11 Commission

The **Browse the CyberCemetery** page (http://govinfo.library.unt.edu/browse. htm) allows the researcher to choose from a list of links to browse agencies by **Branch of Government, by Date of Expiration,** or by **Name.**

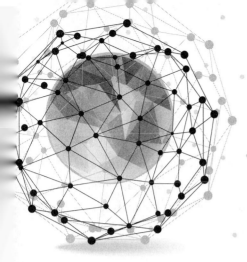

Chapter 13

STATE, LOCAL, TERRITORIAL, AND TRIBAL LAW

This chapter will discuss free resources that serve as starting points for researching U.S. state, local, territorial and tribal law. Most of the resources are in the form of a directory or portal that assembles links to official government websites for the various jurisdictions. Although it is not feasible for this book to provide specific instruction on researching the individual resources of every state, county, etc., in the United States, we will present an overview of the resources described here, along with helpful tips for making the best use of them. In other chapters we have discussed how to find state case law using free commercial case law sites (Chapter 4), free governmental case law sites (Chapter 5), Casemaker (Chapter 8), and Fastcase (Chapter 9).

We will begin by discussing several directory sites that link to each state, local, territorial, and tribal government's home page. These are helpful to determine if the jurisdiction you are researching makes its statutes, ordinances, courts, opinions, and other resources available on the Internet.

USA.GOV

USA.gov is a useful site not only for federal government links, but also for links to state and territorial, local, and tribal government websites. (http://linkon.in/I85y4c)

Links to state and territorial materials are on USA.gov's **State Government** page, located at http://linkon.in/HswSLB. (See Figure 13.1.) The territories, which are listed below the fifty States and the District of Columbia section (not shown in Figure 13.1), include American Samoa, Federated States of Micronesia, Guam, Midway Islands, Northern Mariana Islands, Puerto Rico, Republic of Palau, Republic of the Marshall Islands, and the U.S. Virgin Islands.

Figure 13.1 USA.gov's State Government Page

The page provides links to the official websites of all fifty states, the District of Columbia, and the nine territories listed above. Links on the left side of the page connect to various websites and pages which may be of interest to a legal researcher. For example, the State Governors link goes to a list of the official website of each state governor. The State Legislatures link leads to THOMAS's **State Legislatures Websites** page at http://thomas.loc.gov/home/state-legislatures.html (at some point in 2014, this URL might change when THOMAS is replaced by Congress. gov). The State Courts link goes to the **National Center for State Courts** website at http://www.ncsc.org/Information-and-Resources/Browse-by-State/State-Court-Websites.aspx. We will discuss the National Center for State Courts in greater detail later in this chapter.

USA.gov has a **Local Governments** page, located at http://www.usa.gov/Agencies/Local.shtml. This page provides links to various pages and websites that can be useful to the researcher searching for local government information. The **American Hometowns** link, for example, leads to a fifty-state directory. Each state then links to local government information for that state.

The **Native American and Tribal Legal Resources** page (http://www.usa.gov/ Government/Tribal/legal.shtml) provides legal topics and resources for researchers of tribal law. Examples include links to the **American Indian Probate Reform Act, Indian Affairs Laws, Treaties,** and more. The **Tribal Governments** page on USA. gov (http://linkon.in/I85y4c), provides an A–Z list of the official websites of U.S. tribal governments. Links on the left side of the home page lead to additional resources, such as a **Map of Tribes** and **Regional Tribal Councils.**

In addition to using the links on USA.gov's state, local, territorial, and tribal government pages, you can search the USA.gov website with keywords to find legal and government information for these jurisdictions. For example, in Figure 13.2, the search term was *Guam court*.

Figure 13.2   USA.gov Guam Court Search

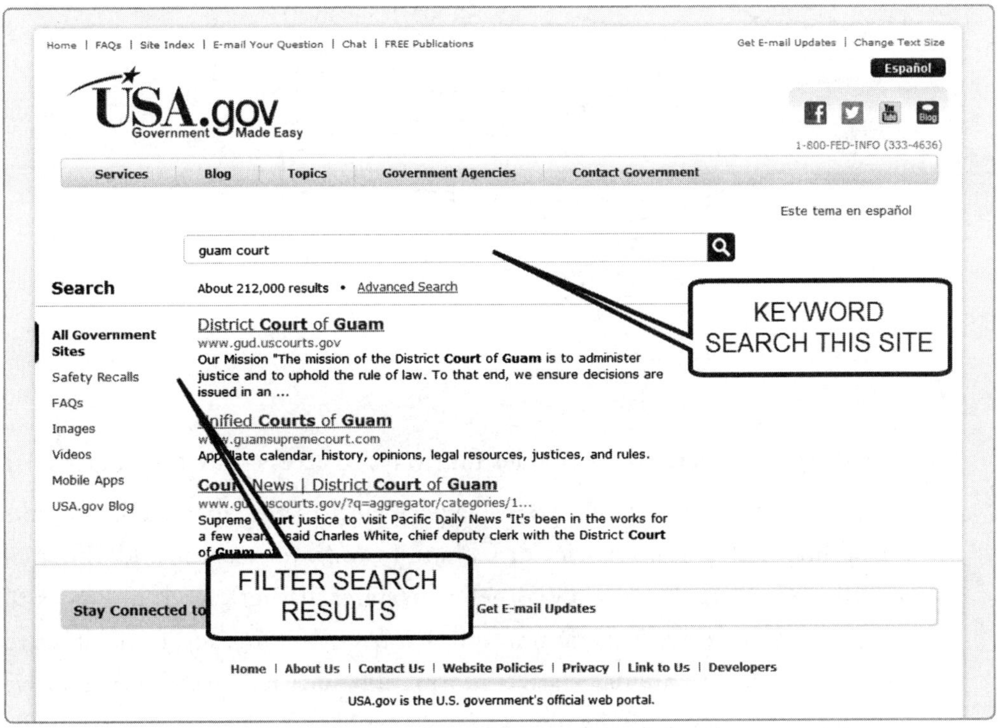

See Chapter 4 on Government and Academic Portals for details on how to use USA.gov's internal search engine, which is powered by Bing.

LII'S LAW BY SOURCE: STATE

We discussed Cornell's Legal Information Institute (LII) in Chapter 4's discussion of Portals, but we would also like to point out its section on state law here. Titled **Law by Source: State** (http://www.law.cornell.edu/states; see Figure 13.3), the section compiles Internet sources for state constitutions, statutes, case law, and regulations for all fifty states, D.C., the U.S. territories and affiliated jurisdictions.

Figure 13.3   LII's Law by Source: State

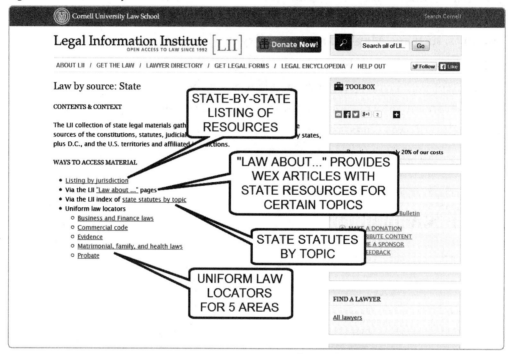

The Law by source: State page provides four ways to access state legal materials:

- A Listing by jurisdiction link goes to a page with an alphabetical list of links for all fifty states, the District of Columbia, U.S. territories, and affiliated jurisdictions (http://www.law.cornell.edu/states/listing). Each link goes to a page for the relevant jurisdiction, and that page contains additional links to sites with statutory and legislative information, judicial sites, administrative law, and more. Figure 13.4 shows the page for New York.

Figure 13.4   LII's Law by Source: State for New York

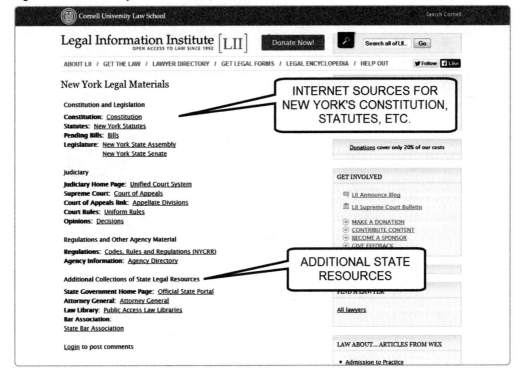

- A "Law about…" link goes to **Wex** (http://www.law.cornell.edu/wex), LII's legal dictionary and encyclopedia. You can browse Wex or search it using the **Search all of LII** search box, and some (but not all) of its topics, such as Divorce Laws and Labor and Employment Laws, list resources for all fifty states, D.C., and U.S. territories.

- A link for LII's index of state statutes by topic goes to an alphabetical listing of links for forty-three topics such as Agriculture, Education, Taxation, and much more (http://www.law.cornell.edu/wex/state_statutes). Each topic link goes to a page with an alphabetical listing of state links to statutes for that topic. (This resource is discussed in elsewhere in this book.)

- The fourth way to access state legal materials on LII's Law by Source: State page is with a list of links to five uniform law locators for the subject areas of Business and Finance laws, Commercial code, Evidence, Matrimonial, family, and health laws, and Probate. Each locator is on a separate page with links to state statutes that correspond to Uniform Laws for the relevant subject areas. Figure 13.5 shows the locator page for Business and Finance Laws (http://www.law.cornell.edu/uniform/vol7.html).

Figure 13.5   LII's Uniform Law Locators: Business and Finance

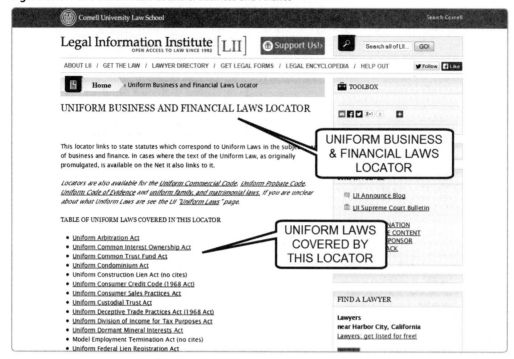

STATE AND LOCAL GOVERNMENT ON THE NET

The **State and Local Government on the Net** (http://www.statelocalgov.net) directory provides access to the websites of thousands of state agencies and city and county governments. Drop-down menus on the left allow you to view directory pages for any state or local government website. You can also link by topic, such as Legislation or Education (see Figure 13.6.). The drop-down menus are labeled: (1) **Select State** (which also includes territorial and tribal choices), (2) **Select Topic,** and (3) **Local Govt.** After selecting from the drop-down menus, you must click on the **Go** button. You cannot select more than one drop-down menu at a time. A search box at the top of the home page also allows you to search by keywords (e.g., marriage records).

State and Local Government on the Net also links to state, local, and territorial executive branches, agencies, and so on. From the home page, click on the **Select State** drop-down menu on the left and choose a state or territory. Then, scroll down to **Executive Branch** (which will list agencies) or scroll down to **Boards and Commissions.** Browse through the list to link to the appropriate entity's website. To find links to local executive branches and agencies, use the **Local Govt** drop-down menu.

For a more thorough discussion on researching executive branch and agency law, see Chapter 12.

Figure 13.6   State and Local Government on the Net Home Page

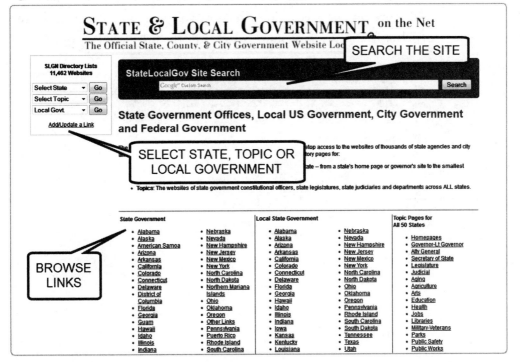

LIBRARY OF CONGRESS

The Library of Congress's **State Government Information** page (http://www.loc. gov/rr/news/stategov/stategov.html) provides links to all fifty states' home pages and to some local government pages. Click the state you want on the map at the top of the page, or select from the list of state links below the map (see Figure 13.7).

Figure 13.7   LOC's State Government Information

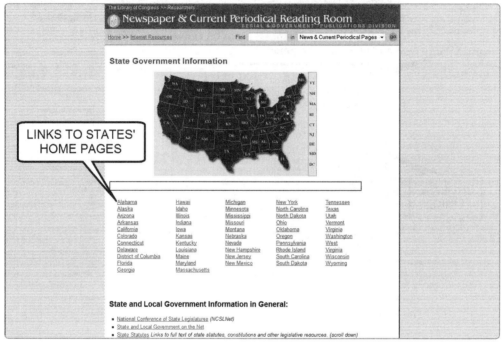

WASHLAW LEGAL RESEARCH ON THE WEB

Washburn University School of Law provides a legal research website titled **Wash-Law Legal Resources on the Web**. This site's **State Resources** section (http://www.washlaw.edu/uslaw/index.html) is quite comprehensive. It provides many links to official state sites as well as extensive resources for local city and county sites. Although our tests indicate some of the links are broken and no updating information is provided, we have included it here as an additional resource. The site appears to be the only one of its kind that is this exhaustive with regard to the resources it has compiled.

Information on the site is arranged by jurisdiction and topic (see Figure 13.8). You can either select the state you wish to research from a menu in the left-hand sidebar, or choose from the multi-jurisdictional material in the main section of the screen.

Figure 13.8   WashLaw Legal Research on the Web

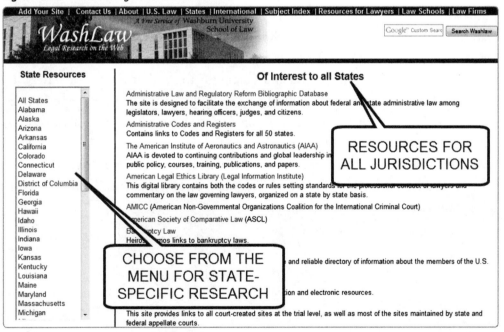

STATUTES AND LEGISLATION RESOURCES

FULL-TEXT STATE STATUTES AND LEGISLATION ON THE INTERNET

The **Full-text State Statutes and Legislation on the Internet** site (http://www. whpgs.org/f.htm) provides access to all states', D.C.'s, and U.S. territories' (American Samoa, Guam, Puerto Rico, and the U.S. Virgin Islands) statutory codes, administrative codes, regulations, bills, constitutions, and local ordinances. The site arranges the material by state name, in alphabetical order. Links for sites that are maintained by governments appear in bold type.

FINDLAW

FindLaw (http://www.findlaw.com/casecode) also provides a directory of state statutory materials. Scroll down to **State Resources** and select a state or territory (see Figure 13.9). The site offers links to all states, the District of Columbia, and to the territories of American Samoa and Guam (at the end of the list of states). By using the directories provided by FindLaw and Full-text State Statutes and Legislation on the Internet (discussed above), you don't have to remember the title of any state's (or territory's) statutory or regulatory material (e.g., New York Consolidated Laws, Arizona Revised Statutes) because the directories make it easy for you to browse through each state's list. A detailed discussion on how to locate state case law is provided elsewhere in this book.

Figure 13.9   FindLaw's State Resources

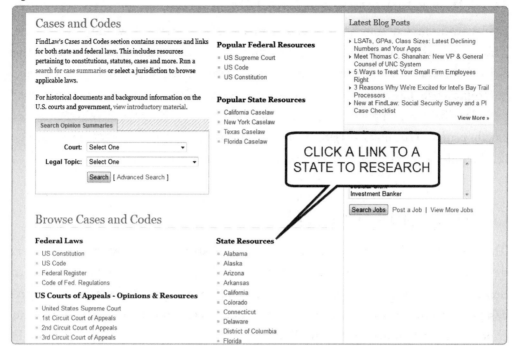

STATE CASE LAW DATABASES

Case law resources are discussed more extensively in other chapters of this book, but we will mention a few sites here.

Justia has a directory of state court links (http://www.justia.com/courts/state-courts). It provides links to all fifty states. When you click a link to a state, you are taken to a page listing all the courts in that state, including federal courts. Selecting a court takes you to a page where you can browse opinions from that court by date.

To locate **FindLaw's** directory to state case law databases, visit http://www.find-law.com/casecode and scroll down to **State Resources**. See Chapter 6 to learn how to search FindLaw's case law databases.

STATE AND LOCAL COURTS: DOCKETS

Some state and local courts have placed dockets online. See Chapter 15 for more information.

TRIBAL GOVERNMENT AND LAW

USA.gov, discussed above, provides resources for U.S. tribal law and government. Another website that provides some helpful links to tribal information is that of the **Wisconsin State Law Library**. The library's **Tribal Law** page (http://wilawlibrary. gov/topics/triballaw.php) provides links to several official and unofficial sites that provide tribal law and government information. Much of this page is Wisconsin-specific, but some of the links—Tribal Court Decisions and Tribal Codes & Constitutions, for example—can be useful to legal researchers from any jurisdiction.

COUNTY AND CITY LEVEL

The **NACO** (National Association of Counties) website (http://www.naco.org/) is devoted strictly to counties. To find basic information about each county, such as demographics and government contact information, along with links to each county's website, hover your mouse over About Counties (as shown in Figure 13.10) and choose **Find a County**. From the Find a County page, you can click the **Sample Codes & Ordinances** link in the left sidebar to go to a search page (http://www. naco.org/Counties/Pages/CodesandOrdiances.aspx). There you can search for various examples of county ordinances and codes by topic.

Figure 13.10 NACO Home Page

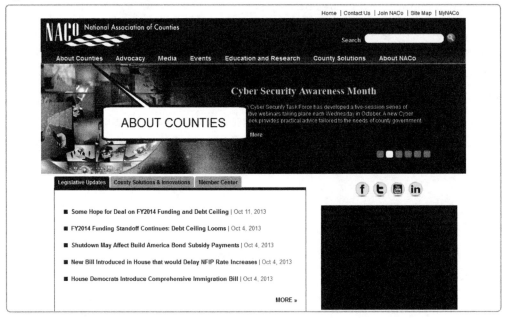

The **State and Local Government on the Net** site (discussed earlier in this chapter) also provides links to both county and city websites, in addition to the states' sites. Select a state from the **Local Govt** drop-down menu on the upper left side of the home page (see Figure 13.6).

LOCAL CODES AT THE COUNTY AND CITY LEVEL

Many local jurisdictions' codes can be found online for free either at the jurisdiction's website or at the websites of one of the three publishers of local codes (noted below). Most of the local codes are full-text, keyword/phrase–searchable, although some only offer the ability to browse by Title or Chapter.

American Legal Publishing offers hundreds of keyword/phrase–searchable local codes in thirty-two states (http://www.amlegal.com/library/; see Figure 13.11). It is the only vendor that offers a free search of all of its state codes together. The option is listed in the middle of the home page (click **View** and **Search ALL the codes in our Online Library**). You can also select just one state from the map or the drop-down menu on the home page labeled **Select a State**. To begin a search this way, select a state from the map or from the Select a State drop-down menu and then choose a city or county.

Figure 13.11 American Legal Publishing

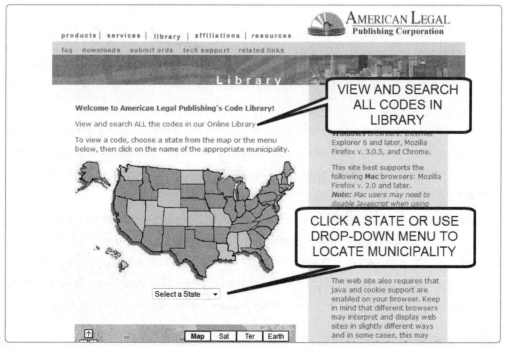

You can also opt to search all the local codes in one state. First, click **View and search ALL the codes in our Online Library**. From there, you can click an **Advanced Search** link near the top of the page, which allows you to enter keywords and phrases into various pre-set Boolean and phrase search boxes (see Figure 13.12). In addition, you can check the **Find alternate word forms (stemming)** box or the **Find synonyms (thesaurus)** box. The Boolean Search page (not shown) allows you to enter keywords and phrases into a single search box and connect them with Boolean and also proximity connectors. Be sure to study the **Search Syntax Summary** listed at the bottom of the Boolean Search page because some of the syntax may be unfamiliar to you.

Figure 13.12   American Legal Publishing Advanced Search

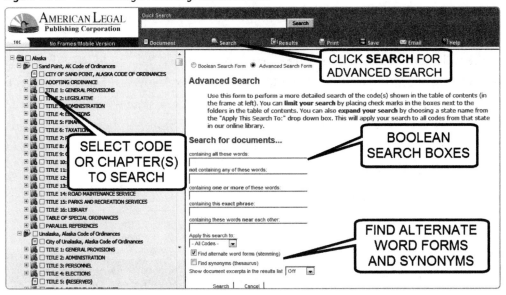

American Legal Publishing allows researchers to create slightly more complex searches than you can at the other municipal code sites discussed below. You can search an entire code or just a specific chapter. You can also browse the codes instead of searching.

MuniCode offers keyword/phrase-searchable codes for over 1,600 local governments in fifty states (http://www.municode.com). Individual codes can be searched for free, but there is an annual fee to search multiple codes. To begin a search, click on the **Code Library** tab at the top of the home page. You can then choose a state from the map or from the drop-down menu and then choose a city or county (see

Figure 13.13). The drop-down menu also provides a Tribes and Tribal Nations option, but only one tribe is listed: the Mohegan Tribe.

Figure 13.13   MuniCode Local Government Search

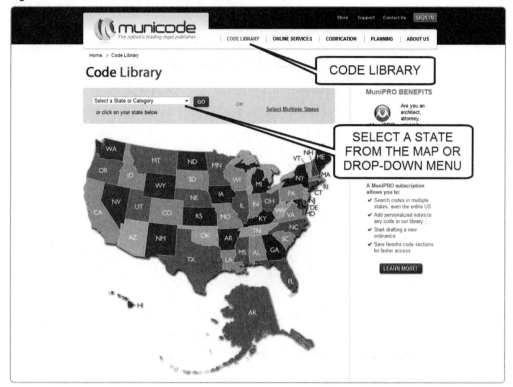

The search page allows you to enter keywords and phrases into a single search box and connect them with Boolean connectors. Use quotation marks to enclose phrases, the plus (+) sign to require words, and the minus (-) sign to exclude words. In addition, you can add an asterisk to the end of a word root to expand the word (e.g., a search for *child** would return *child, children, childish*) or add an asterisk within a word to find variations of words (e.g., a search for *a*n* will bring back results that include *addition, assign*). You can search an entire code, just a specific chapter, or you can browse the codes.

General Code upgraded its E-Codes interface and re-launched as **eCode360** (http://www.generalcode.com/webcode2.html). General Code provides codes for twenty-two states and one city in Canada. Individual codes can be searched for free, but to search multiple codes requires an annual fee. In addition to offering keyword/phrase-searching of local codes (connected by Boolean connectors), you can open an entire chapter or just portions of one and also search by a specific section number.

To begin a search, choose a state from the State Index (see Figure 13.14) and then choose a city or county. You can also browse codes by their Tables of Contents or Indices.

Figure 13.14   General Code's State Index

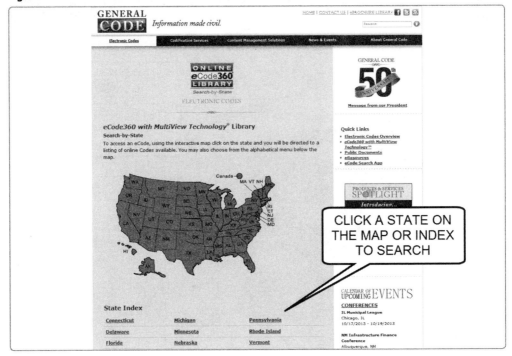

Two other sites we have already discussed also provide links to local codes. **Find-Law** (http://www.findlaw.com/casecode) provides links to some city ordinances. First, select the state you want to research by clicking its name under the **State Resources** heading. Then scroll down the page to the heading for **City Ordinances. Full-text State Statutes and Legislation on the Internet** (http://www.whpgs. org/f.htm) also provides links to some local codes. Scroll down to the relevant state and look for a link such as city codes, municipal codes, or local ordinances; the exact title can vary from state to state.

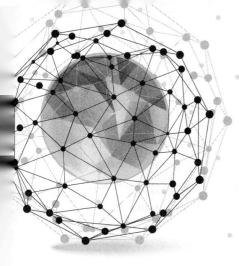

Chapter 14

FOREIGN, INTERNATIONAL, AND COMPARATIVE LAW RESOURCES

Foreign law and international law are two separate but related categories. Foreign law is the national or internal law of any individual nation except the United States. International law concerns the relations between different countries and their governments, organizations, and so on. Comparative law is the study of similarities and differences among the law and legal systems of different countries around the world. This chapter will provide guidance for researching all three of these areas.

The body of information that includes these two topics is large and it has no official structure or organization, unlike the U.S. court system, for example. We will therefore provide several starting points for research that, when combined, cover the majority of the most useful foreign and international resources. We have evaluated the sites discussed here from among the many that are available and believe that these will be especially helpful to you in beginning your research.

This chapter outlines several portals, directories, and academic sites that have helpful sections on foreign or international law. Some of them have been discussed in other chapters, but here we will focus on their foreign and international sections. These sources tend to provide guides and other background materials to help the researcher understand the basics of foreign and international legal research, but they will also lead you to and explain the most authoritative primary sources in this area, such as the websites of the United Nations and the European Union, as well as official resources of many individual countries.

Some of the sources in this chapter may be in languages other than English. To overcome this language issue, you can use **Google Translate** for a rudimentary translation of an entire website by typing its address (or by copying and pasting selected text from a web page or document) into http://translate.google.com. If you're using the Google Chrome browser, you can install an extension that will automatically translate a page for you.

THE LAW LIBRARY OF CONGRESS

The **Law Library of Congress** provides several resources that are helpful for researching foreign and international law. Its **Guide to Law Online** (http://www.loc.gov/law/help/guide.php) is a well-known and frequently used website for legal research generally. Within this guide are some specific sections that are useful for foreign and international legal research. From the Guide's home page, you can link to additional guides for foreign law, international law, and several how-to guides for researching law in specific countries (see Figure 14.1).

Figure 14.1   LOC's Guide to Law Online

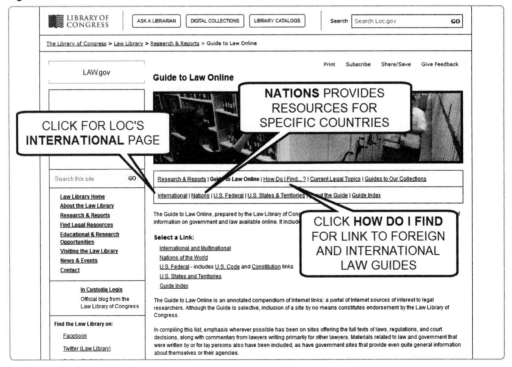

For help researching international law, click the **International** link near the center of the home page to go to the LOC's International page. (Note: the **International and Multinational** link, farther down the page, under the **Select a Link** heading, also goes to the same page.) The International page contains links to sources too numerous to name here, but examples include the LOC's Global Legal Information Catalog, the websites of the United Nations and Organization of American States, guides for Treaties and Multinational Reference, as well as links to guides produced by other organizations, such as the law schools of Columbia, Georgetown, and Harvard.

Another useful resource linked from the home page of the **Guide to Law Online** is the **Nations** page (http://www.loc.gov/law/help/guide/nations.php; see Figure 14.2). You can reach it by clicking the **Nations** link near the center of the page, or the **Nations of the World** link, farther down under the **Select a Link** heading. The Nations page provides an alphabetical list of links for many countries, territories, regions, and other locations. The links lead to a page for each region; that page contains additional links to resources such as constitutions, the country's three branches of government, additional guides, and "general" sources, such as country profiles and more.

A third useful section of the Guide is a bit harder to locate. The **How do I find…?** link is roughly in the center of the Guide's home page (see Figure 14.1). That link goes to the How Do I Find…? page which lists the titles of seven research guides. The fourth title listed is **Foreign and International Law Guides.** Click the **Read More** link under the heading and description to reach the page for the guides, entitled **Foreign and International Law** (see Figure 13.2). You can also go directly to it at http://www.loc.gov/law/help/foreign.php.

Figure 14.2   LOC's Foreign and International Law

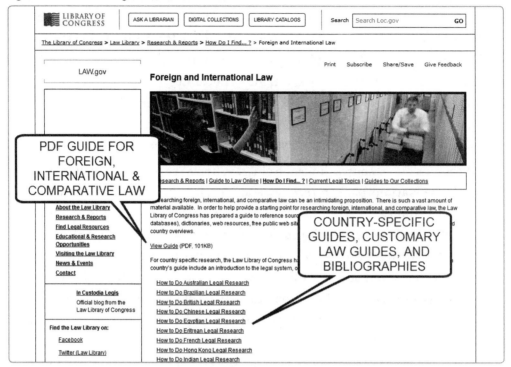

This page provides fourteen country-specific How-to-Do-Legal-Research guides for individual nations. Below the How-to guides are also two bibliographies on Personal Status Laws in Arab Countries and Islamic Law, as well as research guides to customary law in Africa and India and Māori customary law. In addition to the links, the site provides a 2007 PDF guide titled "Researching Foreign, International & Comparative Law."

The Law Library of Congress formerly offered a resource called the **Global Legal Information Network** (GLIN), a searchable database of laws, judicial opinions, and regulations that foreign countries and international organizations contributed (in the original language) to the Library of Congress (http://www.glin.gov). The results list displayed the citation of the document and a summary in English. While searching and viewing the summaries and citations was free, some countries limited access to the full-text of documents to subscribers only. We include this resource because the site states that "An updated web page is forthcoming and will be available soon."

HIEROS GAMOS

Hieros Gamos (http://www.hg.org/) was founded in 1995 by Lex Mundi, a large network of law firms. It was one of the first websites designed to provide information on law and government, and it is still a very useful resource. In addition to its general collection of information, HG has an especially helpful section on foreign and international law.

HG's home page has a Google-powered search box in the upper right-hand corner. The researcher can keyword search the site (see Figure 14.3). For example, when we searched the two words *Dubai escrow*, we retrieved an article titled "Property Development and Escrow Law in Dubai."

Figure 14.3   HG.org Home Page

We also like HG for its links to foreign and international resources. From the home page (see Figure 14.3) you can access several links to pages on the HG site that provide valuable tools for researching foreign as well as international law.

Law and Government Resources

The **195 Countries** link takes you to HG's **Law and Government Resources** page (http://www.hg.org/1table.html), which provides an extensive A–Z list of countries, along with links to each country's entry in these four handy resources (for most countries):

- **GlobaLex.** In its Foreign Law Research section, GlobaLex (www.nyulaw-global.org/globalex) discussed more extensively below) provides research guides for many countries. HG links to each guide that is available.

- **Library of Congress.** When available, HG links to the Law Library of Congress's research guide for each country. See the previous section in this chapter for additional information.

- **World Factbook.** Each country's entry in the CIA's World Factbook (https://www.cia.gov/library/publications/the-world-factbook/) is available. The Factbook is a resource that provides background information on each country, including history, people, government, economy, geography, communications, transportation, military, and transnational issues.

- **Doing Business.** This site (http://www.doingbusiness.org/data) is a joint project by the World Bank and IFC that provides data related to business regulation and the ease of doing business in 185 countries and some cities around the world.

United Nations–World Organizations

HG's **United Nations–World Organizations** page provides a list of relevant links for UN research, including the United Nations website itself, as well as its Treaty Collection, UN Law Reports, and many others. In addition, this page provides a section on NAFTA (which is also linked from the home page) with several related links. Farther down the page are sections with links to **Useful United Nations Publications** and **Other UN and Other International Government Sites** (also linked from the home page).

- **NAFTA.** This link goes to a subsection of the United Nations–World Organizations page, described above.

- **European Union.** The EU page is divided into five sections:

  1. **European Union Institutions** provides links to the websites of important organizations, such as Europa (http://europa.eu/index_en.htm), the

Official portal to the European Union, and the European Parliament (http://www.europarl.europa.eu/news/en/news-room/).

2. **European Law** links to sources of European case law, legislation summaries and other useful resources.

3. **European Union Activities** provides subject-specific links to Europa (http://europa.eu) for thirty-two areas such as Agriculture, Environment, and Taxation.

4. **European Central Banks** lists links for the European Central Bank, as well as the national banks of twenty-seven member nations (Croatia is omitted).

5. **European Law Firms Directory** links to a country-by-country directory of EU law firms generally, and also those that work in international trade.

- **International Law.** This page (http://www.hg.org/international-law.html) also provides links to many useful guides and resources, including Articles About International Law (written by HG contributors), resources for International Treaties, and sections with links to international law organizations, relevant publications, and important websites such as the ABA International Law Section and the International Court of Justice.

- **Other Organizations.** This link leads to the Other UN and International Government Sites section of the United Nations–World Organizations page, described above. It lists links to additional organizations that provide information helpful for foreign and international law research.

THE AMERICAN SOCIETY OF INTERNATIONAL LAW

The **American Society of International Law** (ASIL) is a respected nonprofit educational organization that aims to support the study of international law, as well as promote international relations. ASIL's website (http://www.asil.org) contains two important resources for researching international law.

ASIL's **Electronic Resources Guide** (ERG) is a user-friendly guide to current, important online resources that concern the most relevant areas in international law. The ERG covers such topics as the European Union and International Organizations, as well as several commonly researched subjects such as international commercial arbitration, international criminal law, international environmental law, and international human rights. For the complete list of topics covered, see the guide at http://www.asil.org/resources/electronic-resource-guide-erg.

The second resource that ASIL provides is its **Electronic Information System for International Law** (EISIL), a free online database that provides information about, and links to, resources that include all aspects of international law (http://www.eisil.org). EISIL includes high quality primary sources, as well as research guides and reliable websites. The resources are arranged in an easy-to-use list on the EISIL's home page (see Figure 14.4).

Figure 14.4   Electronic Information System for International Law (EISIL)

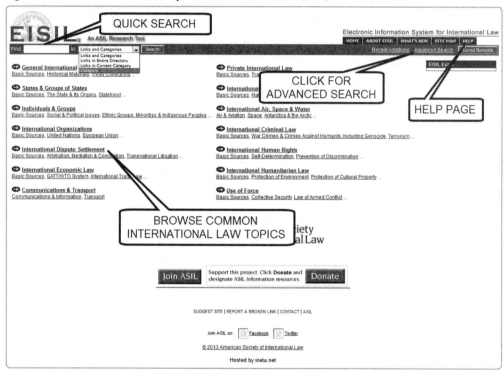

Unlike many foreign and international law resources, EISIL is also searchable. The home page has a **Quick Search** box in the upper left corner (see Figure 14.4). A drop-down menu allows you to keyword search **Links and Categories, Links in Entire Directory, Links in Current Category**, or **Category.**

Click the **Advanced Search** link in the upper right corner of any page to go to a page similar to Google's advanced search (see Figure 14.5).

> **CAVEAT:** Our test searches indicated that EISIL's Advanced Search feature may not always work. We have not been able to get clarification from EISIL about this problem so you may need to rely on the browsing and Quick Search features, which are still quite helpful. Nevertheless, we will explain how the site's Advanced Search should work in case the problem is resolved by the time this book is published.

The different boxes allow you to search all words, with an exact word, phrase or acronym, with any of the words, or without specific words. A Find in drop-down menu allows you to restrict your search terms to any field, to the **Title, Description, Keyword** or **Citation.**

Figure 14.5   EISIL's Advanced Search

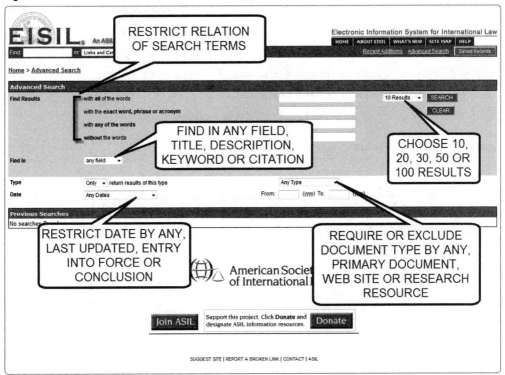

You may restrict the results you receive by Type. A drop-down menu allows you to choose **Any Type of document** or restrict to **Primary Document, Website,** or **Research Resource.** You may also choose to include or exclude these types of documents by an additional drop-down menu that works in conjunction with the Type selection. Choose **Only** or **Don't return results of this type.**

You can also restrict the dates of your search results. First select one of the following from the Date drop-down menu: **Any Dates, Last Updated, Entry into Force (EIF) Date,** or **Conclusion Date.** Then, use a set of two range boxes to enter the year(s) to which you wish to restrict your search.

Finally, you can choose how many search results you receive. From a drop-down menu, you can select 10, 20, 30, 50 or 100 results. Once you have constructed your search, click the blue **Search** button (or **Clear** to start over) on the right side of the page.

The EISIL site allows you to save your search results during a search session. (The results are not retained once you leave the site.) Once you have a list of search results, **Save All (#) Records?** appears at the top of the results list, next to a check box. If you check the box, a pop-up will ask you to confirm that you want to add all records to your saved records list. If you click **OK**, EISIL will save your results. To retrieve them later (but before you leave the site), click the gray **Saved Records** button in the upper right corner of the screen. You will go to a screen like the one in the Figure 14.6, where you can select specific records to retain or discard, as well as print, download, or e-mail your finalized list of results.

Figure 14.6 EISIL Saved Search

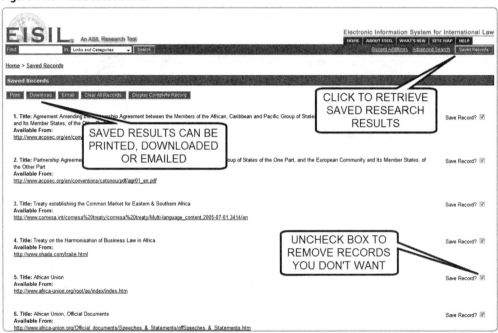

EISIL also provides a **Help** page (http://www.eisil.org/index.php?sid= 488508451&t=help) to assist users with the site's features. Click the **Help** link in the upper right corner of any page on the site, and you will be taken to the Help page. It provides assistance with the following topics: **Browsing, Quick Search, Advanced Search, Search Results,** and **Saving Records**.

NYU LAW'S GUIDE TO FOREIGN AND INTERNATIONAL LEGAL DATABASES

New York University School of Law produces a useful **Guide to Foreign and International Legal Databases** (http://www.law.nyu.edu/library/research/foreign_intl). This is an extensive website that is worth exploring (see Figure 14.7). It links to both "how-to" guides as well as to commonly used sources for foreign and international legal research, such as the websites of the Council of Europe and the United Nations Treaty Collection. Some of the links are outdated, and a few of the databases listed are restricted-use only, but overall, this is a useful resource.

Figure 14.7 NYU Law's Guide to Foreign and International Legal Databases

GlobaLex

One resource that the NYU Guide to Foreign and International Legal Databases links to (see Figure 14.7) is especially noteworthy, and we will describe it briefly here. **GlobaLex** (www.nyulawglobal.org/globalex) is a well-known online publication that the NYU School of Law produces to assist in researching foreign and international law. The guide's home page displays links to different areas for research:

- **International Law Research**
- **Comparative Law Research**
- **Foreign Law Research**

Clicking any one of the links will open a directory to research guides on many subtopics, written by experts whose credentials are described at the beginning of each guide. International Law Research guides include areas such as the **Council of Europe, Human Trafficking, International Criminal Law, NAFTA and CAFTA**, and the **United Nations**. The Foreign Law Research section includes guides for researching 153 countries, from Afghanistan to Zimbabwe.

JUSTIA'S LATIN AMERICAN RESOURCES

In Chapter 4, we discussed **Justia** (http://www.justia.com), a useful legal portal. In addition to the U.S. resources already discussed, Justia also provides sources for researching Latin American law. About halfway down the middle of Justia's home-page (it is a long page, so it takes a considerable amount of scrolling) is a section entitled Latin America (see Figure 14.8). This section has three sub-headings: **Mexico, Central American & Caribbean**, and **South America**. Under each sub-heading are links to various jurisdictions in Latin America.

Figure 14.8   Justia's Latin American Resources

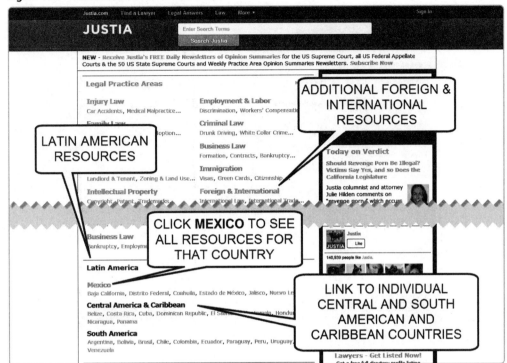

The **Mexico** heading, which is also a clickable link, has links underneath for individual states in Mexico. Clicking **Mexico** will take you to a page (in Spanish) for Mexican federal and state laws (see Figure 14.9). The other two headings on the home page list links for the countries of Central and South America and the Caribbean. They go to similar Justia pages with law for those countries. To access additional foreign and international resources on Justia, click the **Foreign and International** link, near the top of the site's home page, under the **Legal Practice Areas** heading.

Figure 14.9   Justia's Mexican Federal and State Laws

ADDITIONAL RESOURCES FOR SUBJECT-SPECIFIC INTERNATIONAL LAW

Washburn University School of Law (WashLaw) provides a legal research website titled **WashLaw Legal Resources on the Web.** We discuss this site in more detail in the State, Local, Territorial and Tribal Resources chapter. The site also has a useful foreign and international resource, so we will mention it here. The **International Resources** page of WashLaw's site (http://www.washlaw.edu/forint/index.html) provides an extensive A–Z list of subject-specific international law topics along with links to various sources for each. You can browse the topics list, or you can choose the geographic region you wish to research, from a menu in the left sidebar of the page.

For additional resources on specific international law topics, see ASIL's **Electronic Resources Guide** (http://www.asil.org/resources/electronic-resource-guide-erg), discussed earlier in this chapter, as well as **GlobaLex** (www.nyulaw-global.org/globalex) and NYU's **Guide to Foreign and International Legal Databases** (http://www.law.nyu.edu/library/research/foreign_intl).

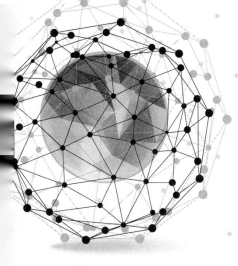

Part VI

ADDITIONAL RESEARCH SOURCES

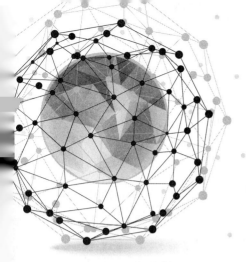

Chapter 15

DOCKETS

Almost all federal courts have placed docket sheets online and often the case documents (pleadings, opinions, orders, and transcripts). Some state and local courts have also placed docket sheets online, but not necessarily the case documents, so you would need to obtain them in person.

If you need to retrieve copies of docket sheets or case documents that are not available online, you can hire someone from **The Public Record Retriever Network** (PRRN) at http://www.brbpublications.com/prrn/search.aspx to visit a court to retrieve them. Some fee-based online docket database companies (such as **Bloomberg Law Dockets, West CourtExpress,** and **LexisNexis CourtLink,** all noted later in this chapter) will also retrieve documents.

Some docket databases can only be searched by docket number, while others can be searched by party or attorney names (and other options). Fee-based commercial docket databases usually offer better search options than free commercial court sites. For example, fee-based commercial docket databases often offer full-text keyword searching, alert services, and litigation history reports.

HOW DOCKETS CAN BE USED FOR LEGAL AND INVESTIGATIVE RESEARCH

Docket searching and reviewing the case documents can be useful for legal research and also investigative (background/due diligence) research. Searching dockets by a person's or company's name could provide you with the following background/due diligence information:

- How litigious a person or company is
- Whether someone has a criminal background
- Whether someone has declared bankruptcy
- What type of allegations have been lodged against a party
- If it is a fresh complaint, you might be able to uncover a good address for service of process.

Some attorneys use dockets for legal research purposes. For example, instead of drafting a complaint or an answer from scratch, some attorneys search dockets to find sample pleadings for cases that are similar to their case. Depending on the court, you can search for a similar case by party name or case number. If you don't know of a particular case, you can search at **PACER** by its **Nature of Suit** (NOS) to find a similar case for sample pleadings. Every filed case is assigned a NOS (e.g., contracts). NOS searches can also be useful to discover which practice areas are heating up in your region.

FEES

Some courts, such as the Los Angeles Superior Court (LASC), charge a fee ($4.75) for a party-name docket search (https://www.lasuperiorcourt.org/onlineservices/ LAECourtOnlineIndex.htm) but a case-number search is free (http://www. lasuperiorcourt.org/civilcasesummarynet/ui). The LASC also charges a fee for the case documents (beginning at $7.50 for up to ten pages, with a cap of $40). One the other hand, the dockets of New York State's sixty-two counties' Civil Supreme Courts (trial level) and other courts can be searched by Index Number, party name, attorney name or firm name for free at its **E-Courts** site (https://iapps.courts.state. ny.us/webcivil/ecourtsMain). You can also receive e-mail updates and appearance reminders. The federal courts offer docket searching by party name and case number (and other options) for a fee at PACER. The fees are a bit complicated, and they are described in more detail later in this chapter.

FEDERAL, STATE, AND LOCAL COURT DOCKET DIRECTORIES

Although **LLRX.com's** docket directory, which links to federal, state, and local court dockets, hasn't been updated since 2011, it is still somewhat useful (http:// www.llrx.com/courtrules). To browse the list, scroll down to **Type of Resource (Federal & State)** and then click **Dockets**. This database can also be browsed by type of court (e.g., bankruptcy) and jurisdiction (e.g., federal or state) or searched with keywords. If you don't find what you are looking for, try a search engine search for the word *docket* and the name of your target court. Another out-of-date, but somewhat useful docket directory is **Legaldockets.com** (http://www.legaldockets. com/index.html). Select a state and then browse the list of federal and state courts to link to docket databases. There will be a notation if the databases are free. One of the free databases that Legaldockets.com links to is **Freecourtdockets.com**, which is not that easy to use (their pay site is more user-friendly). Below is a list of docket sites discussed in more depth in this chapter.

- **PACER (Public Access to Court Electronic Records)** is the government's pay federal docket database (www.pacer.gov). It offers fee-based access to federal court dockets and case documents from the U.S. Courts of Appeal, the Federal District Courts, and the Bankruptcy Courts.

The following sites offer free access to federal court dockets, but on a much more limited basis than PACER, which is why we will spend the majority of this chapter explaining how to use PACER:

- **RECAP** (http://archive.recapthelaw.org) offers access to millions of federal dockets for the: U.S. District Courts (civil and criminal) and the Bankruptcy Courts (some include the case documents).
- **Justia** (http://dockets.justia.com) provides federal dockets for the U.S. District Court dockets (civil only—not criminal or Bankruptcy courts) and the U.S. Circuit Courts of Appeals, back to 2004 (the case documents are not usually available, so Justia provides links to PACER).
- **The U.S. Supreme Court** (http://www.supremecourt.gov/docket/docket. aspx) provides its dockets at its site, but the case documents are not available there.

The sites listed below offer fee-based access to federal, state, and local court dockets (usually with the case documents). They all also offer alert services, litigation profiles, and courier services to retrieve case documents. We will discuss these briefly at the end of the chapter.

- **Bloomberg Law Dockets** (http://about.bloomberglaw.com/product-features/dockets)
- **West CourtExpress** (http://www.courtexpress.westlaw.com)
- **LexisNexis CourtLink** (http://www.lexisnexis.com/courtlink)

TLO (http://www.tlo.com), **Accurint** (http://www.accurint.com), **West's PeopleMap** (http://linkon.in/westpeoplemap), and other pay investigative databases indicate if someone has declared bankruptcy, but do not include the docket sheet or case documents.

PACER AND CM/ECF

FEDERAL DOCKETS (CASE MANAGEMENT/ELECTRONIC CASE FILES)

PACER (http://www.pacer.gov) is the federal government's court docket database, covering over 33 million cases from all the Circuit Courts of Appeals, District Courts, and Bankruptcy Courts. PACER includes the case's docket sheet, its case documents (but not necessarily for all cases), transcripts, and written opinions and orders. **CM/ECF** (Case Management/Electronic Case Files) is the electronic case management and filing system that began to roll out in 2001 and which nearly all of the federal courts have switched over to. A list of courts is available at http://www.pacer.gov/cmecf/ecfinfo.html. CM/ECF is explained by the Administrative Office of the U.S. Courts as "[a] comprehensive case management system that allows courts to maintain electronic case files and offer electronic filing over the Internet. Think PACER for searching and CM/ECF for filing. PACER searches can find CM/ECF documents but you need a separate account to use CM/ECF to file documents" (http://www.pacer.gov).

Dates of Coverage

Although PACER began in 1981, dates of coverage will vary for each court because the courts came online at different times and some courts even uploaded dockets from pre-1981. Coverage dates are indicated at each court's PACER site and also on the Court Information page, but that page is only accessible after you log into PACER (see the tab in Figure 15.1).

Registering or Logging in

From PACER's home page (http://www.pacer.gov) you can **Register** for an account or **Login** if you already have an existing account (see Figure 15.1). Anyone can open a PACER account. For same-day registration, you must provide a credit card.

Figure 15.1   PACER Home Page

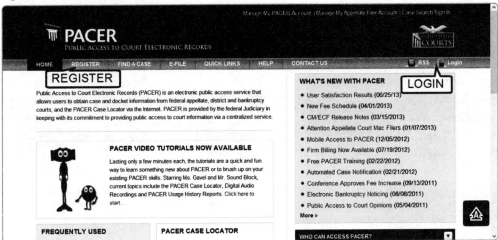

PACER Costs

No annual or monthly fee is imposed; you pay only for actual use. A few years ago, PACER increased its rates from $0.08 per page to $0.10 per page and increased its $10.00 worth of free documents per year to $15.00 worth per quarter.

The following pricing explanation is from PACER (http://linkon.in/IcEfCy):

> "The $.10 per page charge is based on the number of pages that result from each search and each requested report or document. The charge is not based on printing. Here are some examples that may be helpful to understanding how the charges are generated: Enter party name "johnson, t" and receive 2 pages of matches. The charge is $.20. Enter case number 01-10054 and select Docket option. The docket is 10 pages so the charge is $1.00. (You may enter a date range to limit the number of pages by displaying entries for the date range rather than all entries in the report.) Select link within the docket report to view a document. The scanned document is 5 pages so the charge is $.50. Please note that there is a 30-page cap for documents and case-specific reports (i.e. docket report, creditor listing, claims register). You will not be charged more than $3.00 when you access documents or case-specific reports that are more than 30 pages. Please be aware that the 30-page cap does not apply to name search results, lists of cases, or transcripts (when available online)."

Search the Case Locator

After you log into PACER, you are given the option to search **Individual Court Sites** by clicking on a court's link or to search the **PACER Case Locator** (see Figure 15.2), which allows you to search all courts together, multiple courts, or one court.

Notice that there is a link to the **U.S. Supreme Court**, but as noted earlier, that court is not part of PACER. If you click the link, you will be leaving the PACER site and taken to the U.S. Supreme Court's official site.

Figure 15.2   PACER Individual Courts

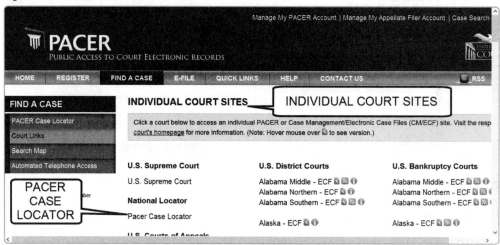

After choosing **PACER Case Locator**, the **Case Locator** page will appear (see Figure 15.3). From there, you first need to click one of the court type tabs at the top: **All Courts** (which will search all federal **Appellate**, **Bankruptcy**, **Civil**, **Criminal**, and **Multi-District Litigation** cases) or click just one of them.

Figure 15.3   PACER Case Locator

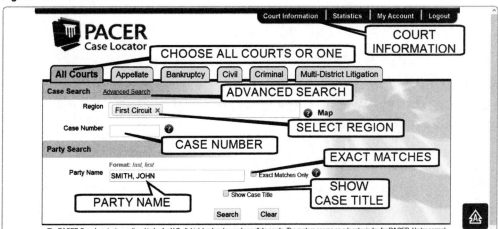

We have chosen **All Courts** (see Figure 15.3). Although the **Advanced Search** link is displayed, this actually means that you are viewing the **Basic Search**. If you want to use the **Advanced Search**, you will need to click the **Advanced Search** link. Depending on which court type you select and whether you select the **Basic** or **Advanced Search**, you will see some different search options. For example, the **All Courts Basic Search** menu displayed in Figure 15.3 allows you to conduct a **Party Name** or a **Case Number** search, while the **All Courts Advanced Search** allows you to also search by: **Case Title**, **Date Filed**, and **Date Closed**. The **Criminal Advanced Search** offers the same search options as the **All Courts Advanced Search**.

Select Region

After you select the court type, then you can select the **Region** (see Figure 15.3). If you selected the **All Courts** tab (to search all federal **Appellate**, **Bankruptcy**, **Civil**, **Criminal**, and **Multi-District Litigation** courts) and you selected the **All Courts Region**, you would be conducting the broadest search possible. Or, you can narrow the region to one or more circuits or states. If you choose a specific state, such as Delaware, this does *not* search Delaware state courts. Instead, it searches all Federal District and Bankruptcy courts in Delaware plus the Third Circuit Court of Appeals. Selecting a particular circuit will search all federal courts within that circuit, so if you selected the Third Circuit, your search would include all Federal District and Bankruptcy courts within Delaware, New Jersey, Pennsylvania, and the U.S. Virgin Islands, in addition to the Third Circuit Court of Appeals. You can also choose to search one specific court, such as the Northern District of California, and you can select more than one region.

Search By Case Number

If you know the case number, enter it into the **Case Number** search box in Figure 15.3. The question mark icon to the right of the box can be selected to see sample case number formats.

Search By Party Name

When you conduct a party name search (see Figure 15.3), you can search by an individual's name or a company name. To search an individual's name, enter last name, first name (or initial). You must insert the comma between first and last names, so your search would look like this: *smith, john*. You can add the * wildcard at the end of a name to indicate that name begins with the letters you typed in. For example, *smith** would bring back results for *smith, smithton, smithly,* etc. Select **Exact Matches Only** if you only want a search by the exact name you have entered.

Be careful about selecting **Exact Matches Only** because if you enter *smith, john* and select **Exact Matches Only**, you will only receive results for last name *smith* and first name *john* and will miss any results for *smith, john j.*

Show Case Title

We usually select **Show Case Title** (see Figure 15.3) so our results show the full title of the case and not just the party name that we entered. This will help you target the correct result(s).

Case Information

To learn the date of the earliest filed and most recently filed case for each court, select **Case Information**. This will also show the court's code (e.g., *almbke* is Alabama Middle Bankruptcy Court's court code).

Appellate and Civil Court Tabs

If you choose the **Appellate** tab or the **Civil** tab and then select **Advanced Search**, in addition to searching by the **All Courts Advanced** search options noted earlier (**Party Name, Case Number, Case Title, Date Filed,** and **Date Closed**), you can also add a **Nature of Suit** (NOS) search (see Figure 15.4). For an explanation of NOS, see the earlier section in this chapter, **How Dockets Can Be Used for Legal and Investigative Research.**

Figure 15.4   PACER Advanced Search: Appellate Court Nature of Suit (NOS)

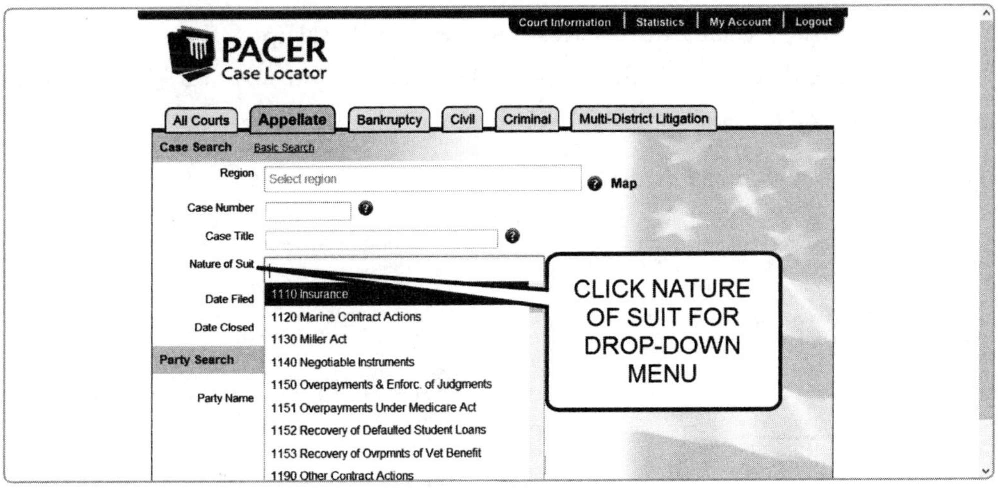

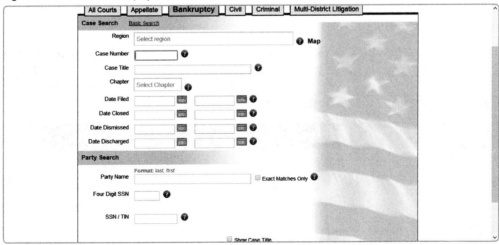

Bankruptcy Court Tab

If you choose the **Bankruptcy** tab and select **Advanced Search**, in addition to all of the **All Courts Advanced** search options, you can search by **Chapter** number, **Date Dismissed, Date Discharged, SSN/TIN** (Social Security Number/Taxpayer Identification Number), and a combined **Four Digit SSN/ Party Name** pictured in Figure 15.5.

Figure 15.5   PACER Bankruptcy Court

When you are unsure where a subject might have filed bankruptcy, PACER is particularly useful because you can search all the bankruptcy courts together (select the **Bankruptcy** tab and then **All Courts** from the **Region** section from the **Case Locator** portion of PACER).

Case Locator Results List

Figure 15.6 shows a **Case Locator Results List** for a Bankruptcy search. (Note: We have redacted the debtor's name in Figure 15.6. When you search PACER, names are displayed.)

Figure 15.6 PACER Case Locator Search Results

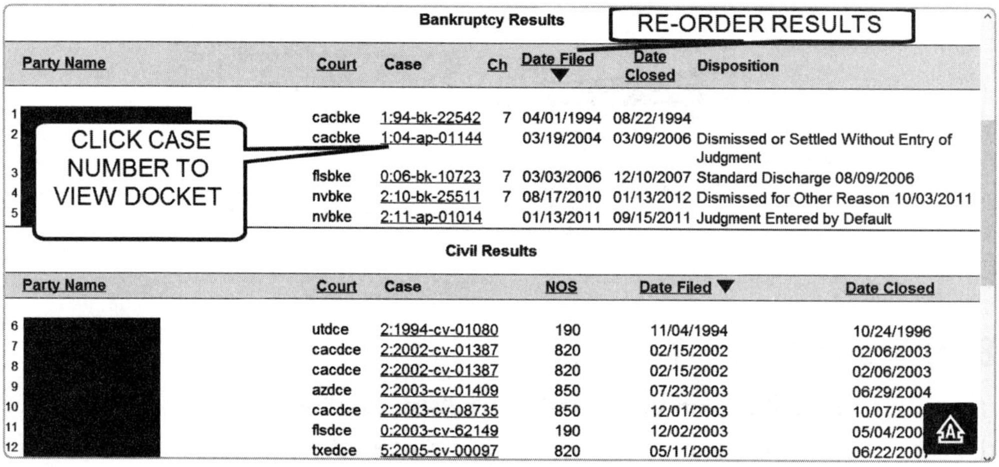

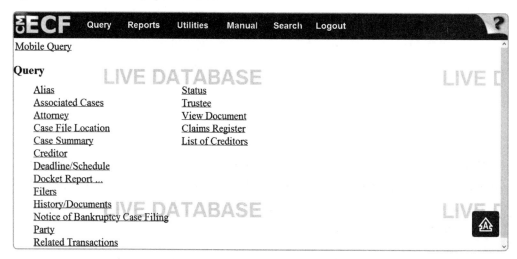

You can re-order the results by clicking on the column heading. For example, if you click the **Date Filed** column heading, the list will display the cases from earliest date to most recent within each court type list. Clicking the **Date Filed** column heading again will re-sort from most recent to earliest. Clicking **Court** will re-sort the list alphabetically by court name within each court type list.

Click the case number to view the **Docket Sheet** (see Figure 15.7) with links to details of that particular case such as **History/Documents**.

Figure 15.7 PACER Bankruptcy Docket Sheet

History/Documents

The **History/Documents** menu allows you to run a **Query** of **All events** or **Only events with documents** and to sort by oldest or most recent. We usually run **All events** so we can see the full list. If the event doesn't have a document, but we need it, we may be able to get it from the court by sending a messenger.

From the **History** list (see Figure 15.8), you can click on any underlined number (to the left of the document description) to display (and print or download) a specific case document. If the number is not underlined, then that event's document is not available online.

Figure 15.8   PACER Bankruptcy History List

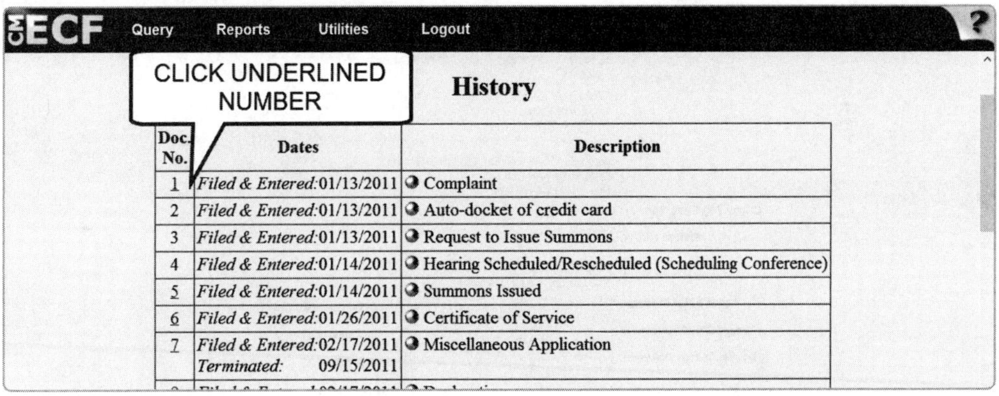

Speaking of redaction, an April 5, 2010 Federal Judicial Study found 2,899 documents with un-redacted Social Security numbers in PACER (approximately one out of every 3,400 court documents), with a greater number found in bankruptcy documents (http://linkon.in/HonEvF). This is despite the Federal Rules of Procedure (Civil, Criminal, and Bankruptcy) requiring redaction (or truncation) of full Social Security numbers by attorneys before filing a pleading.

Searching One Court

After you log into PACER, you are given the option to search **Individual Court Sites** by clicking on a court's link (see Figure 15.2). Figure 15.9 shows the Circuit Court of Appeals' **Advanced Search** menu. If you compare it to the **Case Locator Appellate Court Advanced Search** menu (see Figure 15.4), you will see there are some differences. For example, the Individual Court menu offers searches by **Attorney, Case Type, Origin, Originating Case Number**, and **Docket Activity Between** while the Case Locator menu does not.

Figure 15.9   PACER Advanced Search for One Court Only (Circuit Court of Appeals)

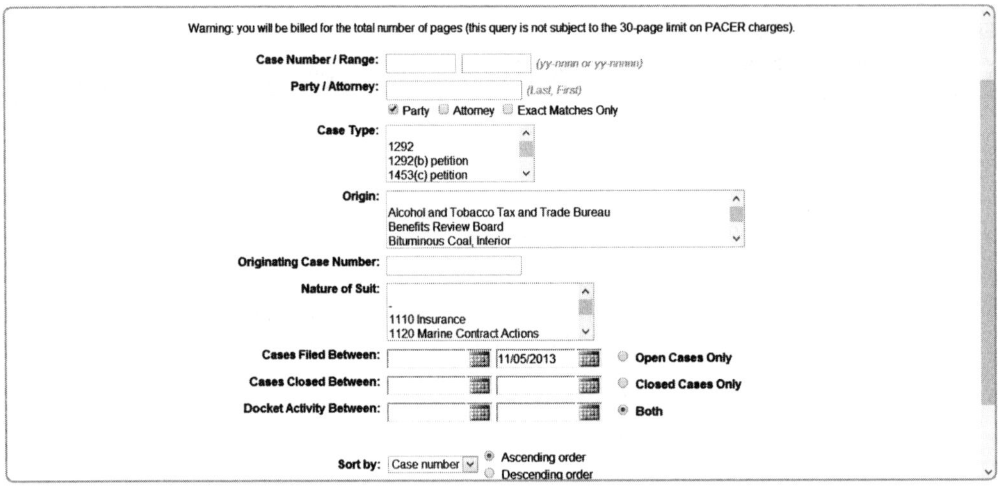

Figure 15.10 shows the **District Courts' Advanced Search** menu. It has most of the same fields to search as the Circuit Court of Appeals but the menu is organized in a different order. To display this search menu, you must click **Query** from the individual district court's home page.

Figure 15.10   PACER Advanced Search for District Courts

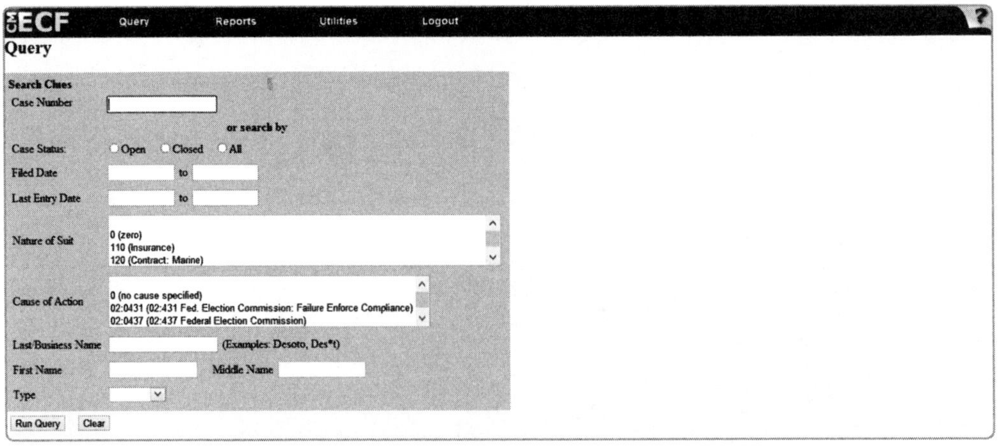

Automatic Case Notification Through E-Alerts and RSS Feeds

Using CM/ECF, each attorney of record (including pro se litigants) receives free e-mail docket alerts with hyperlinks back to the court documents (http://www. pacer.gov/psc/efaq.html#CMECF). To obtain this service, you would log into your CM/ECF account with your court-issued filing login (the PACER login does not work for this e-mail notice service) and supply your e-mail address and the docket number of your case. You can also supply additional e-mail addresses for others to receive alerts as well. You can choose to receive an e-mail alert for each new event related to a filing or a daily summary notice of all filings. One free copy of each document is made available to each attorney of record and to any secondary addressee listed under the e-mail information screen.

Non-parties can also receive notices for cases they are interested in (for free), but they must register for a PACER ID and password, as well as a CM/ECF filer ID and password, and be an approved registrant in a federal court (for more details, see http://www.pacer.gov/psc/efaq.html#CMECF). To view any case documents, the non-party would be assessed the same fees as other PACER users. Information about other docket alert vendors is provided elsewhere in this book.

Some courts now provide free automatic case notification through the use of RSS feeds. To learn which courts have implemented RSS, visit the court links page and select the court's RSS feed icon. Once you subscribe to a court's RSS feed, you will receive notice of all activity in all cases from that court (not just a case that you specify), a summary of the documents filed, links to the document, and the docket report. You can sort the feed results by date or case title. You must log in to PACER and pay the usual costs to retrieve the document or docket report http://www. pacer.gov/announcements/general/rssnews.html.

Audio Recordings

Audio recordings of court proceedings are available online at a cost of $2.40 per proceeding for twenty-six federal district and bankruptcy courts (http://www. pacer.gov/announcements/general/audio_pilot.html). (The cost used to be $26.00 to order a CD.)

Free Federal District and Bankruptcy Court Opinions Via FDsys

Even though court opinions are free at PACER, you still need an account to search for the opinion, and you would be charged for the initial docket search. If you are only looking for an opinion, a better choice might be FDsys because it is free. In 2010, a pilot program was instituted in twelve courts to publish federal district and bankruptcy court opinions via FDsys (http://tinyurl.com/newpacerinfo). The program now includes over fifty Appellate, District, and Bankruptcy courts (http://linkon.in/fdsysops). Details on how to search the new **FDsys U.S. Courts Opinions Collection** are available elsewhere in this book.

PACER Public Access Terminals

PACER public access terminals are provided free at federal courthouses (but only for filings in the courthouse where the terminal is located), with printouts priced at $0.10 per page. (The charge for copies from paper case files at the clerk's office is $0.50 per page.)

Mobile Access to PACER

PACER has announced that they are offering two new services to allow PACER users to access case information via mobile devices such as iOS devices (iPads and iPhones) and Android devices with version 2.2 and higher (http://www.pacer.gov/announcements/general/mobilenote.html).

The first service is a mobile web version to search the **PACER Case Locator.** PACER will automatically detect if users are using supported mobile devices when they visit http://pcl.uscourts.gov and users will be redirected to the **Mobile PACER Case Locator** (or users can visit the **Mobile PACER Case Locator** directly at http://pcl.uscourts.gov/searchmobile).

The second service, the **Mobile Appellate Case Information**, can be used to search appellate cases (using the above devices). You would link to this service from the **Mobile PACER Case Locator.**

Mobile access to district and bankruptcy cases is in a beta testing mode and will be released soon.

Firm Billing Now Available

PACER now offers a **PACER Administrative Account** (PAA) so firms can receive just one invoice for multiple users' accounts (http://www.pacer.gov/announcements/general/paanews.html). The administrator of a PAA can:

- Choose whether to add existing users to the PAA (or leave some users outside the PAA)
- Set up new users and receive their login information immediately
- Activate and deactivate users
- Update user information

Billing back PACER use to individual clients: The down side of the PAA is that the Administrator cannot set the Client-Matter field as a requirement, so if users fail to input the Client name before conducting a search, the Administrator doesn't know which client to bill. Some law librarians, who serve as the firm's Administrator, report that they have opted to have just one account that everyone in the firm uses because this allows the librarian to set the Client-Matter field as a requirement before a user can begin a search.

Help

If you need help, you can call, e-mail, or review **Frequently Asked Questions** at http://www.pacer.gov/help.html. PACER also offers a free **User Manual** (http://www.pacer.gov/documents/pacermanual.pdf) and free training and video tutorials (http://www.pacer.gov/announcements/general/train.html). We found the video tutorials a bit too basic for most legal professionals, but the training site was more useful because it is populated with actual case documents filed between Jan. 1, 2007 and July 1, 2007 from the New York Western District Court. Unfortunately, the training site does not include the Case Locator.

RECAP (PACER SPELLED BACKWARDS)
FREE FEDERAL DISTRICT AND BANKRUPTCY COURT DOCKETS DATABASE

RECAP (https://www.recapthelaw.org) is a "volunteer" federal docket project spearheaded by the Center for Information Technology Policy at Princeton University. According to the founders of RECAP, "We created RECAP in hopes of hastening the day when court records would be freely available to the general public via the Internet" (https://www.recapthelaw.org/why-it-matters). Volunteers who already subscribe to PACER download an "add on" to their Firefox or Chrome web browser. Once installed, each document they retrieve from PACER is then automatically uploaded to a public repository hosted by the Internet Archive where it becomes available for free to any RECAP visitor. RECAP explains this "saves users money by alerting them when a document they are searching for is already available from this repository" (https://www.recapthelaw.org/about).

To download Firefox, visit http://linkon.in/HsyGTR; to download Chrome, visit https://chrome.google.com/webstore/category/apps.

Despite providing free access to millions of U.S. Federal District and Bankruptcy Court dockets and case documents, RECAP is more limited than PACER because its collection does not include every docket for those two types of courts and does not include every case document of included dockets. Also, it is missing the federal appellate courts' dockets and case documents entirely. Because of these limitations, it is advisable to use the RECAP Archive only when searching for a known document.

RECAP includes the PACER court, case number, and docket entry number as the file name (https://www.recapthelaw.org/features), which is a more user-friendly file name than PACER creates.

How to Search RECAP

Even if you are not participating in the donation process, you can search the **RECAP Archive** free at http://archive.recapthelaw.org (see Figure 15.11). While the RECAP Archive offers access to millions of dockets and case documents, you cannot conduct a full-text search through them. Instead, you are searching through the short descriptions on the docket sheet. (This is also the case at PACER.) RECAP hopes to offer a full-text search in the future.

Figure 15.11 RECAP Advanced Search

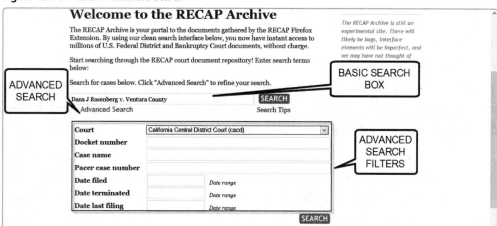

Although RECAP requires you to use Chrome or Firefox to upload a document for the donation process, you are not restricted to those browsers when searching the database.

Notice the **Search Tips** link in Figure 15.11. Some of the tips explain that you can use the asterisk (*) character as a wildcard to extend the root of a word and you can exclude a word by using the minus sign (just as you can in Google). Searching with quotation marks to conduct a phrase search doesn't work. RECAP needs to create a user manual, as you will see from our test searches below.

You can conduct a basic or advanced search by clicking the **Advanced Search** link. Using the basic search box, we entered the case title *Dana J Rosenberg v. Ventura County* and selected *California Central District Court* from the **Court** search box's drop-down list. We received one result: *Dana J Rosenberg v. Ventura County.*

Using the **Advanced Search** and entering *Dana J Rosenberg v. Ventura County* into the **Case name** search box (deleting it from the basic search box), we got no results.

We then conducted three different **Advanced Searches** using just one party name in each search (e.g., *Dana J Rosenberg, Dana Rosenberg, Rosenberg*) and selected the *California Central District Court* from the **Court** search box's drop-down list. The only one that worked was *Dana J Rosenberg.*

Returning to the basic search, we conducted three different searches and instead of entering the case title, we entered just one party name (e.g., *Dana J Rosenberg, Dana Rosenberg, Rosenberg*) into the basic search box. We limited our search to the *California Central District Court* (using the **Court** search box's drop-down list). Our search for *Rosenberg* brought back ten pages of results while our search for *Dana J Rosenberg* and our search for *Dana Rosenberg* brought back the same two results. One result was the case we were looking for, but the other didn't include any of our keywords.

We recommend that you always enter your search (either the case title or one party's name) into the basic search box (above the words **Advanced Search**) and then use the **Advanced Search** boxes to refine your search.

After you run your search, be sure to scroll down to see the link to the case and then click it. The RECAP docket sheet (see Figure 15.12) indicates if a document must be purchased (click **Buy from PACER**) or is available for free (click **Download**). You can also subscribe to an e-mail alert for new case activity or follow the case.

Figure 15.12   RECAP Docket Sheet

JUSTIA

FREE FEDERAL DOCKETS

Justia's **Federal Dockets** database (http://dockets.justia.com) is more limited in scope than PACER because it does not provide access to bankruptcy dockets (it provides access to the dockets of the U.S. Federal District Court and the U.S. Courts of Appeals) and offers case documents only for some dockets (and even then, some documents may be missing from a docket). However, Justia was the first site to offer free federal dockets, with a database back to 2004. The database is no longer displayed prominently on Justia's home page but must be accessed from the home page's **More** drop-down menu http://www.justia.com/ and then you must select **Federal Dockets** from the drop-down list or use the direct URL (http://dockets.justia.com; see Figure 15.13).

Figure 15.13   Justia's Federal Dockets

The database is poorly documented (possibly because it is still in beta mode… and has been for many years), so we have run many test searches to assist you in using it.

At the **Search** page (see Figure 15.13), you can search by one or more of the following criteria:

- **Party Name**
- **Judge**
- **Filed In** (select **All Federal District Courts, Federal Circuit Courts of Appeal** [all], a specific Circuit Court of Appeals (e.g. **Ninth Circuit**), a specific Circuit Court of Appeals (e.g., **Ninth Circuit**) along with its District Courts, or one or all of a state's federal district courts (e.g., **California Federal District Courts–All** or **California Central Federal District Court**), or the **U.S. Court of Federal Claims**
- **Type** (this refers to PACER's NOS designation, such as **Contract**)
- **Show** (choose either **All Case Filings** or **Only Case Filings with Downloadable Opinions or Orders**)
- **Cases Filed** (select **All Dates** or enter a date range)

Our search for the **Party Name** *Riches* and **Filed In** *Ninth Circuit* also brought back results for the party name *Rich* (as shown in Figure 15.14), where *Rich Yi* is one of many defendants in *Brown v. City of Chicago et al.* While many of Justia's docket results provide only a summary of the docket sheet, some include the full docket sheet. Also, if you see a gavel icon (as shown in Figure 15.14), this indicates the opinion and orders are available for free.

Figure 15.14   Justia's Docket Search Results

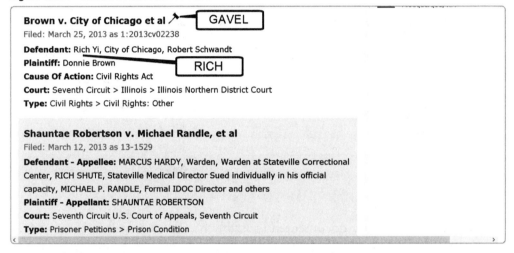

If you click a case title from the results page (e.g., in the above Figure, we clicked on *Brown v. City of Chicago* et al), the full docket sheet and a link to available documents will be displayed (see Figure 15.15).

Figure 15.15   Justia Docket Search, Indivdual Case Details

Some dockets include all of the case documents. This would be indicated by a yellow star icon. If Justia does not have the complete docket sheet or any (or less than all) of the case documents, Justia points users to PACER (discussed elsewhere in this book). In our example (see Figure 15.15), Justia only has one case document available. To download this document, click its docket entry number (e.g., #5). You can also opt to receive free RSS feeds of filings that meet your search criteria by clicking the RSS icon to the left of Follow case documents by RSS.

In addition to searching, you can scroll past the search menu shown in Figure 15.14 to browse by: **Type of Lawsuit** (PACER's NOS designation), **Cases by Circuit**, **Cases by State**, or **Most Recently Filed**.

U.S. SUPREME COURT DOCKETS

The U.S. Supreme Court (http://www.supremecourt.gov) does not participate in PACER's docket or the CM/ECF system and has its own docket database (see Figure 15.16). The Court only offers free access to the current and the most immediate prior terms' dockets.

Figure 15.16   U.S. Supreme Court Home Page

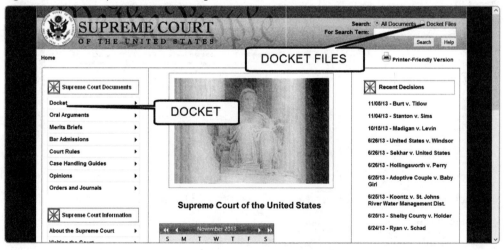

The U.S. Supreme Court's docket database does not include case documents (e.g., petitions, briefs, etc.) unless it's an important/controversial case, but the Court's site does include oral argument audios (http://www.supremecourt.gov/oral_arguments/argument_audio.aspx) back to 2010 and oral argument transcripts (http://www.supremecourt.gov/oral_arguments/argument_transcripts.aspx) back to 2000. For merit and amicus briefs, the Court provides a link to the ABA's site (http://www.americanbar.org/publications/preview_home/alphabetical.html). Additional information on obtaining the Court's opinions is discussed elsewhere in this book.

Although you can enter your docket search into a search box located on the top right-hand side of the U.S. Supreme Court's home page (http://www.supreme-court.gov) by clicking into the **Docket Files** radio button, we recommend that you instead click the **Docket** tab located on the left-hand column of the home page and then select **Docket Search** from the drop-down menu (or use this direct URL: http://www.supremecourt.gov/docket/docket.aspx). We prefer using this search option because various search tips are offered on this page to help you conduct a more effective search (see Figure 15.17).

Figure 15.17   U.S. Supreme Court Docket Search Menu

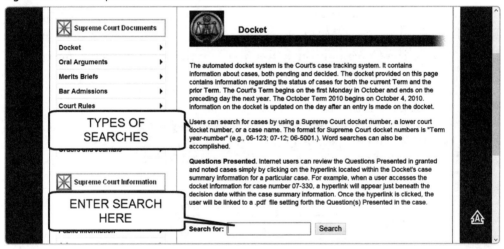

For instance, you are informed that you can search by a Supreme Court docket number (e.g., by term year/number, such as: 06-123), a lower court docket number, or a case name.

Keyword searches can also be performed, but no examples are given on this page. Instead, you will need to visit the **Search Tips** page at http://www.supremecourt. gov/search_help.aspx, where you will learn that:

- Phrases must be placed within quotation marks
- Keywords (and phrases) can be strung together with these Boolean connectors:
  - *AND* (or just leave a space between keywords and phrases)
  - *OR*

- To exclude keywords (or phrases) from your search, use the Boolean connector *NOT*
- The proximity connector *NEAR* (which is defined by this site as within 50 words) can also be employed
- Phrases are enclosed within quotation marks
- A single asterisk (*) can be placed at the end of a string of letters to retrieve words that begin with those letters (e.g., *cert** would retrieve *certify, certificate*, etc.)
- If you use multiple Boolean operators, you can use parentheses to create a more sophisticated search

Although not stated on the Search Tips page, keep in mind that keyword and phrase searching can also include a name search (such as a party, attorney, or expert's name).

See the Pleadings/Briefs/Oral Arguments section elsewhere in this book to learn about sites that offer docket information (including briefs) going back further in time than the official U.S. Supreme Court docket database.

WESTLAW COURTEXPRESS.COM, BLOOMBERG LAW DOCKETS, AND LEXISNEXIS COURTLINK.COM

DOCKETS AND LITIGATION REPORTS

For docket research, there are many reasons lawyers might want to subscribe to the pricier **Westlaw CourtExpress.com** (http://www.courtexpress.westlaw.com), **Bloomberg Law Dockets** (http://about.bloomberglaw.com/product-features/dockets), or **LexisNexis CourtLink.com** (http://www.lexisnexis.com/courtlink) databases.

First, these sites offer much more sophisticated searching than PACER. In addition to the party name, docket number, NOS, and date searching found at PACER, they allow you to search by lawyer name, judge name, subject, and even by a full-text keyword through case documents. Second, these databases can alert you whenever a new docket is filed in a particular court or when a new document is added to a particular docket sheet. You can also set up e-alerts about a particular party, lawyer, judge, NOS, and so on. Third, their archives sometimes go back further than PACER's or state and local courts' archives. Fourth, in addition to federal dockets, these commercial vendors also offer access to various state and local court dockets. Finally, you can order copies of case documents from the vendors if they are not available online. You can usually receive the documents by mail, Federal Express, e-mail, or fax.

Bloomberg Law Dockets also provides dockets for the UK, the Cayman Islands, the EU, and Hong Kong courts, among others.

In addition to dockets, **Lexis** and **Thomson Reuters** offer litigation profile reports of companies, lawyers/law firms, and others. The profiles include litigation history from dockets and cases in addition to graphs and data charts. A report for a lawyer or law firm will show a list of their cases (for whatever time period you select), type of cases they handled (antitrust, banking, etc.), courts where they filed cases, judges they appeared before, outcome of cases (often unknown), and whether they represented the defendant, plaintiff, or other. Bloomberg only provides litigation profile reports of companies.

The lawyer/law firm profiles are useful to learn about opposing counsel or potential hires while the company profiles can be useful for due diligence or client development.

Lexis's product, **CourtLink Strategic Litigation Profiles** (http://www.lexisnexis.com/courtlink/online/strategicprofiles.asp), can be ordered without having a subscription to Lexis (at $165 each) but Thomson Reuters' **Litigation History Reports**   http://legalsolutions.thomsonreuters.com/law-products/westlawnext/litigator/litigation-history cannot be ordered unless you have a subscription to Westlaw.

Each of these companies has sales representatives who should be contacted for more information.

COURTHOUSE NEWS

STATE, FEDERAL, AND LOCAL COMPLAINTS

Courthouse News Service (http://www.courthousenews.com), while not a full docket database, offers access to new civil complaints filed in over 1,600 federal, state, and local courts. The cite also has an e-alert service limited to the federal courts. For information about which courts are covered and for subscription information you will need to call (909) 483-6165 or e-mail csage@courthousenews.com.

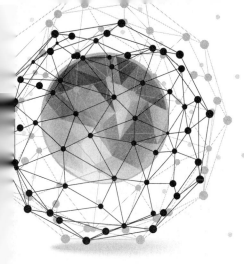

Chapter 16

SOCIAL MEDIA

BLOGS/BLAWGS

Law related blogs are sometimes referred to as "blawgs." For an annotated, topically arranged index of blawgs, see **Justia's BlawgSearch** (http://blawgsearch.justia. com); hover over each blawg title to learn more about it. On the home page, you will also see a list of **Most Popular** blawgs, a keyword search box, a **Featured Blawger**, and **Recent Search Terms** (see Figure 16.1).

Figure 16.1 Justia Blawg Search

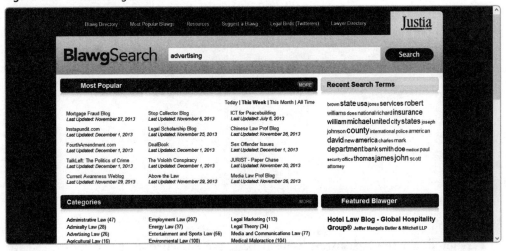

Most blogs allow you to subscribe to their RSS feed, receive an e-newsletter, or follow them on Twitter.

Another source for locating useful blawgs is The ABA Journal's **Blawg Directory** (http://www.abajournal.com/blawgs), arranged by **Topic, Author Type** (e.g., consultant, judge, etc.), **Region** (by court, state, or country), and **Law School**. Also, see the ABA Journal's annual **Blawg 100** list posted every December. To read the one for 2013, see http://www.abajournal.com/magazine/article/7th_annual_blawg_100. The one for 2014 will probably be found at http://www.abajournal.com/magazine/article/8th_annual_blawg_100 sometime in December of 2014.

TWITTER ACCOUNTS

To figure out the best people to follow on Twitter who write about your practice area, visit http://twitter.com/#!/search-home (you can conduct searches there without being logged in) to keyword search through the millions of individual tweets—from (roughly) the last two weeks. You can also use **Twitter's Advanced Search** page (http://twitter.com/#!/search-advanced) to create more sophisticated searches as shown in the Figure 16.2 where we searched for people who tweet about *uk criminal law.*

Figure 16.2 Twitter's Advanced Search

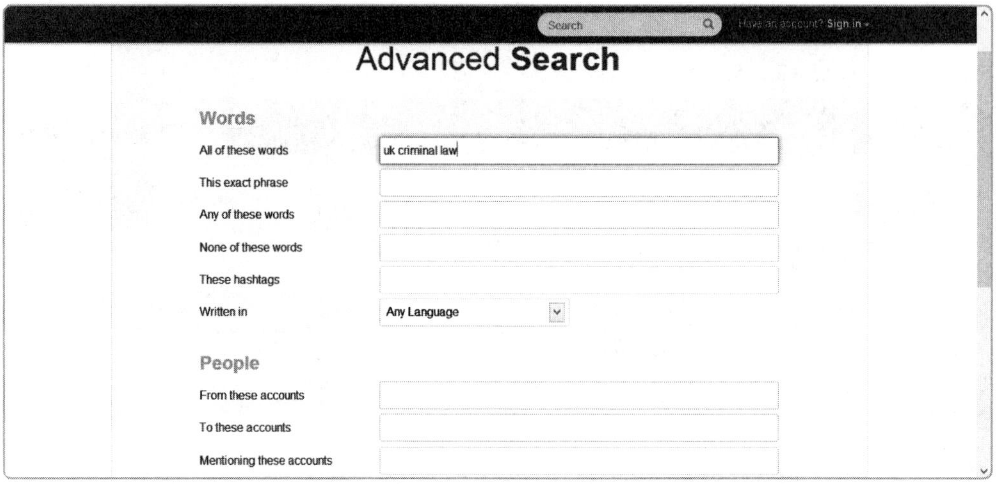

Farther down the **Advanced Search** page are search options to locate tweets: **From these accounts, To these accounts,** or **Mentioning these accounts.** These are a bit misleading because you have to know the user name that an individual tweets under, and many people use a pseudonym or screen name for their Twitter accounts. To learn someone's user name, simply enter their real name into the **All of these words** search box.

For a directory of legal "twitterers" arranged by category/practice area, see the **Justia's Legal Birds** page (http://LegalBirds.justia.com; see Figure 16.3). If you choose a category, the results list will show the lawyer's name (e.g., *Carole Levitt*) and her Twitter name (e.g., *@carolelevitt*). Clicking on the lawyer's name will take you to her profile at Justia and clicking on her Twitter name will take you to her Twitter profile. On the home page, you will also see a list of **Top Legal Birds** and a search box. The categories and the list of results don't always seem to match up. So, for better luck targeting your area of interest, enter key words into the search box. Also, when there is no category for your area of interest, search with keywords; we searched for "hospitality law" and came up with two attorneys who practice and tweet in that area.

Figure 16.3   Justia's Legal Birds ("Twitterers")

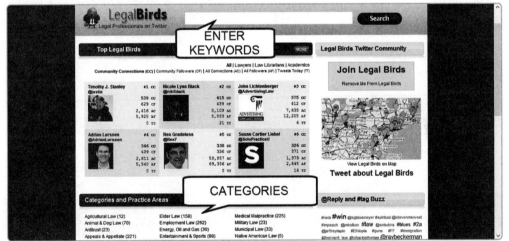

FACEBOOK AND LINKEDIN COMPANY PAGES AND GROUPS

Without being logged into your own account, it is possible to search or browse Facebook and view a results list, but only if you use this URL: http://www.facebook.com/srch.php. When prompted to **Search for Friends on Facebook**, you can enter keywords into the **Person's name** search box to look for Company pages or Groups you are interested in. We searched for *hospitality law* and found one Company page and one Interest Group.

While **Linkedin** (http://www.linkedin.com) does not require you to have an account of your own, you do need one to reach the **Advanced** search page where you can enter keywords into the search menu and narrow down by location, etc. Our search for the phrase *"hospitality law"* brought back fifty-five results.

Chapter 17

RESEARCHING PEOPLE

FINDING BACKGROUND INFORMATION
ABOUT ATTORNEYS, JUDGES, AND
OTHER LEGAL PROFESSIONALS

CONTACT INFORMATION, BIOGRAPHIES, AND DIRECTORIES

It's always a good idea to check into the status and background of an attorney you are opposing or hiring, or with whom you are associating. For information about attorneys' license status, disciplinary action taken against them, and their contact data, check the appropriate state bar site if membership in the state bar is mandatory (commonly called unified or integrated) in that jurisdiction. But if the state bar is voluntary, check the state's attorney licensing site (often the state's supreme court). The **ABA Division for Bar Services** provides a useful color-coded map of the United States to help determine whether a state's bar association is unified or voluntary (http://www.americanbar.org/groups/bar_services/resources/state_local_bar_associations.html). Voluntary bar associations are indicated in green. From here, you can also link directly to the relevant state bar association.

In states with voluntary bar associations, an attorney may still be licensed even if their name is missing from the association's directory. You can determine their status by searching their name at the licensing board for that state. The **Internet For Lawyers** website provides a state-by-state directory of attorney licensing databases (http://www.netforlawyers.com/page/state-state-directory-lawyer-licensing-databases). The directory links directly to the searchable databases of attorney licensing boards (or to the unified state bar association) in forty-five states, as well as the District of Columbia. The directory also includes tips on getting information from the bar associations in the few states that do not offer online searchable databases.

To locate background information about attorneys, there are several free lawyer directories. Three major ones—**LexisNexis Martindale-Hubbell Law Directory** (Martindale; http://www.martindale.com), the **FindLaw Lawyer Directory** (http://lawyers.findlaw.com), and the **Justia Lawyer Directory** (http://lawyers.justia.com)—are discussed below. Several newer directories also exist, and a few of those attempt to offer lawyer ratings, as well; details are provided elsewhere in this book.

Martindale

Martindale (http://www.martindale.com/Find-Lawyers-and-Law-Firms.aspx) allows you to search for a lawyer anywhere in the world (see Figure 17.1). Some judges are also included in their database. Begin by selecting either the **People** or the **Law Firms & Organizations** tab to begin narrowing down your search. Depending upon which category is chosen, the search criteria will vary slightly.

Figure 17.1   LexisNexis Martindale-Hubbell Law Directory

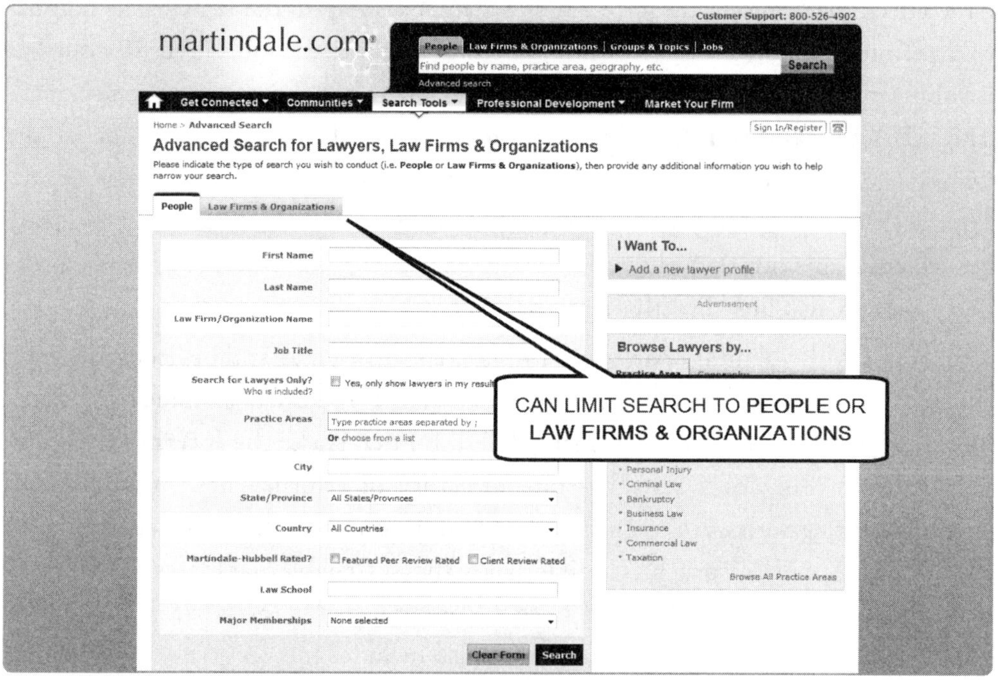

The following types of search criteria are available when using the **Advanced Search** option to search **People** (the default search option): **First Name, Last Name, Law Firm/Organization Name, Job Title, City, State/Province, Country, Practice Areas, Law School/University Attended**, and **Major Memberships**. Check-boxes are also available to limit the results of **People** searches to lawyers only and/or to only individuals who have been peer-review rated or client-review rated. Searches can include a mix of criteria. For example, you can search for all attorneys who practice Family Law in Los Angeles, California, and attended Pepperdine Law School. If you don't know an attorney's last name, you can even search by first name only; just be sure to add other identifying information such as city and state.

If the **Search for Lawyers Only** option is not selected, then search results may include other, non-lawyer legal professionals such as administrators, paralegals, or librarians. Martindale no longer provides separate search options to locate those professionals, however. The site also no longer includes the **Experts and Services** database.

Findlaw

The **FindLaw Lawyer Directory** provides a basic search at http://lawyers.findlaw.com (see Figure 17.2). There are two search boxes where you can search by **Legal Issue** (practice area) and/or **Location** (enter city, ZIP Code, or state). The consumer focus of this database is made clear by the **Do I Need a Lawyer?** sidebar on the right side of the search page. To search by a lawyer's name, click the **Name Search** link to the right of the main search boxes. Other useful links to the right of the search boxes include **Guide Me** and **Help**, as well as options to browse **Lawyers, Law Firms**, and **Types of Cases**. Additional search features are available by clicking the **Advanced Options** link under the two search boxes. The user can search by language(s) spoken and by whether the lawyer accepts credit cards, offers a free consultation, and/or provides a video. The bottom of the search page also provides additional options to browse by **Top Cities, By State**, and **By Legal Issue.**

Figure 17.2 FindLaw's Find a Lawyer

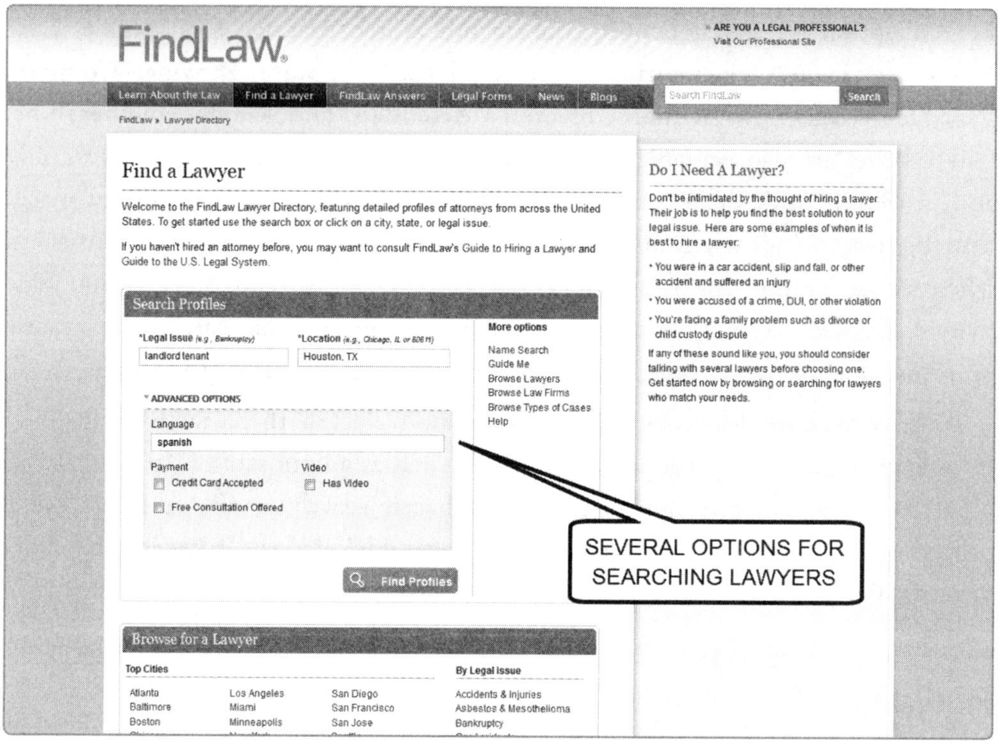

Justia

The **Justia Lawyer Directory** provides a basic search at http://lawyers.justia.com (see Figure 17.3). There is a dual search box at the top of the page where you can search by **Legal Issue** or **Lawyer Name** as well as location. Your city and state are automatically detected and filled in based on your Internet connection but can be easily changed. Using the tabs beneath the search box, you can browse by **Practice Areas, States,** or **Cities.** You can also browse an alphabetical listing of attorney names using the A–Z **Lawyer Name Directory** links at the bottom of the page. No Advanced Search options are offered.

Figure 17.3   Justia Lawyers

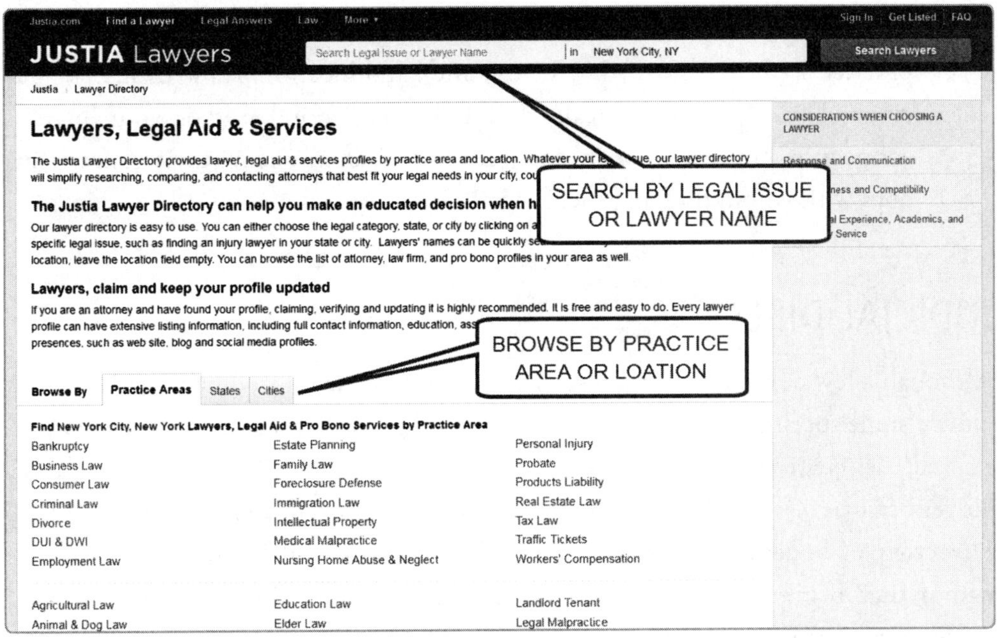

Additional Directories

The following are some newer directories, some of which attempt to create a rating system for the lawyers listed:

- **Nolo** (http://www.nolo.com/lawyers) allows users to browse by **Location** or by attorney **Practice area**. Results include attorney and/or firm profiles and may also include licensing and disciplinary history information.

- **Superlawyers.com** (http://www.superlawyers.com) includes "outstanding lawyers from more than 70 practice areas who have attained a high degree of peer recognition and professional achievement." Tabs and search boxes on the home page allow the user to search or browse by practice area, attorney or firm name, and location. Browsing by **Popular Issues** and **Popular Markets** (locations) is also possible. The **Advanced Search** page allows you to search by **First Name, Last Name, Law Firm/Organization, Practice Area, Language,** and **Law School** as well as by international criteria.

- **Avvo.com** (http://www.avvo.com/find-a-lawyer) is a directory that also includes a rating system for lawyers that employs "a mathematical model that considers elements such as years of experience, board certification, education, disciplinary history, professional achievement, and industry recognition—all factors that are relevant to assessing a lawyer's qualifications." You can search and/or browse the directory by attorney name or practice area (but not by law firm name), and location. As with Justia, your city and state are automatically detected and filled in based on your Internet connection but can be easily changed. Users can also leave reviews for attorneys with whom they have worked.

JUDICIAL DIRECTORIES

Although a few of the resources discussed above provide limited information about judges, some specific sources are available for background information about judges, as well. All current and former federal judges back to 1789, except bankruptcy judges, can be searched by name at the Federal Judicial Center's **Biographical Directory of Federal Judges** site. An A–Z list is also available to browse a list of names that begin with each letter (http://www.fjc.gov/history/home.nsf/page/ judges.html; see Figure 17.4).

Figure 17.4   Biographical Directory of Federal Judges

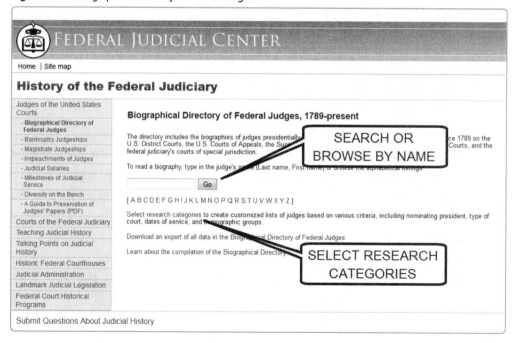

Research questions regarding groups of judges (e.g., How many women judges are there in the federal district courts?) can also be created by clicking on the **Select research categories** link.

There is no directory of all state judges online for free, but some states provide profiles of their state and local judges (or at least contact information) at the court's official site. For example, California furnishes online profiles of its seven sitting Supreme Court justices (**http://www.courts.ca.gov/3014.htm**).

State, local, or specialty bar associations are also good sources for judicial profiles. To locate links to state or local bar associations, see **FindLaw's** page under its **Guide to Hiring a Lawyer** section (http://hirealawyer.findlaw.com/choosing-the-right-lawyer/state-bar-associations.html) or the **ABA Division for Bar Services** site (http://www.americanbar.org/groups/bar_services/resources/state_local_bar_associations.html).

Some bar associations provide information on judges, but some restrict who can access it. **The Los Angeles County Bar Association** (http://www.lacba.org), for example, offers judicial profiles at its site. (A drop-down menu under the **Site Links** tab leads to **Judicial Profiles**.) They are free only to its members, however. Similarly, the **Federal Bar Association** makes the profiles of federal judges that have appeared in past issues of its *Federal Lawyer* magazine available online to its members only, although anyone can view the profiles included in its current issue (http://www.fedbar.org/Resources/Judicial-Profile-Index.aspx). Not all bar associations restrict access, however. The **Dallas Bar Association** provides its collection of judicial profiles to all website visitors (http://www.dallasbar.org/node/110).

ARTICLES BY AND ABOUT JUDGES OR ATTORNEYS

Another way to find useful information on judges, attorneys, and other legal professionals is by locating articles written by and about them. Some public libraries allow free remote access to the **LegalTrac** database, which indexes articles from legal periodicals and legal newspapers. Many of the articles are about lawyers and judges, or are written by them. **LegalTrac** primarily offers abstracts of the articles, although some articles are available in full text. You can use a search engine to find your library's URL and then visit the library's site to learn whether your local public library offers remote access to **LegalTrac** or other legal and general resources containing articles by or about judges and attorneys.

Legal newspapers often profile lawyers and judges or feature articles written by them. **Law.com** (http://www.law.com) provides access to some articles by and about attorneys and judges that have been published in various ALM (formerly American Lawyer Media) legal newspapers. Law.com features a search box on its home page where you can search either the **Law.com Network** or the **Legal Web**. While the search and the brief annotation results from **Law.com Network** and the **Legal Web** are free, access to the full text is available for only some of the articles retrieved. Any search results with a red key icon to the right of the title requires a paid subscription to read the full story. If you have a paid subscription to one or more individual ALM legal newspapers, you can log in to read the stories from those publications. **Legal Web** results will also include links to free blogs or "blawgs."

BLOGS, BLAWGS, AND TWEETS BY AND ABOUT JUDGES OR ATTORNEYS

More and more lawyers and judges are creating blawgs (a play on the word *blogs*, used if the blog is law related). Blawgs may help you learn about a lawyer's practice area or about the lawyer's or judge's personality. To find a blawg (or blog) on a particular topic, visit a site like the ABA Journal's **Blawg Directory** (http://www.abajournal.com/blawgs) or Justia's **BlawgSearch** (http://blawgsearch.justia.com), which can be keyword searched in addition to browsed under **Categories**.

More recently, attorneys and judges have begun microblogging, which entails posting information (short updates) to sites such as Twitter. Justia created a new section on its site called **Legal Birds** (http://Legal Birds.justia.com), a moniker for those who tweet about legal issues, to capture these law-related tweets. A keyword search will return a two-part results screen. The first set of results will list lawyers (if any) who have used the keyword in their Twitter biography; the second set is a list of tweets that include the keyword. The site's information can also be name searched or browsed by topic by using the **Categories and Practice Areas** directory. The front page has a **Recent Tweets** section, as well.

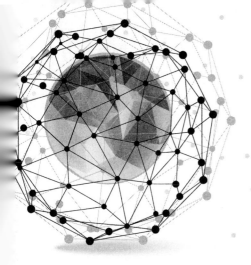

Part VII

CHECKING YOUR RESEARCH

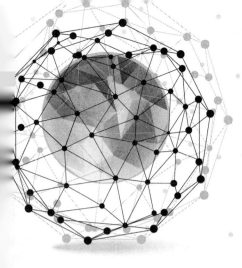

Chapter 18

CITE-CHECKING CASES

FREE ALTERNATIVES TO SHEPARD'S (LEXISNEXIS) AND KEYCITE (WESTLAW)

The final step in a legal research project is to conduct cite-checking to verify that your cases are still "good law." It can also be a first step if you want to expand your research by finding more cases and other materials that cite to your cases. One of the questions that people conducting legal research on the Internet most often ask us is *Can I Shepardize (or KeyCite) cases anywhere for free on the Internet?* The answer, in the strictest sense, is no because the free cite-checking services do not generally offer any editorial treatment (or at least not full editorial treatment). Instead, the free services usually bring back a list of cases that cite to your case, and it's up to you to determine how the citing cases treated your case. You will need to read those cases to decide if a later case overruled, reversed, or affirmed your case. **Casemaker** and **Fastcase's** citator services and **LexisNexis's** "flag" service (provided at the free **California Official Reports** case law database) do provide some limited editorial treatment and have already been discussed elsewhere in this book.

In this chapter we will discuss **Google Scholar's How cited** service for all federal and state cases and **FindLaw's Cite-Check** service found at its U.S. Supreme Court Opinions database and its California Case Law database. In addition to the alternative cite-checking services discussed in this chapter, there is also another citation "option," which we call the "party name as keyword" citation search. It can be used in any jurisdiction, and we will discuss it at the end of this chapter.

In this book we will not be discussing the online cite-checking services that most attorneys are familiar with (Bloomberg's BCite, LexisNexis's Shepard's, and Westlaw's KeyCite). However, we will mention that they offer superior cite-checking to the free resources and to Casemaker's pay citator product because they are the only ones that (1) offer full editorial treatment (indicating if a case has been affirmed, overruled, reversed, or received other negative treatment, etc.) and (2) include citation history for unpublished cases, which is especially important if an unpublished case is later affirmed or reversed by a published case.

GOOGLE SCHOLAR

ALL FEDERAL AND ALL STATES ONLINE CASE LAW (AND ARTICLES)

Previously we discussed the Google Scholar free case law database (http://scholar.google.com/) and mentioned that it includes a rudimentary citation service to update any case found at Google Scholar. To use this rudimentary citation service, begin by clicking the **How cited** link shown to the right of the **Read** link (see Figure 18.1).

Figure 18.1 Google Scholar Mattel Case

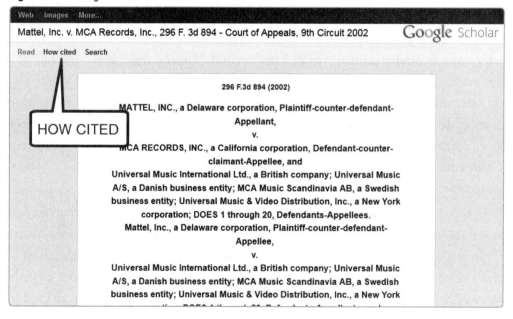

CAVEAT: Unpublished cases are not included in Google's citator (or in Fastcase or Casemaker) so you will need to run a keyword search using the party names to update these cases. FindLaw doesn't have a citator for many of its databases either, so you will also have to use this method for any case that you need to update in FindLaw. Details on how to run a keyword search using the party names are provided elsewhere in this book.

Figure 18.2 shows the citation page. It contains sections labeled **How this document has been cited, Cited by,** and **Related documents.** Google fails to document the differences between these three sections, but we will attempt to explain them here.

Figure 18.2   Google Scholar Citation Page

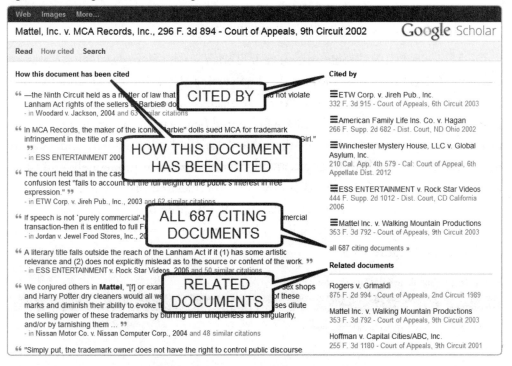

- **How this document has been cited.** A snippet of text is displayed that attempts to show how your case was treated in select citing cases or journal articles. Clicking on one of these snippets takes you directly to the location of the snippet in the citing case—which should be the location of your cited case—if the case is being displayed from Google's collection of free cases. Journal citations are also included in this list. Some journals coming from non-Google sources are in the form of PDFs. In those instances, you're taken to the beginning of the article or to a log-in/payment page of the non-Google database vendor.

- **Cited by.** While the **How this document has been cited** section lists only select documents, the **Cited by** section appears to be comprehensive, at least as to cases. For example, in Figure 18.2, if you click the **all 687 citing documents** link (in the **Cited by** section), it would link to all the cases that cite to the case you're reading, in addition to many books and journal articles. **Cited by** also differs from **How this document is cited** in that clicking on a case citation link takes you to the first page of the case, not to the exact, pinpoint page where your case is cited.

- **Related documents.** This section lists related cases and journal articles that might have similar fact patterns (or could be a countersuit, for instance) but that do not necessarily cite to your document.

On March 8, 2012, Google announced, "Today, we are changing how we present citations to legal opinions. Now, instead of sorting the citing documents by their prominence, we sort them by the extent of discussion of the cited case. Opinions that discuss the cited case in detail are presented before ones that mention the case briefly. We indicate the extent of discussion *visually* [italics added] and indicate opinions that discuss the cited case at length, that discuss it moderately, and those that discuss it briefly. Opinions that don't discuss the cited case are left unmarked." To see this list, researchers must click the **all 687 documents** link indicated in Figure 18.2, or the **Cited by** link listed below the case annotation in the original results list (see Figure 18.3).

Figure 18.3   Google Scholar Search Results

The *visual* that Google is referring to is shown in Figure 18.4 and consists of three horizontal lines to the left of the case name. Two dark blue lines (out of three) show that the first opinion discusses our cited opinion more than the next few opinions (which have only one dark blue line out of three). No lines mean that the original opinion is cited but not discussed.

Figure 18.4   Google Scholar's Visual Results

Rather than reading through each case in the **Cited by** results list in its entirety to find the place where the citing case cites to your case, scan the citing case by using the Web browser's **Find** function. To invoke the **Find** function (a search box that appears at the top or bottom of your browser screen), select **Edit** and then select **Find** from the browser's menu bar at the top of the screen; or simply enter the shortcut **Control F** if using a PC or **Command F** if using an Apple computer. Enter one of the party names (e.g., Mattel) from your cited case to be instantly taken to the place in the citing case where your case is cited. You'll still have to read that part of the case to see how (or if) the new case affects your case, but what do you expect when it's free? **Control F** or **Command F** will also open the **Find** function if you are reading other document files (e.g., Word, PPT, PDF, etc.), as well.

FINDLAW

CALIFORNIA AND U.S. SUPREME COURT ONLY

FindLaw's **California Supreme and Appellate Court Cases** (Powered by AccessLaw) and **U.S. Supreme Court Opinions** databases are the only FindLaw case law databases (http://www.findlaw.com/cacases and http://www.findlaw.com/casecode/supreme.html) that offer a free cite-checking service. However, as noted earlier, there is no editorial treatment to explain how the citing cases affect a cited case.

There are two ways to cite-check a California case at FindLaw. The first way is to go to http://www.findlaw.com/cacases/#dirsearch2 and type a citation into the field box labeled **Cite Check: Find cases which cite another case** (see Figure 18.5).

Figure 18.5   FindLaw Cite-Check Form

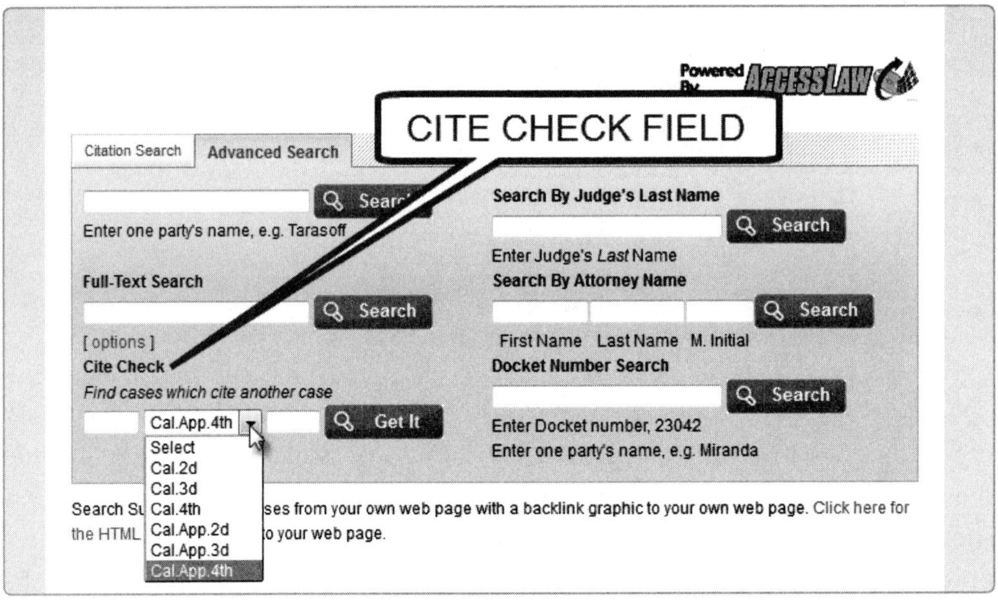

Researchers will need to be logged into their free accounts to view the full text of the case. A list of reported cases citing the cited case will be displayed (see Figure 18.6).

Figure 18.6 FindLaw's Results for a Citation Search

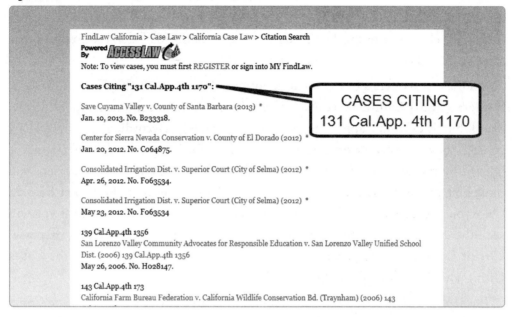

The second way to cite-check a California case at FindLaw is to click the **Cases Citing This Case** link in the upper-left corner of any case that you are viewing. A list of reported cases citing your case will be displayed (see Figure 18.7).

Figure 18.7 FindLaw's Cases Citing This Case

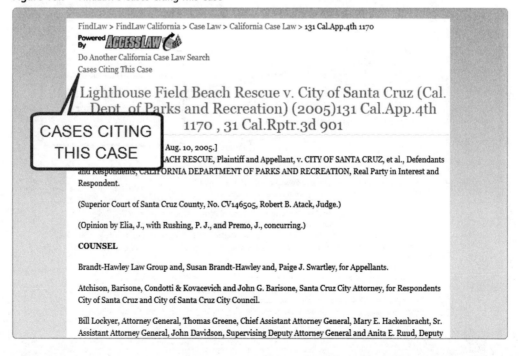

These two cite-checking methods for California cases will only return other California state cases, so you will need to use the "Party name as keyword" search (explained elsewhere in this book) to learn if any California federal courts (or other state or federal courts) have cited to your case.

FindLaw also offers a free cite-check option (**Cases Citing This Case**) at its **U.S. Supreme Court Opinions** database (http://www.findlaw.com/casecode/supreme. html), but it does not appear to be working properly. According to our Findlaw contact, they are working on a fix, so we will describe how it should work in case it is fixed by the time this book is published. To deploy the cite-check option, you must first perform a **Citation Search, Party Name Search**, or **Full-Text Search**. Once you select a result, if there are any applicable cases that cite your case, you will see either a link to **Cases citing this case: Supreme Court** or **Cases citing this case: Circuit Courts** or both (see Figure 18.8). (However, you will never see the **Cases Citing This Case** link if you display a case from the browsing option.)

If you click **Cases citing this case: Supreme Court**, a list of U.S. Supreme Court cases that cite to your case will be displayed. But, if you click **Cases citing this case: Circuit Courts**, a list of Circuit Courts of Appeals cases are not displayed. Instead, it looks as if you need to enter the case name into the search box that is displayed, but when we tried that it brought back only U.S. Supreme Court cases.

Figure 18.8   FindLaw's U.S. Supreme Court Links

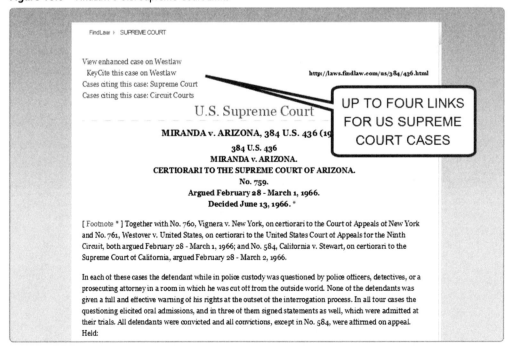

The first two links in Figure 18.8, **View enhanced case on Westlaw** and **KeyCite this case on Westlaw**, take researchers to a screen that states that **Westlaw by Credit Card** is no longer available. (The credit card option used to allow non-Westlaw subscribers to retrieve documents and check citations on an *ad hoc* basis using a credit card.) If you have a paid subscription to Westlaw, you can login to **WestlawNext** or **Westlaw Classic** from here.

"PARTY NAME AS KEYWORD" CITE-CHECKING ALTERNATIVE

The final cite-checking method we will discuss is the "party name as keyword" citation search process. It can be accomplished by searching the party names from the case that you hope to rely on as keywords through a free, full-text searchable case law database that contains cases published after the date of your case. This will bring back results that include later cases that cite to your case. Then, it's up to you to determine how later cases treated your case (i.e., you will need to read the citing cases and decide if a court overruled, reversed, affirmed, harmonized, etc., your case). This process is quite rudimentary and the results do not include the editorial treatment for which the pay services are known. We only recommend using the "party name as keyword" citation search for fairly recent cases because cite-checking older cases with this method might bring back too large a number of citing cases—thousands in some instances—all of which you would have to read to determine if they were at all relevant.

> **CAVEAT:** Unpublished cases are not included in Google's citator (or in Fastcase or Casemaker) so we also recommend that you run a keyword search using the party names to see if an unpublished case has been heard by a higher court and been reversed or affirmed (and possibly become a published case). It would also be important to know if other opinions have cited to your unpublished opinion or if the original court subsequently overruled its unpublished opinion. Since FindLaw doesn't have a citator for many of its databases, you will also have to use this method for cases from FindLaw that you need to update.

To conduct a "party name as keyword" citation search process, follow these steps:

- Enter the plaintiff's and defendant's names from the case you want to cite-check into the keyword search box in quotation marks. Also, if the database has a date range field, add the date of your case's decision as the beginning date and the current day's date as the ending date. For instance, if you wanted to cite-check *State v. Green*, 804 A.2d 810, your search would look like this:

state v. green

You would also need to run another search for "state vs. green" because you never know if an opinion uses *v.* or *vs.*

- Then, if you have too many irrelevant cases (since these are such common words), you can refine your technique. First, add some descriptive keywords or phrases from the case being cite checked. For instance, if the issue in *State v. Green* was about conspiracy to commit murder, you could add the keywords conspiracy and murder and run the following search:

"state v. green" conspiracy murder

- If your search still retrieves a large number of irrelevant cases, try searching for the citation of your original case—in this instance 804 A.2d 810—in quotation marks:

"804 a.2d 810"

Once you have successfully used your citation as a keyword search, you should receive a list of cases that cite to your case, including your case. This last technique can be tricky for two reasons: (1) some case law databases may attempt to convert this to a citation search and retrieve only your original case and (2) some court opinions might not refer to the full citation of your case (e.g., it might just refer to a pinpoint cite).

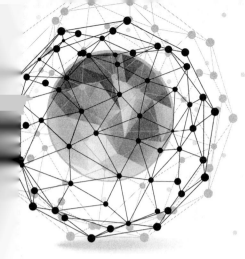

Index

Westlaw CourtExpress, 254, 274
doing business around the world, 240
Doing Business site, 240

E

e-alerts. *See also* e-newsletters
  for docket-related information, 28, 251,
    253–254, 263, 268, 274
  for federal civil complaints, 275
  for federal regulations, 200, 208
  for new cases, 80–81, 136, 148
  for SEC filings, 23
Eble, Timothy E., 12
e-CFR, 203–204. *See also* Code of Federal
  Regulations (CFR)
  browsing, 204
  searching, 204
  update schedule, 204
EDGAR database, 22
e-lawyering, 16
Electronic Information System for
  International Law (EISIL), 242–244
Electronic Resources Guide (ERG), 241–242
employment and labor law, 15
Employment Law Information Network
  (ELIN), 15
employment searches, 42
e-newsletters. *See also* e-alerts
  legal news, 39, 42
  immigration law, 45
  new cases, 38, 39, 97
  practice area, 38
enterprise cloud print plug-in for Fastcase,
  155
ethics, 19–20
ETHICSearch, 20
European Union resources, 240–241
expert witnesses
  directories of, 7–8, 42
  as general legal research resources, 7–8

F

Facebook, 280
family law, 15–16
Fastcase, 69, 139–156
  Advanced Caselaw searches, 142–146
  annotated statutes, 152
  app for, 29, 140
  Authority Check, 150–152
  Bad Law Bot, 150–152
  case law resources, 141
  copying text with citations, 149
  coverage, 140
  enterprise cloud print plug-in, 155
  Federal Appellate Plan, 141
  federal filings, searching, 153
  Forecite, 148
  HeinOnline partnership, 156
  legal forms, searching, 153
  National Premium plan, 141
  navigating, 148–150
  newspapers, searching, 153
  printing, 153–155
  red flags, 148, 150–152
  regulations, 142, 152
  Relevance scores, 146
  reliability issues, 152
  results list, 147–148
  searching beyond case law, 152
  searching case law, 142–146
  search tips, 143
  statutes, 142, 152
    annotated statutes, 152
  subscribers, 139–140, 155
  syncing, 155
federal agencies
  defunct agencies, finding, 216–217
  forms from, 5
  Louisiana State University Libraries
    Federal Agencies Directory, 214
  regulations of, tracking, 208

R

real estate law, 16, 22
  forms, 6
RECAP, 253, 266–268
red flags (Fastcase),148, 150–152
redaction of Social Security numbers in
    PACER, 261
Reed Smith, 11
regulations. *See* Casemaker; Code of Federal
    Regulations (CFR); e-CFR; Fastcase
    administrative law, 199–217
    Federal Register (FR), 199–201
Related Resources for Attorneys (American
    Association for Justice), 66
Report of Current Opinions (RECOP), 93
researching people, 281–288
Research Intelligence Group "New Attorney
    Research Methods Survey," xvii
resolutions. *See* legislative information
Robbins Geller Rudman & Dowd LLP, 13
Rocket Lawyer, 6
Rosch, Mark, xviii
RSS feeds
  blogs, 278
  CasemakerDigest, 136
  CM/ECF (PACER), 263
  Dockets (PACER), 263
  Federal Register, 208
  federal regulations, 208
  Justia, 271
  PACER, 263
Rulebook app, 28

S

sample briefs and pleadings. *See* briefs;
    pleadings
Scholar. *See* Google, Google Scholar
search engines, 31

Bing, 48–50
  Google, 36. *See also* Google, Google
      Scholar
searching (in general)
  Boolean connectors, 36, 49–50, 53,
      86–87, 127–128
  field searching, 121–126, 182
  prefix searching, 182
SEC Info, 23
secondary law websites, 3–9
Securities and Exchange Commission (SEC)
    site, 22
Securities Class Action Clearinghouse
    (Stanford), 9, 23–24
securities law, 22–24
Seller Beware, 11–12
session laws, 126
settlements, 7–8, 13
  Securities Class Action Clearinghouse,
      23–24
Shepard's (Lexis), 82, 112, 133, 152, 291, 292
  alternatives to, 291–300
  positive history, 133, 152
Siegel, Daniel J., 28
social media, 277–280, 288
Social Security number redaction in PACER,
    261
software applications for legal research, 19,
    27–30, 188
Stanford Law School Securities Class Action
    Clearinghouse database, 9, 23–24
Stanford University Libraries Copyright &
    Fair Use site, 17
Stanley, Tim, 33, 39
State and Local Government on the Net, 215,
    224–225
  county and city websites, 231
state appellate decisions. *See* case law
    databases; state case law databases

The Lawyer's Guide to Microsoft® Outlook 2013
By Ben M. Schorr

Product Code: 5110752 • **LP Price:** $41.95 • **Regular Price:** $69.95

Take control of your e-mail, calendar, to-do list, and more with The Lawyer's Guide to Microsoft® Outlook 2013. This essential guide summarizes the most important new features in the newest version of Microsoft® Outlook and provides practical tips that will promote organization and productivity in your law practice. Written specifically for lawyers by a twenty-year veteran of law office technology and ABA member, this book is a must-have.

The Lawyer's Guide to Microsoft® Word 2013
By Ben M. Schorr

Product Code: 5110757 • **LP Price:** $41.95 • **Regular Price:** $69.95

Maximize your use of Microsoft® Word with this essential guide. Fully updated to reflect the 2012 version of the software, this handy reference includes clear explanations, legal-specific descriptions, and time-saving tips for getting the most out of Microsoft® Word—and customizing it for the needs of today's legal professional.

LinkedIn in One Hour for Lawyers, Second Edition
By Dennis Kennedy and Allison C. Shields

Product Code: 5110773 • **LP Price:** $39.95 • **Regular Price:** $49.95

Since the first edition of LinkedIn in One Hour for Lawyers was published, LinkedIn has added almost 100 million users, and more and more lawyers are using the platform on a regular basis. Now, this bestselling ABA book has been fully revised and updated to reflect significant changes to LinkedIn's layout and functionality made through 2013. LinkedIn in One Hour for Lawyers, Second Edition, will help lawyers make the most of their online professional networking. In just one hour, you will learn to:

- Set up a LinkedIn® account
- Create a robust, dynamic profile--and take advantage of new multimedia options
- Build your connections
- Get up to speed on new features such as Endorsements, Influencers, Contacts, and Channels
- Enhance your Company Page with new functionality
- Use search tools to enhance your network
- Monitor your network with ease
- Optimize your settings for privacy concerns
- Use LinkedIn® effectively in the hiring process
- Develop a LinkedIn strategy to grow your legal network

Facebook® in One Hour for Lawyers
By Dennis Kennedy and Allison C. Shields

Product Code: 5110745 • **LP Price:** $24.95 • **Regular Price:** $39.95

With a few simple steps, lawyers can use Facebook® to market their services, grow their practices, and expand their legal network—all by using the same methods they already use to communicate with friends and family. Facebook® in One Hour for Lawyers will show any attorney—from Facebook® novices to advanced users—how to use this powerful tool for both professional and personal purposes.

Blogging in One Hour for Lawyers
By Ernie Svenson

Product Code: 5110744 • **LP Price:** $24.95 • **Regular Price:** $39.95

Until a few years ago, only the largest firms could afford to engage an audience of millions. Now, lawyers in any size firm can reach a global audience at little to no cost—all because of blogs. An effective blog can help you promote your practice, become more "findable" online, and take charge of how you are perceived by clients, journalists and anyone who uses the Internet. Blogging in One Hour for Lawyers will show you how to create, maintain, and improve a legal blog—and gain new business opportunities along the way. In just one hour, you will learn to:

- Set up a blog quickly and easily
- Write blog posts that will attract clients
- Choose from various hosting options like Blogger, TypePad, and WordPress
- Make your blog friendly to search engines, increasing your ranking
- Tweak the design of your blog by adding customized banners and colors
- Easily send notice of your blog posts to Facebook and Twitter
- Monitor your blog's traffic with Google Analytics and other tools
- Avoid ethics problems that may result from having a legal blog

The Electronic Evidence and Discovery Handbook: Forms, Checklists, and Guidelines
By Sharon D. Nelson, Bruce A. Olson, and John W. Simek

Product Code: 5110569 • **LP Price:** $99.95 • **Regular Price:** $129.95

The use of electronic evidence has increased dramatically over the past few years, but many lawyers still struggle with the complexities of electronic discovery. This substantial book provides lawyers with the templates they need to frame their discovery requests and provides helpful advice on what they can subpoena. In addition to the ready-made forms, the authors also supply explanations to bring you up to speed on the electronic discovery field. The accompanying CD-ROM features over 70 forms, including, Motions for Protective Orders, Preservation and Spoliation Documents, Motions to Compel, Electronic Evidence Protocol Agreements, Requests for Production, Internet Services Agreements, and more. Also included is a full electronic evidence case digest with over 300 cases detailed!

Android Apps in One Hour for Lawyers
By Daniel J. Siegel

Product Code: 5110754 • **LP Price:** $19.95 • **Regular Price:** $34.95

Lawyers are already using Android devices to make phone calls, check e-mail, and send text messages. After the addition of several key apps, Android smartphones or tablets can also help run a law practice. From the more than 800,000 apps currently available, Android Apps in One Hour for Lawyers highlights the "best of the best" apps that will allow you to practice law from your mobile device. In just one hour, this book will describe how to buy, install, and update Android apps, and help you:

- Store documents and files in the cloud
- Use security apps to safeguard client data on your phone
- Be organized and productive with apps for to-do lists, calendar, and contacts
- Communicate effectively with calling, text, and e-mail apps
- Create, edit, and organize your documents
- Learn on the go with news, reading, and reference apps
- Download utilities to keep your device running smoothly
- Hit the road with apps for travel
- Have fun with games and social media apps

Twitter in One Hour for Lawyers
By Jared Correia

Product Code: 5110746 • **LP Price:** $24.95 • **Regular Price:** $39.95

More lawyers than ever before are using Twitter to network with colleagues, attract clients, market their law firms, and even read the news. But to the uninitiated, Twitter's short messages, or tweets, can seem like they are written in a foreign language. Twitter in One Hour for Lawyers will demystify one of the most important social-media platforms of our time and teach you to tweet like an expert. In just one hour, you will learn to:

- Create a Twitter account and set up your profile
- Read tweets and understand Twitter jargon
- Write tweets—and send them at the appropriate time
- Gain an audience—follow and be followed
- Engage with other Twitters users
- Integrate Twitter into your firm's marketing plan
- Cross-post your tweets with other social media platforms like Facebook and LinkedIn
- Understand the relevant ethics, privacy, and security concerns
- Get the greatest possible return on your Twitter investment
- And much more!

Virtual Law Practice:
How to Deliver Legal Services Online
By Stephanie L. Kimbro

Product Code: 5110707 • **LP Price:** $47.95 • **Regular Price:** $79.95

The legal market has recently experienced a dramatic shift as lawyers seek out alternative methods of practicing law and providing more affordable legal services. Virtual law practice is revolutionizing the way the public receives legal services and how legal professionals work with clients. If you are interested in this form of practicing law, *Virtual Law Practice* will help you:

- Responsibly deliver legal services online to your clients
- Successfully set up and operate a virtual law office
- Establish a virtual law practice online through a secure, client-specific portal
- Manage and market your virtual law practice
- Understand state ethics and advisory opinions
- Find more flexibility and work/life balance in the legal profession

Social Media for Lawyers: The Next Frontier
By Carolyn Elefant and Nicole Black

Product Code: 5110710 • **LP Price:** $47.95 • **Regular Price:** $79.95

The world of legal marketing has changed with the rise of social media sites such as LinkedIn, Twitter, and Facebook. Law firms are seeking their companies attention with tweets, videos, blog posts, pictures, and online content. Social media is fast and delivers news at record pace. This book provides you with a practical, goal-centric approach to using social media in your law practice that will enable you to identify social media platforms and tools that fit your practice and implement them easily, efficiently, and ethically.

iPad Apps in One Hour for Lawyers
By Tom Mighell

Product Code: 5110739 • **LP Price:** $19.95 • **Regular Price:** $34.95

At last count, there were more than 80,000 apps available for the iPad. Finding the best apps often can be an overwhelming, confusing, and frustrating process. iPad Apps in One Hour for Lawyers provides the "best of the best" apps that are essential for any law practice. In just one hour, you will learn about the apps most worthy of your time and attention. This book will describe how to buy, install, and update iPad apps, and help you:

- Find apps to get organized and improve your productivity
- Create, manage, and store documents on your iPad
- Choose the best apps for your law office, including litigation and billing apps
- Find the best news, reading, and reference apps
- Take your iPad on the road with apps for travelers
- Maximize your social networking power
- Have some fun with game and entertainment apps during your relaxation time

The Lawyer's Essential Guide to Writing
By Marie Buckley

Product Code: 5110726 • **LP Price:** $47.95 • **Regular Price:** $79.95

This is a readable, concrete guide to contemporary legal writing. Based on Marie Buckley's years of experience coaching lawyers, this book provides a systematic approach to all forms of written communication, from memoranda and briefs to e-mail and blogs. The book sets forth three principles for powerful writing and shows how to apply those principles to develop a clean and confident style.

iPad in One Hour for Lawyers, Third Edition
By Tom Mighell

Product Code: 5110779 • **LP Price:** $39.95 • **Regular Price:** $49.95

Whether you are a new or a more advanced iPad user, *iPad in One Hour for Lawyers* takes a great deal of the mystery and confusion out of using your iPad. Ideal for lawyers who want to get up to speed swiftly, this book presents the essentials so you don't get bogged down in technical jargon and extraneous features and apps. In just six, short lessons, you'll learn how to:

- Quickly Navigate and Use the iPad User Interface
- Set Up Mail, Calendar, and Contacts
- Create and Use Folders to Multitask and Manage Apps
- Add Files to Your iPad, and Sync Them
- View and Manage Pleadings, Case Law, Contracts, and other Legal Documents
- Use Your iPad to Take Notes and Create Documents
- Use Legal-Specific Apps at Trial or in Doing Research

30-DAY RISK-FREE ORDER FORM

Please print or type. To ship UPS, we must have your street address. If you list a P.O. Box, we will ship by U.S. Mail.

Name

Member ID

Firm/Organization

Street Address

City/State/Zip

Area Code/Phone (In case we have a question about your order)

E-mail

Method of Payment:
☐ Check enclosed, payable to American Bar Association
☐ MasterCard   ☐ Visa   ☐ American Express

Card Number   Expiration Date

Signature Required

MAIL THIS FORM TO:
American Bar Association, Publication Orders
P.O. Box 10892, Chicago, IL 60610

ORDER BY PHONE:
24 hours a day, 7 days a week:
Call 1-800-285-2221 to place a credit card order. We accept Visa, MasterCard, and American Express.

EMAIL ORDERS: orders@americanbar.org
FAX ORDERS: 1-312-988-5568

VISIT OUR WEB SITE: www.ShopABA.org
Allow 7-10 days for regular UPS delivery. Need it sooner? Ask about our overnight delivery options. Call the ABA Service Center at 1-800-285-2221 for more information.

GUARANTEE:
If–for any reason–you are not satisfied with your purchase, you may return it within 30 days of receipt for a refund of the price of the book(s). No questions asked.

Thank You For Your Order.

Join the ABA Law Practice Division today and receive a substantial discount on Division publications!

Product Code:	Description:	Quantity:	Price:	Total Price:
				$
				$
				$
				$
				$

Shipping/Handling:		*Tax:		
$0.00 to $9.99	add $0.00	IL residents add 9.25% DC residents add 5.75%	**Subtotal:**	$
$10.00 to $49.99	add $6.95		*Tax:	$
$50.00 to $99.99	add $8.95		**Shipping/Handling:**	$
$100.00 to $199.99	add $10.95	Yes, I am an ABA member and would like to join the Law Practice Division today! (Add $50.00)		$
$200.00 to $499.99	add $13.95		**Total:**	$